To Gary

"Lest We Forget"

David L. Israel

The Day the Thunderbird Cried

Untold

Stories of

World War II

by
David L. Israel

Edited by Ruth Israel
Cover and layout design by Great Graphics Services
Cover Sculpture:
    "Liberation Monument" by the late Natan Rapoport is located in
Liberty State Park, Jersey City, New Jersey. The statue depicts an American
soldier/liberator carrying a concentration camp prisoner. Symbolically, the
two figures are joined at the heart. Sculpture photo: Joel Sugarman

First Edition
Published by emek press
Library of Congress Control Number 2005930159
ISBN: 0-9770591-0-3

Includes index, bibliography, glossary, timeline, appendix - 50 black and
white photos, 8 full color photos

1. World War II 2. Military History 3. Germany 4. Holocaust
5. Concentration Camps 6. Dachau 7. Liberation 8. War Crimes Trials
9. Righteous among the Nations 10. GI Bill I. Title

10 9 8 7 6 5 4 3 2 1

Dedication

for
All the GIs of World War II
and
the 60,000,000 souls,
military and civilian,
who perished

1933-1945

Acknowledgements

Without the friendship of the men involved in the stories included in this volume, this book could not have been written. I will be forever grateful to the veterans of the 42nd, 45th, 99th and 106th Infantry Divisions who freely shared their memories, their fears, their passions and their triumphs as we sat together as brothers putting together the pieces of the "story."

In recreating the events of April 29, 1945, primary source material was sought out no matter where it existed. Truth and accuracy were the two criteria that guided the search and were strictly adhered to.

A wealth of information was contributed by Lt. Col. Hugh Foster III who made available many long hidden documents obtained from the military archives in Carlisle, Pennsylvania. Eye witness accounts of the happenings on liberation day and its immediate aftermath were generously shared by Bill Walsh, John Lee, Ralph Fink, Ralph Rosa, Jim Bird, Steve Resheff, Al Panbianco, Dan Dougherty, John Degrow, Robert White, Henry Mills, Karl Mann, Chan Rogers, Col. Van T. Barfoot and Generals Felix E. Sparks and Russell Weiskircher of the 45th Infantry Division.

Tireless research was contributed by Art Lee, Sol Feingold and Don Segel of the 42nd Infantry Division, as were the experiences of Colonel Don Downard, Romeo Figolo, Ken Button, Dee Eberhart, Morris Eisenstein and Ted Johnson of the 42nd. Sincere thanks also to Meyer Shopkow, E.G. McConnell and Mel Rappaport for their knowledgeable contributions about

American armored divisions.

Special thanks to Curtis Whiteway of the 99th Infantry Division, whose squad helped liberate several concentration camps in Bavaria, as well as to Norm Fellman and Winfield Rosenberg, two of the American GI prisoners of war separated from comrades and shipped to the notorious concentration camp, Berga. Whiteway, Fellman and Rosenberg are singled out together with George Oiye and Sus Ito of the 522 RCT due to the uniqueness of their experiences which they were good enough to talk about freely, after 50 years.

I am deeply grateful to each of these men as well as to all members of the 42nd and 45th Divisions with whom I met during the 18 years of gathering the detailed and specific information that went into this book. Knowing these men has enriched my life. Of special importance was the time spent with Curtis Whiteway, Sol Feingold and Art Lee as we tracked the Nazi regime on its path from the so called T4 mercy killings in the euthanasia centers of Germany to the ultimate conclusion of mass murder in the concentration camps of Europe.

John Deh, of Davis California was responsible for the beginning of this long journey. Mrs. Brana Gurewitsch of the Brooklyn Holocaust Center was instrumental in getting the project started and Ms. Topsy Smalley of Cabrillo College, Santa Cruz, California was extremely helpful in locating vital sources of information.

In Germany, Robert Sigel, historian/teacher at the Josef-Effner Gymnasium, Dachau and Hermann Weiss, historian at the Institute for Contemporary History, Munich contributed insightful background on life under the Nazi regine. Ms. Barbara Distel, the curator of the Dachau Memorial Museum, was indispensable in providing information, encouragement and help in bringing the project to fulfillment.

Essential help in translating French and German documents was generously provided by Gunther Baldauf, Johanna Bergmann, Lucia Frank, Elizabeth Jackson, Fred Speer, Gerd Strauss and Pierre C. T. Verheye.

Many thanks to Carol Barrett, Preston Mitchell, Dick Grambow and Paul Peterson for technical assistance.

Ernestine Coryell and Haroldene Aldrich were enthusiastic supporters and provided perceptive feedback. Thanks also to Mary Jane Thornton for her early encouragement and practiced eye.

My deep appreciation to Sue Musolf for dedicated secretarial assistance and to Roberta Great for her patience and skill in book and cover design. Ruth Israel, my editor, kept me on track and pulled it all together.

Thank you!

A note from the author

I must apologize to those readers whose sensibilities may be offended by the visual scenes of the concentration camps. For the unfortunate souls who were prisoners in the camps, for GIs who were liberators, no apologies are necessary. They were there. They saw. They agonized. They cried bitter tears on seeing first hand the depth of man's inhumanity to man. All historical events described within these pages happened. The men and women who served during WWII were witnesses to history. One can only hope that by learning of these horribly haunting events our grandchildren will be better prepared to take the necessary steps to prevent this kind of "history" ever being repeated.

Table of Contents

Book One
Invasion of Sicily; D-Day, Normandy, France

Book Two
Battle of the Bulge, Ardennes Forest, Belgium

Book Three

Liberation of Dachau Concentration Camp to VE Day
(Victory in Europe, May 8 1945)

Book Four

As the War Ends, Prisoners of War, Going Home, GI Bill,
Heroes and Rescuers

Book One

"The past is not dead. It is not even past."

William Faulkner

The Gift

The squad of infantrymen is crouched down, peering across a huge soccer field. German soldiers are looking back at the Americans through binoculars, each waiting to see what the next move will be.

Behind the Germans is a building that looks like a hospital or an institution of some kind. The Americans are amazed to see the Germans talking to a young girl, perhaps five years of age. They see the German soldiers place something in the girl's hands and point toward the Americans.

The blonde haired, blue-eyed little girl starts to skip across the field toward the astonished American GIs. The girl has a blue beret on her head and she is laughing as she gets closer and closer to the American soldiers. Suddenly, one of the soldiers cries out, "Sarge, she's got a grenade in her hands." Other soldiers, focused on the Germans, see them laughing and pointing toward the Americans. The sergeant gasps as he hands a sniper rifle to the squad's sharpshooter and says quietly, "Take her out."

The shooter sights the little girl as sweat pours from his face. With tears in his eyes he shoves the rifle back into the sergeant's hands. "I've got a five year old of my own, Sarge. I can't do it."

The little girl is now 25 yards from the crouching men. The sergeant puts the rifle to his shoulder. He instantly realizes that in another few seconds the girl will take her fingers from the gift the German soldiers have asked her to deliver to the Amis and they will all be blown to heaven.

As his finger reaches for the trigger, the girl suddenly trips...the grenade explodes, instantly tearing her little body into shreds. The American squad races across the field, wiping out the German position, killing all the German soldiers they had been facing. Only then, with tears in their eyes, did they start investigating where they were...Hadamar.

Lucky

It's hard to imagine two men from such different back-grounds forming a lifelong, loyal friendship. They met in bat-tle on the lower East Side of New York in the early 1900's when it was quite normal for young Italians and Jews to get to know each other by fighting with their fists. When Sal and Maier fought, it looked like a foregone conclusion that the older and taller Italian boy would badly whip the younger Jewish kid. The fight didn't turn out that way. The older one, Sal, kept whipping the younger one, but the smaller boy, Maier, kept coming back for more. He wouldn't quit. Finally, the older boy put his arms around the younger Jewish boy and announced that the fight was over. A lifelong, trusting friendship between Sal and Maier began at that moment.

As the two boys matured and became assimilated into the American culture, their friendship grew. Maier Suchowljansky, the younger boy, changed his name to Meyer Lansky; Salvatore Luciana became Charles "Lucky" Luciano.

Lansky left school at an early age, got involved in petty crimes, and eventually became a used truck dealer in the area known as the East Side of New York City. Luciano went into big-ger criminal activities until the prohibition laws came into being in 1918. From then on liquor and its importation and distribu-tion became his main interest. Since trucking was a vital factor in bringing in shipments of liquor from Canada, it was natural that the two friends should merge their business interests.

Lucky Luciano, in time, became the "boss of bosses" in the

New York area, and Meyer Lansky became the mob's treasurer. As time passed, "The Mob" became involved in other lucrative businesses that fit their area of operations. Among these were loan sharking, prostitution, narcotics, union organizing and gambling of all kinds and shapes, including the Black Sox Scandal of 1918 when the Baseball World Series was fixed by the notorious gambler, Arnold Rothstein. When the war started in December 1941, they launched into black market activities in gasoline, tires, meat, sugar and counterfeit ration stamps.

Charles "Lucky" Luciano became the target that New York District attorneys set their sights on. In 1936, after failing many times to get Luciano convicted for his criminal activities, Thomas Dewey finally succeeded where others had failed. Luciano was found guilty on 62 counts of prostitution and pimping and was sentenced to a term of 30 to 50 years. He was sent to a penitentiary in Dannamora, New York, near the Canadian border.

In Clinton State Prison Luciano felt as if he had been sent to Siberia in Russia, far away from his friends and the neighborhoods he had grown to love. When Luciano told Lansky how unhappy he was so far away from "the city," Lansky vowed to rectify the situation.

In 1940, after the fall of France, the US government seized the French luxury liner Normandie. Since 1932, the ship had been cruising the Atlantic Ocean carrying more than 2,000 passengers between Europe and America. On December 24, 1941, the Navy renamed the ship "Lafayette" and began conversion and repairs in order for the ship to be utilized as a troop transport, capable of carrying 15,000 troops and equipment each crossing.

On February 9, 1942, in dry dock at a pier in Manhattan, the Lafayette caught fire. Although millions of dollars were spent in the salvage attempt, the ship never sailed again.

Eventually, it was scrapped. Sabotage was suspected as the cause of the fire, but never proven. The Navy, however, had learned a valuable lesson.

The New York/New Jersey waterfront, with its fishing and shipping operations was vital to the American war effort and would have to be protected against sabotage, strikes and espionage at all costs. American intelligence agencies knew that the waterfront was overflowing with enemy agents and saboteurs looking for ways to foment discontent among the longshoremen in order to tie up the port of New York, the largest and busiest port in the world. Getting information concerning military shipments, committing acts of destruction, signaling U boats waiting offshore, and even supplying those boats from fishing vessels, were actions taken by the sabotage and espionage rings working in the New York and New Jersey port areas. American intelligence agencies faced a daunting challenge; they had to stop the sabotage, and do so with limited manpower.

Lack of security along the waterfront was often cited for the huge losses suffered by Allied convoys to German U boats soon after the convoys left New York's protected shores. Short of tying up thousands of military personnel vitally needed in Europe, the FBI, Office of Naval Intelligence and Counter Intelligence Services were stymied as to how to accomplish this formidable security task. The destruction of the Normandie spurred the intelligence agencies into greater cooperation than had ever existed before. There could be no excuse. The problem had to be solved.

The Naval Commander did not know what to make of the quiet spoken man seated in the office of the U. S. Third Naval District located in New York City. Little more than 5 feet tall, the man was dressed simply but neatly. A small fedora hat rested on the Commander's desk as the visitor shared his thoughts with the Naval officer. Sensing the officer's hesitant attitude, the little man reached for his hat as he rose to leave. At the door he turned to share a parting thought with the officer. There was a half smile on his lips as he said, "If you don't think I can do what we spoke about, check with Dewey."

Before the mysterious man had reached the exit doorway of the building, the Naval Officer was in deep and earnest conversation with Thomas E. Dewey, the New York District Attorney. By the time he hung up the phone, he was convinced that if Meyer Lansky said he could do something, it would be done, no matter how far fetched his claims might sound.

The second meeting between the Naval Intelligence officer, Charles H. Haffenden, and Meyer Lansky took place on a park bench in Central Park; Lansky didn't think it was wise to be seen too often near the office of Naval Intelligence. To show "good faith" on the part of the government, Lansky's first condition had been met; Luciano had been transferred to a prison much closer to New York City. While "Sing Sing" met some of the parameters of what Lansky wanted for his friend, it did not meet all of the specifications Lansky had laid out.

However, to show *their* "good faith," Lansky's men, longshoremen, fishermen and stevedores, had taken over the job of providing security on the docks of New York and New Jersey. From the time Lansky's friends took over surveillance of the waterfronts, there were no major incidents of sabotage or espionage on the docks. The fact that the FBI was constantly arresting German spies and sympathizers undoubtedly added to the "peace" that prevailed along the waterfronts until the end of the war.

By the time the third meeting between Lansky and the Naval Officer took place, Luciano had been moved to a prison more to his liking. Like Lompoc in California where the Watergate culprits would be been sent, Great Meadow Prison in New York

State was where gentlemen criminals spent their time. In a country club atmosphere, Luciano was set up with an office and telephones where he was able to meet with his compatriots and carry on normal business operations while awaiting the end of the war. This was important to him because Lansky had structured the agreement with the government in a way that would set Luciano free when the war ended; the prison sentence would be commuted and Luciano would be deported to his native Sicily. This last clause in the agreement was to become effective only if Luciano was able to contact his friends in Sicily and guarantee that certain arrangements would be taken care of before the Americans began their invasion of the island of Sicily.

As the war progressed and the invasion of Sicily grew in importance in the Allied master plan, the second part of Lansky's vision came into focus. Militarily, an invasion from the sea is considered to be the most dangerous and costly in men and materials for an invading army. Therefore, in Allied projections the invasion of Sicily was expected to be extremely costly. There is no doubt that it would have been without the cooperation of Meyer Lansky and Lucky Luciano's Sicilian Mafia contacts.

On July 10, 1943, the invasion of Sicily, code named "Husky," began. What happened in the first few hours of that day shocked and amazed the world. With American forces keyed up and tensed for a bloody battle, the men hit the water on the run as the ramps descended. Expecting the worst, the American forces were stunned by the sight that met their eyes.

No enemy fire was directed at them. Debris floated all around the boats, obviously from underwater obstacles that would have entangled them in a death trap had they not been removed beforehand by someone. "It was a cake walk," one of them remembered. "There wasn't even much firing going on. We were completely surprised at how easy it all went down."

The Allies committed 467,000 British and American troops to the invasion of Sicily. They were opposed by 60,000 Germans who had been totally and completely misled as to when and where the invasion forces would hit. The American invasion force never knew that the underwater installations set up to deter the invaders had been removed before the GIs stormed the beaches. They were unaware that all the defensive fortifications had been pinpointed by Luciano's friends and that German troops had been lured to another part of the island leaving only Italian defenders who put up token resistance.

Meyer Lansky had been sure his promises to the Naval Commander would be carried out to the letter since contact had been established with Vito Genovese, a New Jersey mob boss. Vito had been living in Italy for many years, hiding from indictments against him filed by the New York District Attorney's office. Lansky banked on his Italian Mafia contacts coming through, and the Office of Naval Intelligence banked on Lansky.

On May 8th, 1945, the day the war in Europe was declared officially over, Luciano's attorney submitted a petition asking for clemency from the United States government in its case against Charles Lucky Luciano. The petition cited Luciano's patriotism and contributions to the United States war effort. In February, 1946, Luciano was duly deported to his native Italy.

The papers involved with Luciano's deportation were locked away in District Attorney Dewey's private vault until after his death. Examined by top Navy officers in 1954, it was decided that releasing the papers could "jeopardize operations of a similar nature in the future and could embarrass the Navy public relations wise."

The last few years of his life, Luciano spent many hours every day sitting at an open air bar in Naples waiting for any American sailor on leave to sit with him for a bit while sipping beer and talking about how things used to be. Among the sailors, the Red Lantern Bar was known to be a great meeting place where "this guy Luciano would always pick up the tab for a couple of beers."

Luciano believed he had led an exceptionally exciting life. He tried to interest Hollywood in the idea of making a movie about his experiences. Getting no response, Luciano decided he would get his own writer and produce his own movie. While waiting for the writer at the airport in Naples, Luciano suffered a fatal heart attack. The movie was never made.

In a book written shortly before he died, Luciano also claimed that he and his associates were responsible for setting the fire that destroyed the Normandie. This was to give notice to the American authorities of just how important a personage they would be dealing with. This claim has never been substantiated.

To this day the Pentagon and Office of Naval Intelligence deny any knowledge of a deal being made with Meyer Lansky or Charles Lucky Luciano during World War II. J. Edgar Hoover claimed there was no such thing as a Mafia in America, so it certainly could not have happened. What cannot be denied however is that the invasion of the island of Sicily, code named "Husky," launched the beginning of the Italian campaign on July 10, 1943. Furthermore it cannot be denied that the Allied troops met little opposition during the amphibious landings, and that the Sicilian invasion eventually led to Italy's surrender. It will never be known how many American lives were saved by the preparations made prior to invading Sicily.

State of Terror

From the beginning of Hitler's ascension to power in 1933, he intended to identify and persecute groups of people he considered to be undesirable or racially inferior. Hitler's ultimate goal was to first isolate and then destroy for all time those "untermenshen," Slavs, Jews, Gypsies and Asocial Germans, groups he described as people unworthy of living.

In March of 1933 the first concentration camp was established in Bavaria to imprison those people branded as enemies of the state. For their own safety, the people of Germany were told, these unworthy people had to be placed in "Protective Custody" to save them from the wrath of the German people. The camp was built on the grounds of an old munitions factory from World War I, approximately 10 miles northwest of Munich, in the heart of the province where Nazism was born (Bavaria). The first prisoners were political dissidents of any party that disagreed with Hitler's policies. Communists, Socialists, Social Democrats. Masons and Jehovah's Witnesses were mixed in with so called racially dangerous groups. Citizens with mental or physical diseases were imprisoned as well.

In order to devise the most efficient methods of achieving Hitler's aims, German doctors and scientists applied their "cleansing methods" to the physically deformed, the mentally disturbed and the intellectually handicapped. Under the guise of the Law for the Protection of Hereditary Health, "mercy-killings" became the accepted method of exterminating people said to be biologically inferior. Hadamar became one of the first of these extermination centers to be inaugurated under what came to be known as the Euthanasia Program. Hitler promoted the program as a stimulus to national health and the racial integrity of the German people. As the war progressed Hitler showed less and less restraint in using extermination methods to do away with "undesirables."

The German public was bombarded with a propaganda barrage aimed at convincing the population that they were being forced to carry an unnecessary economic burden by allowing these "types" to remain among them. The Law for the Prevention of Progeny with Hereditary Diseases was passed so that sterilization became mandatory for all persons suffering from mental illness, retardation, physical deformity, epilepsy, blindness, deafness or severe alcoholism. The first step was to gain public acceptance for keeping these individuals from having children. The sterilization program began in January 1934. It is estimated that 300,000 to 400,000 sterilizations were carried out in the hospitals and mental institutions before Step Two was introduced. This inaugurated the era of indoctrinating school children and adults into the Nazi way of thinking. In schools and movie houses, the German people were shown stereotypes of racially inferior types of people usually grouped together with rats and rodents.

At the same time, Hitler's scientists devised methods of identifying racially superior, or perfect Germans, with blue eyes, blonde hair and superior bodies. These "Aryans" were glorified in films, books and schools. It took only a short time for the law abiding German people to identify, respect and salute the superior modes and to discriminate and persecute those groups thought to be inferior.

When the German government began exterminating the "inferiors," there was little opposition, for by then the people had accepted the concept of isolating and destroying inferiors for the good of the greater German people. Ever law abiding, they enthusiastically participated in the program without dissent. All Germans now stood with outstretched arms, swearing allegiance, not to the German Reich, but to their Fuehrer, Adolf Hitler. The extermination program could now proceed without any fear of opposition.

The beginning of the state of terror.

In the Beginning

The great American writer William Faulkner is often quoted for his description of the past. "The past," he wrote, "is not dead. It's not even past." World War II and the Holocaust confirm Faulkner's perception. Sixty years after the events took place they are still discussed as if they were happening today. To those who lived through the era, to their children and grandchildren, memorable events took place during the years of 1933 to 1945 that are neither forgotten nor dead. The concentration camps of Nazi Germany aptly fit into this category.

Adolf Hitler assumed the role of Chancellor of Germany on January 30, 1933. Knowing the character of the German people well, he and his henchmen wasted little time in passing new legislation and amending the old Constitution. Hitler knew that the German populace would accept these changes readily.

On February 28, one month after taking office, Legal Bulletin #17 was proclaimed. Reich Bulletin #17 invalidated Articles 114, 115, 117, 118, 123, 124 and 153 of the German Constitution and specified the implementation of restrictions on the freedom of individual rights. Among the rights now restricted were:

Freedom of the Press	The Right to Assembly
The Right to Free Speech	The Right to Form Groups

No longer permitted were secrecy of the post office, telegraph, or telephone communication. House searches by police would be legal. Confiscation and limitation of property ownership would now be permissible. Those who endangered human life in opposition to police direction would be sentenced to penal servitude. Violation of any of the new laws could result in being sent to a concentration camp.

The camps were all the same. The camps were all different. Built to fit the prototype of the first concentration camp, Dachau, each acquired its own individual character depending on the commandant of the camp.

The concentration camp era in Germany began in March 1933, three months after Hitler was elected as Chancellor of Germany. In February 1933, Hitler issued a decree of the President of the Reich for the protection of the country's loyal citizens. This decree gave the authorities permission to imprison all political rivals without judicial sentence for an undefined period of time.

Two weeks later, the Reichstag in Berlin burned to the ground. Before the blaze was fully extinguished, a Nazi spokesman announced to the world that Communists had set fire to the German Parliament building and would face immediate arrest. They would be placed in "protective custody" for their own good.

Social Democrats and union members were arrested under the same justification, as were any other political dissidents who had disagreed with Hitler and the Nazi agenda. Citing Hitler's "decree," the authorities then proceeded to arrest all political opponents and churchmen who offered any opposition to the new, legally elected government. The problem then became where to put all those arrested under the guise of "protective custody."

In the southern German province of Bavaria, the birthplace of Nazism, Heinrich Himmler was the leader of the SS. In his haste to carry out Hitler's edict, thousands of protective detainees were arrested with no thought as to how many jails were needed to accommodate them. On March 22, 1933, the problem was solved. Barbed wire fences were erected around a former ammunition factory in the village of Dachau. This became the home of the "protective custody" prisoners and the first concentration camp in Germany. Fifty-four policemen from the nearby city of Munich were charged with guarding the prisoners in Dachau.

Newspapers throughout Germany carried the story of the new policy of "protective custody," but little attention was given to the announcement by the rest of the world. The Jewish Central Association in Germany issued a statement saying, "We do not believe our German fellow-citizens will let themselves be carried away into committing excesses against the Jews." The Jewish Central Association was guilty of wishful thinking. Silently they hoped the Nazis would not carry out their often-stated policies against the Jews. In many cities, a boycott against Jewish businesses had already begun, and the Jews were included in the campaign of violence against Socialists, Communists and other Nazi opponents.

In New York City, less than a week after Dachau opened its gates, a meeting of American Jewish organizations took place in Madison Square Garden. The American Jewish War Veterans were calling for a worldwide boycott of German products. Some of the representatives who attended this meeting called for restraint. However, Rabbi Stephen S. Wise, president of the American Jewish Congress, counseled, "The time for prudence and caution is past. We must speak up like men. How can we ask our Christian friends to lift their voices in protest against the wrongs suffered by Jews if we keep silent? What is happening in Germany today may happen tomorrow in any other land on earth unless it is challenged and rebuked. It is not the *German* Jews who are being attacked. It is the Jews."

On March 27, 1933, all Jewish organizations in America held simultaneous protest rallies in New York, Chicago, Boston, Philadelphia, Baltimore, Cleveland, St. Louis and 70 other locations throughout the country. Former New York Governor Al Smith and several Christian clergymen called for an immediate cessation of the brutal treatment being given to German Jewry. Rabbi Abba Hillel Silver, in a voice that rolled like thunder over his audience, called for an immediate boycott of German products. His voice shook with rage as he spoke of the atrocities taking place in Germany and those that would surely follow if Hitler were not stopped then.

On April 1, 1933, German propaganda minister Goebbels announced that all good Aryan Germans must immediately boycott all Jewish-owned businesses. Moreover, he threatened the annihilation of German Jewry if American Jews continued their boycott of German products. To underscore his threats, Jewish-owned stores had their windows smashed by SS troops as they tossed in foul-smelling chemicals, driving the customers into the streets where they were beaten by other SS men, standing by to administer punishment to the unfortunate customers. Urged by Jewish organizations to protest, the American government issued a statement delivered by Secretary of State Cordell Hull. "Unfortunately, incidents have indeed occurred, and the whole world joins in regretting them; however, the reports of anti-Jewish violence were probably exaggerated."

During the early thirties, although unknown to Secretary of State Hull or anyone else in the American government, German espionage agents were being placed in vital manufacturing plants throughout America. Shipyards, aircraft factories, chemical plants, automotive facilities and utility operations were prime targets for these long-term undercover agents. Hitler, in 1933, did not know when these espionage agents would be called upon to commit their acts of sabotage against America, but he was certain that at some point in the future Germany and

America would become antagonists. What was known for sure was that in less than three months after gaining power, Hitler had effectually eliminated the civil rights of all German citizens. This was the beginning of the catastrophe that was to affect not only Germany, but the entire civilized world.

On Sunday December 7, 1941, Japan carried out its treacherous attack upon the United States at Pearl Harbor. A day later President Roosevelt addressed the American Congress:

"Yesterday, December 7, 1941 – a date which will live in infamy –the United States of America was suddenly and deliberately attacked by naval and air forces of the Empire of Japan. I believe I interpret the will of the Congress and of the people when I assert that we will not only defend ourselves to the uttermost, but will make very certain that this form of treachery will never endanger us again. Hostilities exist. There is no blinking at the fact that our people, our territory and our interests are in grave danger. With confidence in our Armed Forces – with unbounded determination of our people – we will gain the inevitable triumph. So help us God. I ask that Congress declare that since the unprovoked and dastardly attack by Japan on Sunday, December 7th, a state of war has existed between the United States and the Japanese Empire."

On December 9, 1941, Germany declared war on the United States.

Oradour-sur-Glane

A rusty old bicycle lies at the side of the road; next to it, the charred wreckage of a baby carriage leans against a broken, blackened bed frame. An old, barely readable signpost tells strangers they are looking at the monument of "Oradour-sur-Glane." A monument of skeleton-like buildings, it has been left as a memorial to the 642 men, women and children who were burnt and slaughtered in their French village, Oradour-sur-Glane, by German troops the week of the invasion of Europe in June, 1944.

Two hundred seven children, two hundred forty five women and one hundred ninety men were murdered and their village set ablaze on June 10, 1944, four days after the Allied armies stormed ashore on the beaches of Normandy. Suspected of helping resistance fighters, the Germans marched the villagers into the village church, which was then set on fire. Anyone trying to escape was shot by machine gunners who surrounded the grisly scene.

French historians, with newly released archival records, now claim that it was all a tragic mistake. The Germans had intended to attack the nearby village of Oradour-sur-Vayes that had been a stronghold of resistance fighters in the past. Oradour-sur-Glane was burnt to the ground in error.

By order of Charles de Gaulle, President of France, the skeleton of the village was left as the Germans left it, serving as a memorial to the suffering of all the people of France under the German occupation.

Sixty years later, in June 2004, a French teacher, Vincent Reynouard, 33 years of age, was sentenced to two years in jail and banned from teaching in France. Reynouard had produced a film entitled "The Tragedy of Oradour-sur-Glane." In the film, Reynouard claimed the massacre never happened, and that if it did, the villagers themselves were to blame for helping the Resistance. Reynouard also wrote a revisionist book in which he questioned German guilt for what had taken place in the village. The book was entitled "The Oradour Massacre: A Half Century of Theatre." The appeals court that turned down Reynouard's appeal said that his views insulted the memory of those who had been massacred.

The tragedy that took place at Oradour-sur-Glane was not unique. Many villages in Russia, Poland and Czechoslovakia unfortunately suffered the same fate. On June 10, 1942, two years to the day before the Oradour-sur-Glane massacre, the village of Lidice in Czechoslovakia disappeared from this earth. All of the residents of the village were slaughtered with the exception of 90 children who were dispersed through Germany to be renamed and raised as German children. When the massacre and deportations were completed the SS leveled the entire area.

In Russia, some 70,000 towns and villages were obliterated by the Germans. In Poland, more than 200,000 children were taken to be screened, and when found to be "racially pure" were deported to Germany where they were adopted and raised as Germans. Approximately 20,000 of these Polish children were traced after the war and returned to Poland. The massacres that took place at Lidice and at Oradour-sur-Glane were repeated in almost every country dominated by the Germans before they were finally defeated.

Violins

On June 1, 1944 a coded message was broadcast by British Broadcasting to French resistance fighters in France. It was standard operating procedure for the British to send hundreds of messages over the open airwaves alerting the resistance as to the status of the war, where certain ammunition and supply drops would be made, and the most important message of all, when the invasion of the Allied Forces would begin.

The Germans were well aware that the messages were being sent. Hundreds of communication specialists worked around the clock desperately trying to decipher the meaning of groups of words which by themselves meant nothing. Everyone knew that an invasion was imminent. Knowing where and when it would come could mean the difference between victory or ultimate defeat. The Germans recorded every word coming over the airwaves. Only the French knew which particular message would be *the* one that would finally unleash them after three years of German occupation.

Mixed in with hundreds of words which meant nothing, the French listeners could hardly believe their ears when the words from a nineteenth century French poem came out of their radio receiver. "The long sobs of the violins of autumn." They immediately sprang into action, knowing that this was only the first part of the message they had been waiting for. They were aware that their organizations had been penetrated by hundreds of French collaborators who would gamble everything in order to give the Germans the date of the invasion.

"The long sobs of the violins of autumn" was part of the most important message resistance fighters would ever hope to hear. Keyed up, they now awaited the second part, which, by arrangement understood by all, should come within a 48 hour period. At precisely 10pm on June 5th, the anxious listeners heard the last half of the message... "wound my heart with a monotonous languor." The last half of the message was now clear. D-Day, the invasion by Allied forces, would begin in the early hours of June 6, 1944.

That date would go down in history and be part of the memory of all who participated in the momentous effort by the Allies to get a foothold on European soil. The French rejoiced that their forced inaction against the German forces had come to an end. The long awaited invasion of Europe was about to begin.

A prayer service aboard ship on the way to Normandy for D-Day.

Telephone Red Sash

On D-Day, June 6, 1944, the American 4th Infantry Division landed at Utah Beach in Normandy. Although an Infantry Division is composed of more than 15,000 soldiers, few of the Americans were aware of the six Native Americans who were busily talking over walkie-talkies as infantrymen encountered some of the heaviest fighting in World War II. Two Comanche code talkers were assigned to each of the three regiments with the 4th Infantry Division. The first message sent out on June 6th was, "Five miles to the right of designated area. Five miles inland. The fighting is fierce and we need help." Sent to the Naval forces shelling enemy forces, the message meant, "We are here – shoot somewhere else."

The Comanche code talkers on Utah Beach were part of a group of seventeen who were trained in code talking by Lieutenant Hugh Foster, Jr. Given the assignment by the Army Signal Corps, Foster recruited seventeen Comanche volunteers to learn a military code he had created to be used with Native American words. Although a dozen other Indian tribes partic-ipated in "code talking," only the Comanches, in Europe, and the Navajos, in the Pacific, went through intensive periods of training. Using harmless words, like sewing machines, turtles, stovepipes, the Comanches were describing machine guns, tanks and bazookas. Similarly, a pregnant plane indicated a bomber. The record of messages sent by the Comanche code talkers was impeccable. Unfamiliar words were sent out word by word, or when necessary, letter by letter. There were no mistakes.

Code talk training was so secret that few in the Army knew of the unit's existence. Moreover, during actual combat, infantrymen were too busy to think about the elements put together by the Army that aided in their successful operations.

Hugh F. Foster, Jr. retired in 1975 as Commanding General of the Army's Electronics Command. Honored by the Comanches he had trained, he was called "Telephone Red Sash" – referring to the red sash Army officers wore in the 1800's. Foster was made an honorary member of the Comanche tribe.

When the Comanches mentioned "Posah-tai-wo" to each other, they were saying "Crazy white man" – the code name for Adolf Hitler.

Major General Hugh F. Foster, Jr. developed the codes used by the Comanche code talkers.

Ritchie Boys

The story is told about a paratrooper outfit that was set to jump over Normandy one day before D-Day, June 6, 1944.

As the first man was about to jump from the plane, he whispered to the Sergeant standing behind him, "You know, I've never jumped before!" As the Sergeant prepared to push the GI from the plane, he whispered back, "It's tradition; the new guys always go first," then quickly added, "You Ritchie Boys can do anything. Think how much experience you'll have under your belt for the next one. Go!!"

The Sergeant was only half kidding. The Ritchie Boys had what were generally considered to be abrasive attitudes. The group of young GIs, referred to as "Ritchie Boys," was made up of German Jewish refugee teenagers who had been lucky enough to escape from Nazi Germany in the years prior to the beginning of the war. As the Allies advanced into the heartland of Europe after D-Day, these youngsters, each of whom had received special training at Fort Ritchie, Maryland, became a vital link to Allied Intelligence. They helped to acquire and evaluate information received from German servicemen as well as from civilians as the Allies advanced across Europe.

Thanks to the American decision to train "these valuable assets" in psychological warfare, methods of interrogation of prisoners, writing and editing anti-Nazi propaganda leaflets, radio broadcasting to the enemy in their native language and the internal methods utilized by the Wehrmacht and SS in their everyday activities, the group of Ritchie Boys made their presence and value to the Allied cause known from the first instant the Allies landed on European soil.

Often riding in GI trucks with loudspeakers pointed at enemy lines, the Ritchie Boys were able to persuade untold numbers of German soldiers to surrender. This tactic worked well until the Battle of the Bulge when American troops were warned of masquerading Germans in American uniforms. Unfortunately the accents of the Ritchie Boys were exactly the same as the German infiltrators. The Ritchie Boys over-came this danger to their lives by stationing themselves at outposts with men they had known before the Battle of the Bulge broke out.

There were several instances when the German speaking Americans warned higher-level intelligence that a major thrust from the Germans should be expected in mid-December. However, Allied Intelligence had been lulled into complacency and disregarded the warnings of imminent danger. On the morning of December 16, 1944, 2,000 German artillery pieces opened up on the unprepared American lines. The greatest bat-tle of World War II had begun at precisely the weakest seam in the American lines. The Germans penetrated exactly where America's most inexperienced troops were positioned. Before the battle ended, Allied troops suffered 80,000 casualties.

Book Two

"Those who can't remember the past are condemned to repeat it."

George Santayana

Bourgeois

The basic weapon of the U.S. Army has always been the individual infantry soldier with his rifle. He is the ultimate weapon. After all the bombing, after all the artillery, after all the light and heavy mortars have done their devastation, the infantryman is still the one who has to go in, under withering machine gun fire, to occupy the fought over territory. The entire structure of the Armed Forces is designed to support the infantryman in accomplishing his mission.

During lulls in fighting while squad members were cleaning their weapons, they would often talk about the hardships of infantrymen. Maybe the griping made them feel better. Maybe men needed to build up their confidence for the next time things got hot and heavy. Either way the "infantry talk" came up time after time in bull sessions. Invariably one of the squad members would disagree with the facts as presented.

"If a squad is made up of 12 men, how come we've got only 8 guys? How come?" Or, "If the authorized strength of a platoon is 41, how come we've got only 30 in ours?" Or, "If a Rifle Company has an authorized strength of 193, how come we've got only 150?"

No amount of explaining about casualties could convince the "doubter" in "I" Company, 3rd Battalion of the 157th Regiment of the 45th Infantry Division. The "doubter" was nicknamed "Bushwah." It is uncertain how many in the company knew his real name. The only thing that was certain was that at the tail end of any talk or discussion he would add his inevitable comment, "Bushwah!!!" A kid who had gone to college for a year before being called up, once tried to make sense of the comment by asking, "Do you mean 'Bourgeois'?" to which he got a quick grunt of a reply, "That's what I said, 'Bushwah'."

In 1918 American soldiers fighting in France picked up the word "bourgeois." To the French this was a derogatory term that originated during the French Revolution and described the hated ruling class. The Americans adopted the word and used it to mean "baloney" or "bull." Back home, after the war, "Bushwah" was heard frequently. The youngsters who used it were unaware that they were speaking French when they announced their disbelief in what had just been said. "Bushwah" said it all.

As the Captain assembled the company to give them a final pep talk before the assault on Munich was to begin, he ended with words of caution about the citizens of Bavaria and the fact that Munich was the gateway to Austria and Hitler's Eagles Nest.

"Wouldn't it be great if we were the ones to capture Adolf Hitler? Let's go men! Let's go get him!"

The loud whisper was heard by every member of the company, although not one head turned to see who the whisperer was. Only one word was uttered, "Bushwah."

Kilroy

During World War II, a name emerged among the troops, no matter where they were, which brought a smile to almost everyone's face. No one knows where "he" originally came from. There are hundreds of stories claiming to know the origin of "Kilroy," but only one thing is sure. No matter how or where he originated, "Kilroy" became a part of every GI. He took part in every encounter, in every occupation, in every training camp, in every country Americans encamped. He was in every factory, every shipyard and every airport that worked in the American war effort. "Kilroy" was as American as any American imaginable. And he was everywhere any American had ever been, and what is even more important, he was there first!

Of the many hundreds of stories about "Kilroy was here," one of the most accepted was about James A. Kilroy, a shipyard inspector in World War II. Kilroy put his mark of approval on sections of hundreds of ships before they left the shipyards. GIs and sailors liked the graffiti and, as a joke, started writing "Kilroy was here first" on anything they came in contact with. If anyone asked about the symbol or the writing the GIs would swear it had been there when they arrived. The idea was accepted unconditionally by GIs all over the world, and always brought smiles to newly arrived personnel who were inevitably greeted with "Kilroy was here first."

One of the best "Kilroy" stories took place during the post war conference between Truman, Churchill and Stalin in Potsdam, Germany. As the President of the United States, the

Prime Minister of England and the Soviet Premier discussed the post war future of the world, Stalin excused himself to attend to a personal matter. A new restroom had been built for the exclusive use of the three heads of state. The first one to use the new facility was Stalin. Emerging from the restroom, Stalin whispered to his aide, "Who is this Kilroy?"

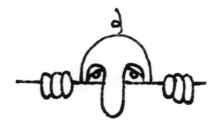

KILROY WAS HERE - FIRST

Kilroy drawing: Joe Giulie

Badges worn by some of the 32 different categories of prisoners in Dachau Concentration Camp, Germany (1933-1945).

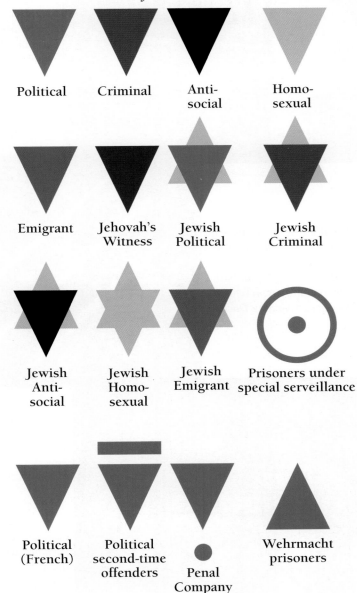

Political   Criminal   Anti-social   Homo-sexual

Emigrant   Jehovah's Witness   Jewish Political   Jewish Criminal

Jewish Anti-social   Jewish Homo-sexual   Jewish Emigrant   Prisoners under special serveillance

Political (French)   Political second-time offenders   Penal Company   Wehrmacht prisoners

The author at Dachau, April, 1995 (fiftieth anniversary of liberation). The sign points to the Dachau Memorial Museum.

The author at the award winning Dachau Monument created by Abraham Borenstein of Kibbutz Ein Hashlosha, Israel. The sculpture represents the fences surrounding Dachau.

Main gate at Dachau; "Arbeit Macht Frei" means Work Makes One Free.

Curtis Whiteway, infantry squad sergeant, in Germany for the 50th anniver-sary of liberation.

The author researching material for this book.

Barbara Distel, Director of the Dachau Memorial Museum.

General Felix E. Sparks with the author, 1993.

The Bulge

Part I

The formal name for the area was simply "Replacement Depot," but in the language of GIs it quickly became "Repple Depple." Thousands and thousands of newly trained recruits shipped to Europe waited in the Repple Depple tents until their names appeared on a shipping list. They then discovered which outfit they were being assigned to and where in the European Theatre of Operations they would serve. Shortly after arrival, by ones, twos and threes they picked up their duffel bags and disappeared, to be replaced by another recently arrived group of raw recruits.

Repple Depple areas all looked the same. The rows of tents stretched for miles and miles in every direction. Only the names of the camps were different. In the Le Havre area of France the names were "Lucky Strike," "Phillip Morris" and "Chesterfield." During the few days the new recruits remained there, they passed on the latest rumors about how the war was going, where they were headed and what kind of an outfit they would join.

Combat veterans stationed in other areas of the vast complexes would make their way to the tents of the new recruits to tell them stories of what combat was really like, while at the same time trying to sell the newcomers German war booty of every description. Usually these were items of little value that the replacements "had to have."

Few friendships were made among the men. Each one was too deeply involved with his own thoughts and fears about the future. Few, if any, realized that while the German army replaced whole units at one time, the American system was to send in one or two men at a time. Within a short time, especially at the time of the Bulge, the replacements would generally end up on the casualty lists, before learning even the basic fundamentals of what real combat was all about.

Most new recruits felt isolated after joining a squad. Veteran infantrymen looked upon the new men as untrained, untried, awkward kids who were being sent up to the front to fill in empty spaces that would soon, more likely than not, have to be refilled by yet another green recruit. The older veterans at the front often did not know the name of the new recruits or where they came from before they became casualties and, once again, had to be replaced. Experience had taught the veteran infantrymen not to get emotionally involved with the newcomers since it was most likely they wouldn't be around that long and the better they knew them the harder it was when they got hit.

The casualty rate among replacements was extremely high. They simply did not have time to learn the necessary skills needed to stay alive on the front lines. Where they were being sent, the front line was everywhere. Men who had survived thus far were deeply involved in seeing that they continued to survive until the damned war came to an end. They had little time or interest in teaching survival skills to new men who, in all probability, would soon become casualities.

While waiting in the Repple Depple, each recruit felt like an individual piece in a game of chess, a game in which he did not know the rules. Isolated from the other chess pieces, he was completely on his own while he waited for someone, someplace, to move him somewhere else. One thing was for sure, he had no choice or voice in the matter. He didn't even know how long the wait would be as he sat alone and apprehensive among the thousands of others in the same situation.

The longer the men waited, the more they wanted to move on to whatever lay in store for them. For the infantrymen, that meant into combat, into whatever unknown terrors lay ahead. The urge to move on, to get it over with was very strong. Even the unknown was better than sitting and waiting for what seemed an endless amount of time.

At night, to cover their feelings of fright and anticipation, the younger GIs would call out to no one in particular, "Let's get these men out of the hot sun – let's move it!!" This would be followed by nervous laughter from many tents as the young men tried to hide their anxiety and feelings of being totally alone. One youngster expressed his feelings by saying he felt like one of the cigarettes in a pack. Slowly the other cigarettes disappeared. Eventually, he knew his turn would come, and then he too would go up in smoke. As he lay on his cot in the huge Repple Depple tent, he wondered if that was the reason the army had named all these places with cigarette names.

On December 1, 1944, the 106th Infantry Division arrived in Europe. Trained in the states, they had been sent over as a unit. Known as the "Golden Lions," the division was sent to a region on the Belgium-Luxembourg border to replace the combat-experienced 2nd Division. The section of the front that the 106th was responsible for stretched 21 miles in length, while the entire front facing the Germans encompassed an area 80 miles in length.

The men of the 106th, now in Europe a total of 10 days, had no idea that a division under combat conditions, facing the enemy, was normally given an area 5 miles long to guard. However, this particular zone was classified as a rest and rehabilitation area where new recruits could get used to hearing the sounds of battle and get some combat experience by being sent out on relatively safe patrols. Officers in charge felt the area was a quiet one, suitable for training men who had never experienced real combat conditions. The 106th Division dug in around the village of St. Vith awaiting their baptism of fire. The forest where they crouched down in their foxholes facing the Germans was known as The Ardennes.

The men of the "Golden Lions" Division were American youngsters averaging 22 years of age. They were among the youngest American infantrymen in the European Theatre of Operations facing the German army. Less than six months before they had been civilians working in gas stations, soda fountains and local markets. They had been carpenters, plumbers, bus drivers and high school students. They had been ordinary American citizens. Now they crouched in the mud awaiting they knew not what.

Three times in the past, German armies had successfully advanced through the Ardennes to capture the important Belgium port of Antwerp. In September, 1944, Hitler was informed that this area was thinly held, and that there was a seam or junction between the American and British forces precisely in the area where German forces had successfully attacked in 1870, 1914 and again in 1940. Hitler envisioned another Dunkirk-like defeat, one that would be so great that the Americans would be forced out of the war. Dunkirk, when France fell in 1940, had been such a defeat. Only a miracle had helped the British Expeditionary Forces escape to England.

The overall code name "Watch on the Rhine" was adopted by the Germans to hide the true purpose of the attack from the spying Allies. In the northern sector the Germans would go up against the American 99th Division. The center and weakest part of the line would be defended by the newly arrived 106th Division. In the south, elements of Patton's Third Army would come into contact with the German 150th Panzer Brigade.

Secrecy became the key ingredient of Operation Grief, which had as its ultimate goal the capture of General Eisenhower.

At 5:00am on the morning of the 16th of December, 1944, the Germans began their artillery barrage. Two thousand artillery pieces flung salvo after salvo onto the unsuspecting American lines. Centered at precisely that area guarded by the 106th Division, the German tank battalions broke through the American lines in force. Well-trained veteran German fighting units completely overran the over stretched American forces. Along an 80-mile front the American troops fell back. The 106th Division, in the center of the line was completely over-run. The three German armies using the skills and experience they had gained in 5 years of fighting the Poles, French, British and Russians quickly broke through the American front lines. The American replacement troops were unable to contain the massive blow the Germans had thrown at them. Taken completely by surprise by "Watch on the Rhine," the Americans retreated along the entire 80-mile front. Before the battle ended in January, 1945, one million men had been involved.

Historians would later refer to the biggest battle of World War II as "The Battle of the Bulge" wherein the Germans suffered 100,000 casualties killed, wounded or captured, with the Americans losing 81,000 men killed, wounded or captured. The 106th Division, at the very center of the breakthrough, was decimated on the first day of battle and ceased to exist as a military unit from then on.

As the Commanding General of the 106th Infantry Division received the battle reports in the afternoon of the 16th of December, the magnitude of the German breakthrough began to sink in. The General's eyes misted as barely audible words formed on his lips. Those standing closest to him thought they heard him mumbling over and over, "I've lost my entire division in one day."

Part II

Shocked by the strength of the German onslaught, the American GIs retreated, trying to hold the enemy off until more American reserves could be brought forward. The retreating newcomers were forced to leave the deep and well fortified fox-holes that had been prepared previously by the 2nd Division men. Decimated squads, platoons and companies tried desperately to hold out until more replacements arrived. Often in a state of shock, never understanding what was happening all around them, the GIs crouched on the frozen ground under the trees, as the German artillery hit the branches above them and sent murderous, stiletto sharp shafts and razor sharp splinters into their unsuspecting bodies.

At night they were terrified because they couldn't see more than a few feet from their foxholes. By day, the fog rolled in and it rained or snowed, making visibility again impossible. The coldest European winter in 50 years made their conditions even worse. Dressed in inadequate clothing and shoes, they froze on the muddy ground as they tried desperately to keep their eyes open. They quickly learned that their shallow foxholes offered little or no defense against the German 88's that were zeroed in on them.

Placing their arms around tree trunks offered the best solu-tion to avoiding the knife like projectiles that rained down from above, killing many of them before they learned how to cope with the situation. Unable to use their trenching tools in the frozen ground to dig deeper holes, they used grenades and explosives to help soften the earth, often without visible signs of success. Suffering from frozen toes, frozen fingers, despair, rage and confusion, often without officer leadership, the men followed anyone who was capable of taking decisive actions. In tiny, small groups the men fought back and held. For fifty years after the Battle of the Bulge, historians would be heard to ask,

"Where did we get such men?"

Nineteen thousand GIs paid with their lives for their heroism in the Ardennes. Thirty nine thousand Americans were wounded during the Battle of the Bulge. The twenty three thousand Americans who were captured during the Bulge were marched to prisoner of war camps in Germany. Infantrymen and tank crews that survived fired until their ammunition ran out, then used captured enemy equipment and supplies until American reinforcements came up in quantity. As the shells dropped around them, soaking the white snow with deep red American blood, the earth shook and rumbled as individual heroes encouraged others to stand, hold and go forward.

As the weather gradually cleared, Air Force planes were able to drop desperately needed supplies to the Allied fighting men. In addition, fresh replacements were thrown into the battle. When the scope of the German breakthrough was analyzed, it became evident that the Allies had to achieve three major objectives. First, by December 27th, 634 enemy aircraft were destroyed, versus 292 Allied planes. The second objective was to isolate the battlefield by destroying the enemy's supply lines without knocking out the bridges over the Rhine River. Five targeted railroad bridges had been destroyed, three damaged beyond possible use, and one identified as damaged. The third objective was the destruction of the German army on the ground. More than 600 enemy tanks and armored vehicles, 4,000 motor transport vehicles, 1,500 rail cars, 60 locomotives and 399 gun positions were knocked out of action in the first two weeks of fighting in the Bulge. Since most of these losses took place at the tip of the German thrust, Hitler's attempt at a breakthrough had been blunted and contained. What was left of three defeated German armies limped back towards Germany. Allied commanders had turned defeat into victory.

Part III

At the crossroads where five roads intersected, named "Five Points" by the GIs, German tanks suddenly came upon a group of 140 Americans from the 295th Field Artillery Observation Battalion. The American prisoners were lined up in the field and two German machine guns mounted on tanks began firing at them. At the sound of the first shots, the Americans scattered in all directions, most of them heading for the nearby woods. When the machine guns ceased firing, individual German soldiers walked among the bodies in the field firing their rifles at anyone still showing signs of life.

Eighty-six Americans were massacred at the crossroads. Forty-four men escaped and were able to make their way to the American lines. First Army Headquarters heard of the massacre at about 4:00 in the afternoon. Within hours, every American in the European Theatre of Operations was aware of what had taken place at Malmedy. When Hitler had ordered the offensive to begin, he specified that operations be carried out ruthlessly and without pity. His objective was to put fear into every American serviceman and to cause panic in the ranks.

However, the opposite occurred. The Malmedy Massacre, more than any other single event of the European war, acted as a catalyst which spurred the American infantrymen on to final victory.

Immediately after the war ended, American forces made an all out effort to locate the perpetrators of the Malmedy Massacre. The Germans were captured, tried at Dachau and proved guilty by William Denson, American Chief Prosecutor. In December, 1945, all were sentenced to be hung or long prison sentences.

By 1948, however, sympathy for the German soldiers convicted of war crimes began to build up in the American Midwest, an area populated by many immigrants who had come from Germany. Solicited by veteran and church groups from Germany, this group of Americans wanted leniency shown to the German soldiers. In a petition to the Supreme Court, Major Willis Everett alleged brutalities were committed against the German prisoners and that the trial itself was filled with irregularities. By 1949, several American newspapers became involved, as well as Senator Joseph McCarthy who was running for re-election in Wisconsin, a state with a large population of German-Americans. McCarthy complained that, while in jail, the German prisoners were not allowed to spend time "with their ministers or rabbis." After another review by the Secretary of the Army in 1949, the death sentences were commuted to imprisonment. Finally the case was brought before the Senate Armed Services Committee for further consideration. With McCarthy leading the attack, the Committee began to investigate a possible case against the U.S. Army.

The Committee went to Germany to investigate the allegations first hand. Returning to the states in September, after five months of investigation, the case was adjourned. As the years passed, all prisoners were released. The Cold War with Russia had come into being and the role played by the Germans in the Malmedy Massacre had shrunk in importance compared to the need for a change in attitude towards Germany and its well-trained army. The charges against the U.S. Army were eventually dropped.

Senator Joseph McCarthy went on to win worldwide television fame when he claimed he had evidence to show that hundreds of Communists were employed by the State Department and other governmental agencies. A famous quote from the Army-McCarthy Hearings came from Joseph Welsh who was the Defense Counsel for the Secretary of the Army. After McCarthy reneged on an agreement between the two attorneys,

Welsh sighed, "Sir, have you no sense of decency?" McCarthy died three years after he was censured by the United States Senate. He was 48 years of age at the time of his death which was brought on by complications of alcoholism. It was said of Senator Joe McCarthy that he was the most gifted demagogue ever bred in the United States.

The Battle of the Bulge took place during the coldest European winter in fifty years.

American antiaircraft gunners watch a dogfight during the Battle of the Bulge.

The Game of Life or Death

Part I

In October 1944, Generaloberst Jodl, Chief of the German Army Forces Operations Staff, summoned Lt. Col. Skorzeny to his office for a secret conference. Skorzeny, who was chief of the German Sabotage Service and SS Jagdverbaende, was shocked to find a third man at the conference. The third man was the Fuehrer, Adolf Hitler.

The three men bent over map tables discussing the coming German offensive in the Ardennes and emphasizing the need for secrecy, deception and the role Skorzeny and his sabotage specialists would play in the opening hours of the battle. This battle, code named "Watch on the Rhine," would be the greatest battle of World War II.

Otto Skorzeny's exploits were known to every German. Beginning his career as a member of Hitler's personal SS bodyguard regiment, he went on to fight as an SS officer in France, Belgium and the USSR. After studying British commando tactics and organizing a special operations unit in the Waffen SS to create havoc behind enemy lines, his importance among German military leaders grew. Skorzeny's greatest coup had been in rescuing Italian dictator, Benito Mussolini, from an impenetrable mountain prison, Gran Sasso, in 1943. Skorzeny described his exploit as "a mission impossible."

Following the July 20th plot against Hitler's life in 1944, Skorzeny virtually took control of the German Army. He not only helped guard the Ministry of War in Berlin, but was also deeply involved in finding evidence of the plot and capturing many of the military conspirators. Three months later, Hitler personally picked Skorzeny to head Operation Grief during the upcoming offensive in the Ardennes forest which would be known forever by historians as the "Battle of the Bulge." In time, Skorzeny would come to be known as "the most dangerous man in Europe."

Operation Grief, the infiltration of the American lines, was to begin in mid-December, 1944. Under cover of darkness, German troops dressed in American uniforms, and using American vehicles and equipment, were to create chaos among the American forces. In addition to vital bridges, other targets included radio stations, supply and ammunition dumps and the occupation of important road intersections.

Wearing American MP uniforms, the Germans were to pinpoint crucial road intersections to take over and control. By altering or removing road signs, the Germans could infiltrate and ambush the unsuspecting American troops. In addition to causing confusion, commanders of localized units were to use their discretion to create total havoc, mayhem and destruction behind the American lines. Codenamed "Condor," it was one of the best-kept German secret operations of the war.

Pleased with the plan and honored to be picked by the Fuehrer, Skorzeny's mind raced ahead with plans for securing the necessary specialized manpower and a training timetable that would allow him to carry out this monumental operation in the allotted time frame. Failure was unthinkable. Assured by Hitler that he would receive total support from the German military and Gestapo, Skorzeny proceeded in transforming the amalgam of thoughts and ideas about Operation Grief into reality. The target date was set for December 16, 1944. No one who was there would ever forget it.

Utilizing 2,500 English speaking German troops with special capabilities, Skorzeny organized the 150th Panzer Brigade, devised as the ultimate program of deception. Made up of volunteers from the German Army, Navy, Air Corp and SS, the men picked to serve in this ultra-secret unit had to possess several skills, most importantly, the ability to converse in English. They received special training in American dialect, military terminology, physical fitness, mental alertness and close combat fighting methods. Tapping into American telephone wires and the use of passwords were emphasized in the training sessions.

The candidates were tested for their English fluency and were told that they would be in a special training program, code named Operation Grief. The men assumed they would be used as interpreters as they entered the super secret area called Schloss Friedenthal. The best linguists in the group were selected for special training while the others were given general field training. The special linguists were assigned to work with Lt. Stielau, Commander of the group. Their unit was called Einheit Stielau (The Stielau Group).

Fifty of the most fluent of the volunteers were assigned to infiltrate Prisoner of War Camps where their objective was to mix with the American prisoners, familiarizing themselves with GI slang and American customs. These men observed how GIs opened a pack of cigarettes, how a knife and fork were utilized in the mess hall, how a GI placed a bath towel on his shoulder while washing and how cigarettes were lit. Special attention was paid to idioms and general, all-purpose expressions such as "shut up," and "damn it." The specialists were taught not to respond to German expressions or orders. They utilized U.S. Army manuals to learn military terminology, markings, unit designations and organizations. Special attention was paid to hand signals and movements under combat conditions. Night combat was simulated using anti-tank weapons and firing of captured U.S. equipment.

Once the German volunteers entered the training facilities, they were never allowed to leave the area. Secrecy was the most important element of the operation and the Germans utilized every method to protect it. The Germans were methodical in making their preparations for the breakout on December 16th. Those selected to act as American officers were issued identity cards with photographs and fingerprints. Drivers were issued American Army Driving Licenses and all carried facsimile dog tags. Uniforms, boots and dog tags were taken from prisoners of war or from packages innocently delivered by the American Red Cross. In addition, the disguised troops carried carbines or M-1's, rode in U.S. jeeps and weapon carriers and even utilized two captured Sherman tanks.

In the final preparation phase, the German troops were given the best foods available in Europe. Everything that could be done in the way of providing comforts for the men was done. However, no communication of any kind was permitted between the chosen troops and the outside world. Any member caught trying to subvert this order was imprisoned or, in some cases, executed. This order of secrecy was considered to be so important that all volunteers were required to sign a secrecy pledge which was to be in effect even after the war, under penalty of death. Those that refused to sign just disappeared.

For two weeks prior to December 16, 1944, no German patrols or radio messages had been sent out in the entire Ardennes area. These precautions severely disrupted American intelligence gathering.

The three major sources of Allied information about German plans had been the capturing of German prisoners, questioning civilians traveling through the area and listening to German radio messages. Now, all three sources were totally cut off. American Intelligence was effectively blocked from receiving vital information. Totally unaware, the Americans were taken by surprise on December 16th. After a barrage from 2,000 artillery pieces, three German armies overran the thinly manned American lines.

Advance German units, in small groups had been given the mission of destroying fuel dumps and bridges and changing directional signposts. Spreading confusion by misdirecting American units, these Germans, dressed as Americans, caused havoc among the legitimate American troops. In order to recognize their fellow Germans, captured American tanks had yellow triangles painted on the rear and artillery pieces were pointed at nine o'clock.

Germans dressed in American uniforms created confusion and chaos among the American troops. Most devastating of all were the German soldiers who had been brought up in America, spoke English as well as the GIs, and tapped into American communication lines. They then issued false instructions to the Americans who, in the beginning, were unaware of the infiltrators. The Germans were able to direct American troops into ambushes, had them withdrawn from vital areas by issuing orders supposedly from Allied headquarters, and in general were a serious obstacle to American officers trying to contain the German advance.

However, despite all German Intelligence precautions, a German officer was captured on December 16th by men of the 106th Infantry Division. Although orders concerning Operation Grief were to be transmitted only verbally, this officer was carrying written secret orders outlining the entire operational plan. American counter intelligence (CIC) quickly disseminated the captured plan to frontline units. Armed with this information, the Americans developed effective methods to identify and capture impostors. The discovery of the elaborate German plan, the effectiveness of the CIC and the fortitude of the American GIs resulted in a decisive Allied victory in the Battle of the Bulge.

Part II

Few people, other than military, were aware of the role played by the CIC in World War II. Created as a counterintelligence force in 1917, it was called the Corps of Intelligence Police (CIP). In September 1939, when Hitler invaded Poland, America's peacetime force of counter intelligence police had dwindled to a mere 16 men. While U.S. congressmen were debating conscription and whether or not we should be preparing to enter the conflict in Europe, the U.S. Secretary of War decreed that intelligence agents would not and could not intercept or read other nations' mail or telegraph traffic since "gentlemen did not read other gentlemen's mail." In spite of this naïve attitude, after Germany's attack on Poland in 1939, the number of intelligence agents began to increase.

When the first draftees started training, prior to Pearl Harbor in December 1941, they used broomsticks to simulate rifles, eggs instead of hand grenades and trucks, with hand painted signs, designated as tanks. By December 7, 1941, Congress had authorized the Corps of Intelligence Police (CIP) to attain a strength of 588 men. Immediately after Pearl Harbor in January 1942, the CIP name was changed to the Counter Intelligence Corps (CIC), with an authorized strength of 1,026 men. By VE Day (Victory in Europe, May 8, 1945), having proven their value many times over, CIC authorized strength had been increased to 7,500 men.

American counterintelligence agencies evolved slowly while Congress debated why, how and when the United States would become involved in World War II. Rivalries developed between Army, Navy and civilian agencies, such as the FBI, regarding which agency would be responsible within a specific area of jurisdiction. CIC activities were many and varied, bridging a gap from psychological warfare to capturing enemy plans and maps and placing agents in strategic locations in order to follow enemy troop movements and operations.

Recruiting reliable agents in Sicily, Italy, Belgium, Denmark and France had been relatively easy for American intelligence agencies. As the war progressed closer and closer to German borders, the task became increasingly more difficult. By this time, General "Wild Bill" Donovan had created and implemented the Office of Strategic Services (OSS) and the counter espionage mission in Europe involved the CIC, OSS, and a third entity, the Criminal Investigation Division.

Part III

As word spread among front line troops, there were many varied incidents of infiltrators being captured by ordinary GIs. An infiltrator who identified himself as belonging to C Company of the 394th Cavalry was advised to come forward, at which time he was immediately arrested and sent back to the CIC for interrogation. Cavalry units in the U.S. Army were not called "companies," but "troops," a fact of which the unfortunate infiltrator was obviously unaware.

Some of the Germans, wearing American enlisted men's uniforms, wore American pistols and carried carbines. They were immediately identified as impostors; the GIs knew that in the American Army only officers carried these weapons.

Another case involved a Lieutenant Colonel who had all the proper documentation. He claimed he was born in Chicago, Illinois.

"What is the capitol of Illinois?" the GI on guard asked.

"Why, Chicago, of course," came the Colonel's reply. He was immediately placed under arrest since the guard came from Springfield, Illinois and thought that someone who had reached the rank of Lt. Colonel should know his geography better.

Men assigned to outposts were extremely conscious of the danger from impostors and devised innovative methods of recognizing the Germans. Changing passwords after every challenge became necessary since the visibility was so bad the Germans could hear and observe everything that was taking place at the checkpoint.

"Who was Mickey's mate?"

"What is the Yankee Clipper?"

"Who is known as 'The Babe'?"

"I'm Bud Abbott – who are you?"

"Me Tarzan – who are you?"

"Who delivers fireside chats?"

"Where do the Dodgers play?"

"Who is Joe D?"

"Who was the last guy to hit 400?"

"What kind of car did Jack Benny drive?"

"Why is Walt Disney famous?"

"Who won the World Series last year?"

Each person who approached the American lines was asked a different question. Any slight hesitation in answering any of these questions or hundreds of others made up on the spot became a game of life or death. Stragglers who were not knowledgeable about baseball, comic strips or American radio shows were detained and turned over to CIC for further interrogation. In most cases, those who could not answer correctly were found to be members of Operation Grief.

Although captured members of Stielau Group told of plans

to kidnap the Allied Commander, Dwight D. Eisenhower, in Paris, they never got close enough to execute this part of their mission. Eighteen of the infiltrators were captured and executed as spies. The Commander of the 150th Panzer Brigade served a jail term and then escaped. He was then heard from in Spain where he helped many Nazis escape to the Middle East and South America. Unknown to Skorzeny and the Nazis controlling these "Rat Lines" of escape, the Germans had forced Jewish prisoners of the camps to forge passports and other documents. The records kept by those who survived later became vital when the Israelis began their campaign of identifying, tracing and plotting the elimination of Nazi war criminals.

Long after the Battle of the Bulge, the game of life or death became a standard part of relaxation for the men who had lived through the ordeal of The Bulge. One man would come up with a phrase or question that everyone knew or should have known the answer to.

"Who is Fala's master?"

"How many senators are from each state?"

"Who is the King of Swing?"

"Who is the King of Swat?"

"Who is the All American Boy?"

"Who is Johnnie calling for?"

Almost everyone knew the answers to the questions.

Even 60 years later when veterans got together, they would reminisce about the passwords and countersigns of life and death. Memories of the Battle of the Bulge stayed with the men for the rest of their lives.

Answers to Challenges

Mickey's mate...Minnie
Yankee Clipper..Joe DiMaggio
The Babe ....Babe Ruth
Bud Abbott ....Lou Costello
Me Tarzan ....You Jane
Fireside Chats ....Franklin D. Roosevelt
Joe D ....Joe DiMaggio
400 hitter ....Ted Williams
Jack Benny's car ....Maxwell
Walt Disney ....Mickey Mouse
Fala ....F.D.R.'s dog
Senators ....Two
King of Swing..Benny Goodman
King of Swat ....Babe Ruth
All American boy ....Jack Armstrong
Johnnie calling for ....Phillip Morris

What a Waste

The huge field was covered with 400 bodies, carcasses of 400 slaughtered horses.

The German Army depended heavily on the use of horses to pull their larger guns and artillery pieces. They, and the Russians, were still using methods dating back to World War I. In that war, horses were used extensively. It was inconceivable to the Germans that the 400 horses would not be a valuable resource for the Americans. Therefore, as the Americans rapidly advanced toward the German positions, the German Command gave the order to shoot all the horses.

GIs who came upon the scene were stunned. One was heard to whisper, "What a waste."

The "victorious" German Army in full retreat.

Fagedaboudit

It all happened in a flash. Literally. One minute guys were marching forward, up toward the front, and the next minute the soldier found himself in a foxhole with a badly injured GI he had never seen before. A medic was working on the wounded man. Some GIs continued forward, while others ran back to their own lines. The ones going forward were grabbing weapons, munitions and equipment from the GIs running away from the front. Words were not exchanged. The GIs going forward just grabbed whatever equipment they could lay their hands on to have something to fight with. Dazed, the young GI heard the medic saying, "Keep him talking – if he stops talking, we'll lose him. I've got to get some morphine. I'll be back as soon as I can, but for God's sake, don't let him stop talking!!" Then the medic was gone.

"Where you from, buddy?"

"Nebraska."

"No kidding, I never met anyone from Nebraska before. What do you do for fun in Nebraska?"

"Well, we've got cattle – lots of cattle. And we've got snow – lots of snow. Had fun in New York before we shipped out. Had one whole day in New York and that was fun."

"What did you do?"

"Well, we took a subway ride to that Coney Island. Had Nathan's hot dogs and they wouldn't let us pay for a thing.

When we reached for money to pay the man he just said 'Fagedaboudit', whatever that means. Then we went to this steeplechase place and rode all kinds of rides and things and no one would take any money from us. Then we went to that place in Brooklyn where they play baseball and a guy they said was a scalper came up to me and handed me a ticket. 'Box seat,' he said. 'Sojer, have yourself a good time'. You go into this gigantic sized room these people in Brooklyn called a 'rotunda' and then there were ramps leading to the field and when you went down the ramp it opened up on a huge baseball diamond and the grass was the greenest I ever saw and it looked like an emerald shining in the sun and the ball players were all dressed in white uniforms and the bases and home plate and everything were white and it was fantastic. People were all buying the soldiers hot dogs and pretzels and beer and when we went to pay the vendors they all said 'Fagedaboudit.'   There was a lot of yelling and shouting and cheering. You talk about fun, that was it."

"Then somebody said we should go into Manhattan and we rode the subway. But, before we got uptown, somebody else said we should go out to see 'The Lady' in the harbor. So we took the ferry out to the Statue of Liberty and we all climbed the steps to the very top in her crown where we could look out on the harbor and all of New York and New Jersey. And there were tears in our eyes.

Then we got back on the subway and ended up in this place called the Automat. You ever been there? It's a big room with walls made of glass blocks where you can look through and see the food back there and you stand and look and someone says, 'what would you like, soldier?' and they shove some nickels in a slot and out pops the food and nobody will take any money. Then you go over to this thing that looks like a cow's head and its got a lever like on a big slot machine and someone says, 'you want some coffee, soldier?' Just put your cup on the ledge and pull down on the lever,' and before you know it, your cup is filled and everyone around is smiling and someone asks if you want some doughnuts. And right then and there, they plop some coins into the glass wall and out pops two doughnuts. When I reached for some money to pay, a voice called out 'Fagedaboudit.'

"You ever been to Times Square, New York City? They call it the crossroads of the world. These three avenues, which they call Avenoos, come together at this place called Times Square. I mean these are big Avenoos, named Broadway, 42nd Street and 7th Avenoo. There's a skinny building there called the Times Building and it's got these lights going around flashing the news. Can you believe that? And people stand around in crowds reading the news from the Times Building lights."

"Then there are the theatre and movie houses like the Paramount and the Capitol. Movie houses bigger than anything you ever saw. Then there are hotels, too, like the Astor Hotel where there's a big old clock right outside the front door and all kinds of people meet right there at the clock in front of the Astor. Restaurants like you wouldn't believe are all over the place. One, called Lindy's made a kind of cheesecake. People came out with dishes piled high with pieces of cheesecake and gave samples to all the servicemen passing by. I never tasted anything like that Lindy's cheesecake.

You remember Jack Dempsey? The heavyweight champ? He's got a place there on Broadway, too. A man came out with a plate of spaghetti for me. I must have looked hungry or something. Boy, was that good spaghetti. Then we were standing near an Italian place where they made canollis. Did you ever taste a real Italian canolli? You think you're in Heaven or something.

Then a guy set up a little three-legged table right there on the sidewalk where we were standing. He started flipping these cards. Someone said it was a game called Three-Card-Monte. It looked easy. He showed you the two Queens and an Ace and then flipped them face down, daring anyone to guess which card was the Ace. It looked so easy. I had two dollars in my pocket. I bet the whole two dollars. The dealer, who had a hat on his head sort of gave me a wink, and with his eyes he told me which card to turn over. Would you believe it? I picked the Ace and the dealer smiled as he handed me four dollars. When the people standing around saw how easy it was to play this game they all started putting money on the table. They all wanted to guess which card was the Ace. I said to the man with the hat, 'Sir, I'd like to play this game again.' The man whispered to me, 'Fagedaboudit.' From that minute on, he flipped the cards so quickly no one else was able to guess which card was the Ace. Then as quickly as he had appeared he picked up his little table and moved on. As he walked by me he whispered, 'good luck, sojerboy.'

"Then some guys said they were going to the Empire State Building to see the view. We could see for miles in any direction and it was beautiful. And then someone said we could all go up to the Stage Door Canteen. You wouldn't believe it; there were movie stars and food and drinks and it was all free and it was fantastic. Real, live movie stars and they were serving us food and stuff and I wanna' tell you, there was nothing you couldn't order. We stayed there dancing and singing and kidding around 'til the place closed down. Then we got back on the subway that took us to the trucks waiting to take us back to camp. You talk about fun – that was some day."

Just then the medic jumped into the foxhole and jabbed the Nebraska man with a hypodermic needle. As the morphine took effect and the wounded soldier's eyes closed, his face relaxed into a big smile. The medic said, "Boy, you saved this man's life. He owes you plenty. How did you keep him talking so long?"

"No problem. He was just telling me what life was like in Nebraska."

Willie Peter

The squad was lost. In the woods the trees all looked alike.
No one knew for sure where they were, but they all had confidence that the Sergeant would figure out a way to get them back
to Allied lines.

"We're out of water, Sarge. Can we send someone back to
that little lake we passed, to fill some canteens?"

"Send the new man and tell him to be very quiet. These
woods are full of Germans."

The Sergeant did all kinds of things the men did not understand. Those W.P. grenades he always made them carry was a
case in point. No other squad in the company carried them.
Some of the other men even made fun of them. "Willie Peter
Boys," they mocked. But the Sergeant insisted they carry them
always, and carry them they did. New men coming on line were
always told about the W.P. grenade order. Although none of
them had ever been trained in their use in Infantry Basic, they
learned quickly that when this Sergeant gave an order it had
better be carried out.

Five minutes later, the Sergeant sent two men back to the
lake to make sure the new man hadn't run into any trouble. As
they reached the lake they heard voices. They knew immediately the new man had company. The voices they heard were
not speaking English. As they surveyed the situation, they too
were taken prisoner.

The Germans forced the three Americans to strip. Pointing

to the water, the Germans pushed the three GIs in until water covered their waists. Then, laughing, the Germans called out "tanz, tanz." As the Americans took a few steps the Germans began shooting into the water, obviously not trying to hit the Americans, but the shots were close enough to get the GIs moving in a comical dance step. Suddenly, a cloud of fog rose between the squad of Germans and the Americans in the water.

"Willie Peter – Willie Peter – take off, you guys!" a familiar voice rang out. The Americans needed no further explanation. They moved as the Germans, covered with smoke, were temporarily blinded. By the time the smoke lifted, the German squad knew they were surrounded. They gave up without a shot being fired. On that day the Germans learned about white phosphorus, the chemical the GIs commonly called "Willie Peter" or smoke.

The new man, while thanking the other squad members, said the smoke reminded him of crop dusters flying low over the fields while emitting chemicals. "Yeah," said one of the old timers as he finished tying up the German prisoners who kept muttering, "vas is dos Villie Peter?"

Most infantrymen carried one or two bandoliers which crisscrossed their bodies with extra ammunition; each bandolier contained 80 bullets which could easily be utilized when needed. The squad the new man had been assigned to was different. In addition to two Browning automatic rifles carried by the squad , each man carried two white phosphorus hand grenades. Most often used by artillery outfits or shot out of mortars, very few infantrymen came into contact with Willie Peter hand grenades.

As the men nervously spoke about the narrow escape they had just lived through, the Squad Sergeant took a long swig of water from his canteen. For him it had been just another day's work. His job was to keep his men alive and healthy. As the new man said, "Boy, we were sure lucky we had those smoke grenades today."

The Sergeant took another swig and said, "Yeah, `we were sure 'lucky'."

The Hat

After the Battle of Aschaffenburg, obvious changes took place in the American battle plan. Many new replacements filled the gaps in the infantry units and German prisoners multiplied by the thousands. Von Lambert who had hung anyone who wouldn't fight in Aschaffenburg and then rode around on the hood of Colonel Sparks' jeep using a bullhorn to tell his men to surrender, acted as a catalyst. German soldiers began surrendering by the hundreds and then by the thousands as the Americans converged in Bavaria, the birthplace of the Nazis.

One of the replacements coming into the squad was barely five feet tall. Quite naturally, he picked up the name of "Shorty." Some thought his name was Melvin, others Milton, but none bothered to find out his real name. When word went around that Shorty had volunteered to get into the infantry outfit, the attitude of the old timers toward him softened a bit. Some of the old timers went so far as to carry Shorty's piece on the more strenuous marches. It was very obvious, however, that Shorty would never become a "real" infantryman.

Two days drive northwest of Munich, a strange incident took place that would affect all the men in the squad. While resting in one of the hundreds of farm towns the unit had gone through, a slave dressed in a striped uniform dared to come close to the American GIs stretched out in reclining positions in a shaded area of the town. All of the members of the squad warned the slave away, fearing the spread of disease or contamination of some kind from the scarecrow looking survivor. All except one waved him away. Shorty motioned him closer.

Some whispering took place and then Shorty was seen empty-ing his pockets of cigarettes, food and any other items of value that he had been carrying. He placed all the items in a neat package and offered them to the sorrowful collection of skin and bones that stood before him. The slave bent his head in thanks, then silently left the area.

As the squad was leaving the rest area, the skeleton looking slave appeared a second time. Finding Shorty, he thrust some-thing into the surprised GI's hands, whispered some unintelli-gible words and then just as suddenly disappeared behind some shrubbery.

"Hey, wha'd the guy give Shorty?" was whispered from GI to GI as they mounted trucks to speed up their advance. Once the rout began, the advances were measured in miles, 30, 40 and 50 per day. The German troops wanting to surrender were waved back to M.P. units in the rear. Meanwhile, the men in the truck were crowded around Shorty, anxious to see what the scarecrow like individual had given the GI. To everyone's amazement the gift turned out to be a Russian officer's cap with a huge bill on the front extending out several inches. As Shorty put the cap on for a laugh, one of the other guys yelled out, "Hey! I've got the perfect thing to make Shorty look like a general." Taking the cap in his hands he affixed a five-pointed silver star to the cap's front. Then, he placed the cap back on Shorty's head as the whole squad broke into laughter. "I'll be damned," one of the squad quipped, "Shorty looks like a God damned general with that cap on!" As he squashed the cap into his backpack, almost everyone on the truck tried to touch his arm, saying things like "nice goin" or "good show." It was a genuine show of accept-ance by the old timers in the squad. Then the cap was forgot-ten. There was still a war going on.

A few miles out of Dachau, the squad found themselves in a firefight. Suddenly a white flag was seen on the German side.

The Sergeant went out to meet the German to see what message was being delivered. The Sergeant was laughing as the squad gathered around him, waiting to hear what was going on. "There are 200 men in there that want to surrender. The problem is they will only surrender to an officer of equal or higher rank than their Colonel." The Sergeant had told the Germans it would take one hour to get an American officer on the scene at which time the Germans could surrender. "In the meantime," the Sergeant said, "someone get Shorty and make sure he brings his General's cap."

The surrender went off without a hitch. The German Colonel saluted Shorty, who answered with a grunt. The Colonel clicked his heels then unbuckled his pistol that he handed to Shorty. His subordinate officers unbuckled their pistols, handing them to the Sergeant. Shorty shouted something that sounded like "farshtunkonah something or other," turned on his heels and walked away as the squad gathered the 200 German soldiers at gunpoint. The Americans were unable to keep straight faces as they went through the formal arrest procedures. They were bursting with laughter, pride and curiosity.

The pistol the German Colonel had handed to Shorty was silver plated and reflected in the sunlight with a blinding light. Back in the truck, everyone wanted to get a look at the regal looking pistol that Shorty happily passed around for everyone's inspection. No one had ever seen anything like it. The pistol was passed around to each of the men. There were lots of "oohs" and "aahs" until the pistol finally reached the Sergeant. "Men," he said, "I've seen only one other pistol like this one. A Sergeant from the 99th Division name of Whiteway took it from a Kraut General. It was silver plated like this one, and had never been fired. It's called a Walther PP and is usually carried by police undercover agents, in other words, Gestapo officers. My guess is it will be worth plenty of bucks back home." There were a lot more "oohs" and "aahs" and "wows."

Every outfit had a guy called a shvitzer. He was usually from a big city in the states like New York or Chicago or Los Angeles or Denver or St. Louis. He knew more than any of the other guys. He could do everything better than anyone else. He was a blowhard and a braggart and in German he was called a shvitzer. The squad had a shvitzer, too, and he was furious at the attention Shorty and his special pistol were getting. He silently fumed and plotted. When the next situation arose, he would be ready.

Events unfolded rapidly. In the woods right outside Dachau, the lead scout named DeGro signaled for the Sergeant to come up for a pow-wow. The lead smelled trouble ahead. Within minutes the squad was engaged in a firefight. As soon as the firing stopped the shvitzer made his move. He knocked Shorty to the ground and quickly took "the" cap from Shorty's knapsack. As he put the cap on his head, he announced to anyone interested that he would take charge of this surrender and get himself a fancy war trophy to boot.

While the Sergeant was trying to figure what the Germans were up to, DeGro spotted a glint high up in a tree. As he directed the Sergeant's attention to the sniper, a shot rang out. The German sniper had spotted an officer wearing a cap. Too good a shot to miss. The white flag could wait a few seconds before making its appearance. But one thing was for sure, the officer with the star on his cap would not be around to accept the surrender of the German troops.

No one was interested in the cap after the surrender. German troops dug a grave for the shvitzer's body. The cap with the now deformed star was buried together with the last man who wore it.

As the men of the squad stood around the grave, the radio brought them the message about a place called Dachau which had some VIP's or something. The camp, or whatever it was,

was to be sealed until an International Committee could be brought up to inspect the situation. This would be different from any other action the squad had ever been involved in, but no one could dream how different it would be.

The Quiet Man

The squad gathered around the Sergeant as he drew a map of the surrounding territory in the dirt with a tree branch. The battalion had been advancing more than 25 miles a day. There appeared to be little danger, but the Sergeant had posted lookouts as per standard operating procedure. It was clear to almost everyone that the war was winding down. The end was near. Unhurriedly, the Sergeant spoke about Bavaria, the gateway to the Austrian Alps where it was said, "Hitler would make his last stand." A sudden motion in the branches of a nearby tree caused the Sergeant to look up just as an object fell to the ground just a few feet from the squatting men. "Grenade!!!," the Sergeant yelled as the long, oblong object rolled towards the men. "Grenade!!!" Eight men dove for the ground...one flung his body over the grenade just as it exploded. Stunned, the Sergeant reacted with a flurry of shots into the rustling branches of the tree. The sniper's body fell to the ground from the upper branches.

The men quickly ran to the body of the man who had saved their lives. Covered with blood, he lay writhing with pain. His right leg had been blown off. His left arm lay detached alongside his body. His eyes were open. He was still alive. "My God," one of the new men whispered, "Who is he anyway?"

He was known to the older men of the company as the Quiet Man. He never spoke unless he was spoken to directly. No matter what was asked of him, he did his duty, never complaining. He never spoke about his past life until that one night only a week ago...right after the battle of Aschaffenburg.

New replacements had come up to the line and were being introduced and encouraged to say a few words about themselves. They would say where they were from, what they wanted to do with their lives after the damned war was over...things like that. After the first few comments, there was a long silence. Then the one they called the Quiet Man spoke up.

He grew up in one of those orphan homes they had in New York City. He had no family, no relatives of any kind. He liked being in the army, especially in this infantry squad. These men were his family. He loved them all, he said. "When one of our boys goes down, it tears up my insides," he said. He loved to hear their stories about going to school, going out on dates, about brothers and sisters and moms and dads. He had never spoken before at one of these "talk" sessions. He would usually just hug his knees and absorb every word that was spoken with a kind of blissful expression on his face.

The 157th Infantry Regiment was part of General Alexander Patch's 7th Army. The General was a quiet, capable military man. He was not the flamboyant type of officer, eager to pose for photographers or public relations people. He was assigned tasks and, with great assurance and courage, these assignments were satisfactorily carried out. The veterans of the 7th Army respected their general greatly. In spite of his caution and concern for his men, a casualty rate of 75% had been inflicted on the 7th Army by the fighting German troops.

"I" company of the 3rd battalion had the same percentage of casualties; 75% of the men had been killed, wounded, captured by the enemy or were missing in action. Having been in continuous action for almost 500 days since the invasion of North Africa, these types of statistics were inevitable. Sicily, Anzio, Naples, France, Belgium, and now, Germany...all landmarks where the outfit had served with distinction. The Quiet Man had heard many stories since wading ashore in North Africa.

He had seen many good men fall.   In spite of his long period of service, he had never once spoken of his own experiences. Now, finally, something someone said, brought his memories to the surface.

From the time he was able to leave school and get away from the orphanage, he had worked as a parking attendant in a garage on Jerome Avenue in the Bronx. Everyone knew where that was…just a few blocks from Yankee Stadium. The two words brought visions of the huge stadium where Joltin' Joe would be belting out homeruns or roaming the vast stretches of center field, running like a gazelle, gracefully grabbing any ball that was hit his way. The garage was a local hangout for the men of the neighborhood, who would stand around smoking, pitching pennies, talking baseball, discussing the war and talking about friends and relatives who were away "for the duration."

One of the steady parkers was a tall, distinguished looking elderly man who parked his car on the second floor of the garage. His car was a shiny, black 1940 Pontiac four-door sedan with the familiar Indian head ornament on the hood. The car belonged to the man's nineteen- year-old son who had worked and saved for three years before he was able to buy this most precious possession…his own car.   Two months later, the Japanese attacked Pearl Harbor. The boy was one of the first in line to enlist.

The day after the naval battle at Midway, the old man received a telegram from the Navy Department with the fatal words, "We regret to inform you…." For three months after receiving that telegram, the car with the Indian head symbol remained untouched in its spot in the garage.

The Quiet Man droned on as everyone leaned forward in order not to miss a single word. One Saturday morning, the old man showed up at the garage with a small suitcase under his arm. As he unpacked, he expertly eyed every inch of his son's automobile, making sure there were no nicks or scratches. When he was satisfied that the car was in perfect condition, he began to rub and polish the big, black car with the wide rimmed white tires. He spent several hours lovingly stroking and polishing the big car with the proud Indian head hood ornament. Occasionally he stopped to wipe away the tears that ran down his face.

Finally, the old man was satisfied that the shine just couldn't be brought out any brighter. He slid in behind the wheel, hit the starter and took the Pontiac out for a ride. Twenty or thirty guys were watching this solemn, almost religious ceremony. A word wasn't said. Silently, a few guys fell into line behind the Pontiac to see where the old man was headed. Up Jerome Avenue, he drove for about ten blocks. At 181st Street he turned right, heading up the long, steep hill to the Grand Concourse. Heads turned at every corner as the shiny, black Pontiac with the white-rimmed tires drove by. There was a lot of "oohing and aahing." When he got to Tremont Avenue, he turned right again and, in another minute, was back to Jerome Avenue and the garage. As he exited the car, his face was beaming. He did one final dust off and left the garage with a jaunty step.

Every Saturday after that, like clockwork, the old man followed the same routine. Two hours of polishing and preening, and then the same short trip to the Concourse and back to the garage. The old man didn't know that as soon as he left the garage, the Quiet Man would put huge sheets of corrugated cardboard over the four door handles to protect the car from getting nicked and scratched by other doors opening nearby. Every car in that garage had those telltale nicks and scratches. Every car except that big, black 1940 Pontiac.

The crowd gathered every Saturday to watch this ceremony

of love and devotion. But, each week there were fewer and fewer onlookers as the war continued on relentlessly, devouring young people. As the old man toiled, never a spoken word was uttered by the onlookers. They all agreed that when he left the garage, his step was always lighter than the one he had come in with. It was hard to understand how a tough group of boys could get a charge out of watching an old man rub and stroke that big, black Pontiac.

When it was the Quiet Man's turn to go, he left explicit instructions with his replacement of how and why that Pontiac was to get special treatment for as long as it was parked in that garage. "One day," he told the new attendant, "I'll get my own car, and when I do, I'll take care of it like the old man takes care of that big, old Pontiac." This was the story the Quiet Man told the men of his squad just one week before he threw his body onto that German grenade.

The Sergeant leaned over the wounded boy; he had seen many men die. He knew it would be only a short time before the one they called the Quiet Man would pass on. Tears welled up in the Sergeant's eyes. He had never seen anyone die more heroically, thinking only of the squad, his family.

No, the boy signaled with his eyes, "but, it's funny isn't it," he whispered with great effort, "that when I finally get my car, I won't be able to polish it like I always wanted to…like the old man polished his son's."

The men of "I" company who lived because of the heroic action of the Quiet Man went back to their homes and loved ones in the states. They went to Vermont and Colorado, and New Jersey and Oregon, and Texas and Massachusetts, and Illinois and Pennsylvania. Not one of them ever forgot the Quiet Man.

Medics tryings to save the life of a wounded GI.

In Flanders Fields

In Flanders fields the poppies blow
Between the crosses, row on row
That mark our place; and in the sky
the larks, still bravely singing, fly
Scarce heard amid the guns below.

We are the Dead. Short days ago
We lived, felt dawn, saw sunset glow,
Loved and were loved, and now we lie
In Flanders fields.

Take up our quarrel with the foe:
To you from failing hands we throw
the torch; be yours to hold it high.
If ye break faith with us who die
We shall not sleep, though poppies grow
In Flanders fields.

The poet John McCrae (1872-1918) was a Canadian physician who served as a soldier and later in the medical corps in France in World War I. He died in 1918 while on active duty. "Flanders Fields" became the best known poem of World War I and was read and recited by both soldiers and civilians.

Flanders is a name used for the Flemish (Dutch) areas of Belgium; it includes the Ardennes Forest where bloody battles were fought in World War I and again in World War II. In 1944, during the Battle of the Bulge, American forces suffered 81,000 casualties.

J Companies?

Part I

It is ironic that while America and its Allies were waging an all out war against Hitler's racist ideology, that our own American Army was practicing its own brand of racism against American GIs. The worst case of discrimination in our armed services undoubtedly was against our Black soldiers who could not get a blood transfusion in combat unless the blood came from another Black soldier. Placed in segregated units, the Black GI often felt that he was fighting two battles at the same time; the first against the Germans and their ideology, and the other against the bias of the white officer corps of the U.S. Army.

While it may be hard for youngsters today to believe, racism was unashamedly a government-sanctioned policy in the military services of World War II. Taking its lead from the southern congressmen who controlled American military appropriations, large numbers of southerners became the nucleus of the white officer corps, bringing with them their deep-seated prejudices and beliefs. Even in the all Black segregated units the officers were most often white southerners who treated the enlisted men with contempt and hatred.

One million Black soldiers ultimately served in World War II. Among the ones who saw combat nearly 25% were killed or wounded. However, regardless of their education, training or background they were considered incapable of functioning on a level equal to white soldiers.

In battle, when a Black unit became undermanned, white GIs could not be sent to reinforce the unit. In Italy, when Black units suffered heavy losses, the remaining men were attached to another segregated group, the Japanese-American 442nd Infantry Regiment.

Toward the end of 1944 when the Allies had developed new and formidable weapon systems that were brought to bear on the Nazis, Black units were still using handoffs of white fighting units. For example, in the area of transportation, Blacks were supplied with 372 mules that were acquired from Italian peasants.

During the Battle of the Bulge, Americans suffered a tremendous loss of personnel. Eisenhower, desperate for fighting men, allowed Black GIs to volunteer for service in front-line infantry units. 4,000 Black soldiers volunteered. From this number, 2,000 high school graduates were picked and transferred out of their Black units. These Blacks lost all rank previously attained and were put into special companies designated with the letter "J". These "fifth" platoons helped stem the tide and were a vital part of the American offensive that eventually reclaimed all the territory lost in the "Bulge."

In most cases the Blacks were then returned to their original outfits, with no mention made in their records of their "temporary duty." One group of Blacks however remained with the infantry units that eventually hooked up with the Russians at the Elbe River. However, Army Signal Corps films of the happy event never showed any of the Black troops. When the victorious infantry troops returned to the United States, the Blacks were not allowed to march in the homecoming parades with the white troops with whom they had fought. Eventually transferred back to Black units, there was never any mention made in their Army records of the time served in the infantry. They were, however, allowed to resume their former rank.

During the Battle of the Bulge, Black troops fought along-side the white troops. In the 1st, 9th, 69th, 99th and 104th Infantry Divisions they were designated as "J" companies. In addition to the five infantry divisions Black GIs were also assigned to the 12th and 14th Armored Divisions as fifth pla-toons of the infantry companies. Veterans of these outfits would be the first to verify the truth of "J" companies and to the fighting abilities of the Black infantrymen. Of the courageous volunteers 38% came from engineer outfits, 29% came from quartermaster outfits and 26% came from transportation troops whose drivers were referred to with great respect as "The Red Ball Express."

To this day, many veterans will laugh and say that there was no such designation in the American Army as "J" company. They are correct. However, during the Battle of the Bulge the Black infantrymen who were organized as a fifth platoon were so designated.

Prior to World War II the Army was completely segregated; there were very few Black men in American military service. In 1939 there were only 3,640 Black soldiers in the army. Of these, five were officers, three of whom were chaplains. During the Battle of the Bulge there were no official records of racial fric-tion between the Blacks and the whites, although they lived in close quarters and shared the stress of battle.

Prior to the Battle of the Bulge Black troops were used in supply units of the Quartermaster Corps or as truck drivers. They were responsible for getting munitions and supplies to the fighting troops but were not considered capable of doing actual fighting. A Black tank outfit, the 761st, did see action toward the end of the war.   Moreover, there was also a squadron of Black fighter pilots that protected American bombers on their missions to and from Germany. Stories continued long after the war's end about the Black fighter pilots and how, once under their protection, American bombers were never shot down.

Part II

Hitler's hate for Blacks dated back to the 1936 Olympics in Berlin when America's great Black runner, Jesse Owens, won several track events that Hitler had boasted would be won by his German Supermen. When the American was awarded the Gold Medals, Hitler left the Berlin stadium in a rage. Few Blacks were ever taken prisoner by the Nazis; they were shot on the spot.

This hatred of Blacks was multiplied in geometric proportions when Joe Louis, a poor Black boxer from Detroit, defeated Germany's Max Schmeling in a rematch prizefight that determined the championship of the world. In that second Louis-Schmeling fight, Louis hit Schmeling with a blow to the body that was so hard it caused Schmeling to cry out in pain. The scream was heard by the more than 70,000 fans in Yankee Stadium that evening; the fight was over in the first round. Joe Louis had become the heavyweight champion of the world. From then on, Hitler's feelings were well known to the German people. He equated Blacks, Jews and Slavic peoples with insects.

Under battle conditions many Black soldiers performed heroically, but their actions were never recognized or recorded. Regardless of how great their sacrifices, not one Medal of Honor was issued during World War II for their actions. The Congressional Medal of Honor was reserved for white personnel, with the exception of one medal awarded to a member of the Japanese American 442nd Infantry Regiment. It was said at the time, Black soldiers just "melted away" after combat along with their fighting records. This phrase was originated by

Truman Gibson, the War Department Special Assistant on Negro Affairs. During a 1945 interview he used the words "melted away" in an off-hand remark to describe the way Black military actions in World War II were forgotten by the white establishment. Most of the Black GIs who fought in the Battle of the Bulge were left only with memories of the heroic actions they had performed along with their white counterparts.

Fifty-five years after the fact, a Congressional Medal of Honor was awarded to Lt. John Fox for his heroic action in Tuscany, Italy against superior German mountain troops in December, 1944. With two platoons of Black soldiers and the help of 25 Italian partisans, Fox held up the German advance until the Americans ran out of ammunition. It was then that Fox called for an artillery barrage to be brought down on his own position. Disregarding orders to abandon the position, Fox and his men fought off the Germans in hand-to-hand combat until artillery shells wiped out the entire area. As the Germans advanced, they systematically set every house on fire, knowing the American dead and wounded were still inside the structures. His best friend, Otis Zachary, who was at the other end of the line recorded Fox's last radio message. "They're coming after us. Please, when you get back to the states, tell my wife, my kids and my mother that I love them." The German advance had been held up long enough for American reinforcements to successfully stage a counter attack.

Researchers who heard about the heroic actions of the Americans from Italian peasants who witnessed the battle, could find nothing in official archive records, not even a list of the men who had died that day in the small village of Sommocolonia, Tuscany. Although the Italians remembered, as far as the Army was concerned, Fox and his men had just "melted away."

Sitting at the end of the line on December 26th 1944,

Zachary remembered the events well. He took the message from his best friend, which called for a barrage on the outpost's coordinates. For fifty years he and Fox's family, together with Black veterans' organizations, tried to get the Pentagon to recognize the exploits of the Black soldiers. The response was always the same. The official book on World War II honors had been closed in 1952. Only an act of Congress could reopen the book.

Veterans of the 92nd Infantry Division and Fox's family never stopped trying. In 1996, Colin Powell, the Black Chairman of the Joint Chiefs of Staff, added his support. It was at this point that Congress decided to honor Black soldiers for their actions in World War II. On January 13, John Fox and six other Black American Soldiers were presented with the highest honor our nation has to offer, the Congressional Medal of Honor.

Fifty-six years after the event, John Fox and the men who defended a tiny mountain village were honored at the spot where they fell. In a joint ceremony presided over by the mayor of the village and U.S. diplomats, a park was built and dedicated to the American heroes who had laid down their lives so that the people of the village could one day live in peace. John Fox's best friend Otis Zachary was present, representing the 92nd Infantry Division.   Fox's wife, Arline, their daughter and two grandchildren were also at the ceremony. The Peace Park was dedicated on July 17, 2000.

Lt. John Fox, was awarded the Congressional Medal of Honor 56 years after the event.

Jesse Owens won several gold Medals in the Berlin Olympics, 1936. Hitler left the stadium in a rage; a black man had defeated his "Aryan supermen."

Major Lambert's War

Barely three months after the Battle of the Bulge and the Malmedy Massacre, the American 7th Army attempted an assault crossing the Rhine River on a 15-mile front between the cities of Gernscheim and Mannheim. The date was March 26, 1945. One day earlier, Patton's Third Army had crossed the Rhine even further north. Now, Lt. Colonel Felix Sparks, commanding a Battalion of the 45th Infantry Division was approaching what was to be known as the Schweinheim-Aschaffenburg complex on the Main River.

When the Germans retreated, they had systematically blown up all the bridges crossing the Main River, all except one railroad bridge that remained intact. This bridge lay directly opposite the twin cities of Schweinheim-Aschaffenburg. Capitalizing on this stroke of luck, the 3rd Army's 4th Armored Division seized the bridge intact and established a bridgehead across the river on the evening of March 28, 1945.

Without prior notice, on March 26th, Supreme Allied headquarters had ordered a change of strategic areas between General Alexander Patch's Seventh Army and General George S. Patton's Third Army. Simultaneously, with their crossing of the Rhine, Patch's 45th Division (due to the changeover) found the Schweinheim-Aschaffenburg complex under its jurisdiction.

Prior to the changeover, Patton had requested permission to send a 3,000 man task force fifty miles behind German lines for the purpose of liberating an American Prisoner of War camp located at Hammelburg. General Bradley had turned down the

request on the grounds that the entire force would in all probability be destroyed before being able to accomplish its mission.
Patton continued to push for the mission and was finally given
permission to send a force of 300 men. Bradley, at the time, was
unaware that Lt. Col. John Waters was reported to be one of the
prisoners in the camp at Hammelburg. Col. John Waters was
General Patton's son-in-law.

Under utmost secrecy, a task force was hastily assembled.
Captain Abraham Baum was placed in command of the mission.
Baum's total task force consisted of 294 men and 53 vehicles.
Task Force Baum was launched from Schweinheim with the
men in the group knowing they had to cover a distance of 100
miles, wholly in enemy territory without being able to carry
enough fuel for the 50 mile return trip. In addition, because of
the lack of transport, the Task Force men knew that they would
be able to save no more than a few prisoners, even if they were
lucky enough to obtain additional gasoline for the return trip.

After fighting a pitched battle to clear the path for Task
Force Baum, on the night of March 26th the 4th Armored
Division withdrew to its newly assigned territory back across
the Main River. Task Force Baum was left to shift for itself. The
arriving 45th Division was advised only that Patton's men had
cleared the Schweinheim-Aschaffenburg complex area. No one
was told about Abraham Baum and the 294 volunteers headed
for Hammelburg, deep behind the enemy lines.

Lt. Col. Felix Sparks, Commander of the 3rd Battalion,
157th Infantry Regiment of the 45th Division wrote in his
memoirs, "The assigned mission was to secure the ground for
the anticipated advance of the 45th Division through the area
on the following day. It seemed to be a simple, uneventful mission. I was told nothing about Task Force Baum, then operating somewhere in my assigned area. My orders, however, did
include one bit of curious information. I was told I must not

fire on any American tanks that I might encounter to my front."

As Sparks' men approached the railroad bridge leading to the twin city complex, they were aware of a deadly silence that covered the area. Expecting to find some elements of the 3rd Army, they were surprised to find no one. Sparks wrote, "it was a setting in which any infantryman could smell trouble."

As the lead scouts reached the end of the bridge, they were engulfed by mortar and small arms fire. The German fire was precise and devastating. It immediately became evident that, if indeed the complex area had been cleared, it would have to be cleared again. German civilians informed Sparks' men that some 3,000 troops were dug in to defend the twin towns and they had been given orders to fight until death. The civilians showed the Americans pamphlets distributed by the commander of the German Forces, Major Lambert:

"Soldiers, Men of the Wehrmacht, Comrades,

The fortress of Aschaffenburg will be defended to the last man. As long as the enemy gives us time, we will prepare and employ our troops to our best advantage. This means....Fight! Erect dugouts! Make barriers! Get supplies! And win!

As of today, everyone is to give to his last. I order that no one shall rest more than 3 hours out of 24. I forbid any sitting around or loafing.

Our belief is that it is our mission to give the cursed enemy the greatest resistance and to send as many as possible of them to the Devil.

Signed, Lambert, Major"

Task Force Baum, defying all odds, created havoc behind the German lines. Believing the small force to be a feint, the

Germans plotted the course of Baum's group as it approached the prisoner compound at Hammelburg, 50 miles beyond Aschaffenburg. Shooting their way into the camp, Baum's men were able to rescue only a small portion of the 1,000 wildly cheering American prisoners. Col. John Waters was seriously wounded during the fighting and could not be evacuated. As Baum and what was left of his Task Force headed back towards Aschaffenburg, many of the other prisoners took off on foot in the direction of the American lines. By then, the composition and mission of Baum's force had been fully determined by the Germans who effectively sealed off the escape route. All members of the Task Force were killed or captured, as were all of the freed prisoners who had taken off on their own. The Task Force was annihilated some 30 miles short of reaching its goal at Aschaffenburg. The Prisoner of War compound at Hammelburg was liberated a few days later by units of Patch's 7th Army.

The advancing 3rd Battalion of the 157th Infantry Regiment came under even heavier and more accurate mortar and small arms fire. As squads moved up into built-up areas of the cities, they found themselves in hand-to-hand combat with ferocious defenders. In some buildings, the Americans occupied basements while the German troops occupied the upper floors. German snipers were dug in under the rubble and were taking a deadly toll of the slowly advancing American infantrymen. Many buildings captured during the day were retaken by infiltrators during the night, only to be retaken by the Americans the next day. Casualties were heavy on both sides.

Concrete casements and pill boxes previously used in training SS officer candidates were now effectively being used to thwart any American advances. American intelligence was unaware that an SS Officer Training School had been located in Aschaffenberg. In an effort to cut down on their losses, American GIs attached mirrors to the ends of their rifles which were then extended out of windows to spot snipers and inspect buildings where mortars had been emplaced.

Sparks sent in additional bazooka teams, which zeroed in on the snipers as they shot at the extended mirrors. The bazooka teams eliminated the snipers and entire floors of buildings where the snipers had been hidden. Nevertheless, the fighting continued on a room-to-room and building-to-building basis. By March 31st, most of the Americans were recalled to the outskirts of the twin cities while fighter-bombers and heavy concentrations of artillery reduced the cities to rubble.

On two separate occasions, the Germans were asked to surrender. They were told that they were surrounded and that to continue fighting was useless; the civilian population would be killed needlessly. Lambert, the German commander, gave his answer by hanging both civilians and military personnel who showed any signs of weakness. The bodies were strung up on lampposts with signs attached identifying them as traitors.

As the Americans watched from the hills surrounding the twin towns, the Air Force dropped its devastating bombs until the rubble resembled a landscape of death. By April 1st, the Germans had been driven out of Schweinheim a dozen times, only to have them infiltrate back again at night to establish new positions in the skeleton like structures that still remained standing.

The 7th Army Bulletin for April 2nd read:

"Schweinheim, twin city of Aschaffenburg, was cleared last night in a tooth and claw fight, after infantrymen of the veteran 45th Division fought room to room into the town. At 15:00 yesterday, more than 600 fanatically resisting German soldiers of the garrison town were forced from their training center barracks and taken prisoner in a move that broke the back of the town's defenses." One man describing the action said, "If you watched the company going up the street, you would see a whole platoon go into a house. Then, there would be shots and grenade bursts. Then, about twenty minutes later, you would see forty Krauts come marching out of the house with one of our boys for a guard. Then the casualties would be brought out - ours, and the Germans. And then, the platoon would go into the next house and the whole process would be repeated again."

Major Lambert, who had given the order to hang anyone who surrendered, eventually gave up. He then was driven through the twin cities, on the hood of Colonel Sparks' jeep, ordering all remaining German soldiers to surrender. Fourteen hundred German civilians in Aschaffenburg died needlessly; on May 8, 1945, Germany surrendered unconditionally.

The 7th Army had been delayed for more than a week by Major Lambert and his die-hard SS troops. Now Lt. Colonel Sparks and his Third Battalion were able to continue their rout of the German Army as they headed south towards Munich, the jewel of Bavaria.

No one will ever know how many souls perished needlessly in Dachau, as the prisoners awaited the American advance. To the men of I Company, 3rd Battalion of the 157th Regiment, 45th Infantry Division, looking at their route of march on a map spread out on the ground, the name Dachau meant nothing. They had no way of knowing at the time that they would be the lead troops into a kind of terror impossible to envision.

The 522nd

Headquarters Battery of the 522nd Field Artillery Battalion came to be known as the most decorated unit of its size in the history of World War II.   The 522nd was made up of Nisei, Japanese Americans.

Although there was strong sentiment against the Asian soldiers by the upper echelons of the American military establishment, the men of the 522nd proved themselves in battles in Italy and France.   In November 1944, near Brugeres, France, they were assigned a rescue mission.   The 36th Division, isolated and surrounded by German troops, was referred to as the "Lost Battalion."   The situation of the desperate men, mostly from Texas, was thought to be hopeless.

The Japanese Americans were given the job of breaking through the German lines to rescue their fellow Americans.   In two weeks of bloody fighting and at great loss to their own men, they accomplished their mission.

The Japanese American soldiers suffered more than 800 casualties while rescuing the 211 Texans.   The chains of prejudice were broken forever on that day.   The men of the 522nd were made honorary citizens of the state of Texas and were recognized as American heroes.

In April, 1945 the 522nd Field Artillery Battalion crossed the Danube River and entered what would come to be known as the Holocaust Corridor.   This area of Bavaria was the home of the notorious Dachau Concentration Camp and its 240 sub-camps. The men of the 522nd were headed for Munich and then to the Austrian Alps, where Hitler was thought to be planning his last stand. They found themselves on the shores of the Lech River in Germany, surrounded by a group of 11 concentration camps which were among the worst in the entire German system. Within the Kaufering system, the prisoners were housed in underground bunkers, their sleeping quarters dug into the earth. Other than buckets, there were no sanitary facilities. In their efforts to live even one more day, they would steal whatever they could from each other. Shoes were vital for existence. The only place shoes could safely be kept from being stolen during the night was under their heads. When the slop buckets ran over, they had to walk in the filth that was all over the floor of the sleeping area. There was no ventilation in the bunkers. Staying alive, if only for a few days, was a major accomplishment. Living under these conditions was the nearest thing to Hell that man could imagine.

Those were the nighttime conditions. The day of labor was worse. Given some gruel that served as soup, they lived on a diet of 250 calories a day until they were too weak to do heavy work. The death rate from disease and starvation, which reached catastrophic proportions, was of no interest to the concentration camp Commanders since new bodies were constantly available. The pervasive smell of death was everywhere.

This was the scene that greeted the men of the 522nd as they traveled through Bavaria. They simply were not prepared for the sights they encountered in the German concentration camps. None of the American GIs were prepared for what lay immediately ahead. They walked into the camps as boys. They came out with memories that would stay with them until they took their last breath. They became witnesses to atrocities that were impossible for the human mind to comprehend.

The Japanese American GIs were, as a group, reticent to

speak about their wartime experiences. Upon discharge they immediately set to work to make up for the time lost in military service. In the Japanese culture, education is of prime importance. Although some went into farming on the west coast, most continued their education by going to college and attaining degrees. For the most part, the Japanese Americans in America prospered. Marrying among themselves, they raised families in many of the major cities in the country while advancing in their chosen professions. Contact was maintained with former army buddies through military organizations but little, if anything, was discussed with family members about their military exploits.

At a reunion of the 522nd Field Artillery Battalion in 1992, some pictures were being passed around to the men who were now in their seventies. Forty-seven years had passed since the end of the war. One old timer looked at a picture and asked, "What is that?" He was looking at a pile of bodies in a snow bank near a barb-wired fence.

"Don't you remember?" someone answered. "Those are the bodies of the slaves we found as we headed down to Austria. The slaves who had been in the concentration camps."

Part II

A reporter standing nearby heard the by play and smelled a story...he was right!

A small story appeared in the *San Francisco Chronicle* about the reunion and the role played by the 522nd in liberating concentration camps. Eric Saul, a San Francisco resident, saw the story and smelled a potentially much bigger story. He took it upon himself to contact the historian of the 522nd, George Oiye of Los Altos, California, to find out more about the exploits of the Japanese Americans.

George Oiye had been a forward observer for his artillery team.   During those last hectic weeks of the war, his jeep roamed 30 and 40 miles ahead of the artillery men. George was a prolific photographer, taking numerous photos of the area he was traveling through.   Not used to talking about his army experiences, he let his pictures tell most of the story. When Eric Saul saw a picture with the word "Dachau" in it, his mind raced ahead with untold possibilities.   He contacted a local Jewish organization in the San Francisco area and within weeks Saul set up a breakfast for an upcoming Sunday morning. The publicity for the breakfast advised that it would be attended by survivors of the Dachau Concentration Camp and their liberators, the Japanese Americans of the 522nd Field Artillery Battalion. George Oiye, himself, had no memory of ever liberating the Dachau Concentration Camp, but that didn't stop Eric Saul. The "bagel and sushi breakfast" story was picked up by the major networks and newspapers. News of the event spread like wildfire.   The Jewish organizations in the area were delighted with the opportunity to thank the Japanese American liberators for what they had done to help the Jewish survivors of Hitler's death camps. This was really a good story.

There was one slight problem. Eric Saul could not find any men of the 522nd who remembered liberating the Dachau Concentration Camp. However, by this time "the story" had taken on a life of its own. Some veterans of the 522nd, invited to be on radio and television stations and newspapers all over the country, elaborated on the story of the Dachau liberation. Eric Saul was hailed as a historian while he desperately searched for someone, anyone, who remembered liberating Dachau.

Finally, Eric Saul found the man he was looking for. Located in Oakland, California, the former member of the 522nd said he remembered shooting the locks off the gate at Dachau. Eric Saul neglected to find out that this particular veteran had joined the 522nd as a replacement in March, 1945, less than 6 weeks before the war ended. In addition, the historian neglected to find out that this talkative GI was known by the other men in the outfit to be a perpetual liar. Saul had his eye-witness now and the story continued to grow.

On September 24, 1995 the *San Francisco Chronicle* ran a long, elaborate article about the 522nd and the role they had played in liberating the Dachau Concentration Camp. It was a good article that was entitled "The Conflict Behind the Battle Lines." The Japanese Americans who fought in World War II were engaged in another, private battle against prejudice. While they were fighting in Europe, their families were behind barbed wire in internment camps in the United States.

A major part of the Chronicle article was devoted to the liberation of Dachau by the 522nd. Its message was picked up by the major newspapers throughout the country. By now, other old timers began to "remember" things about the day of liberation. As the frenzy grew, members of other military outfits began to dream up their own memories. Before long, veterans from some 20 military outfits all claimed they were the first ones into the main concentration camp of Dachau, and that they were the liberators. The newspapers loved the stories, especially when those claiming to be liberators belonged to minority groups. Such stories were dramatic and had great reader appeal.

Part III

The last few weeks of the war in Germany were chaotic. Nine months earlier, in the Anzio campaign in Italy, advances by the Allies had been measured in feet and yards. Now in March and April of 1945 the Allies were advancing 30, 40 and 50 miles a day. The Germans were retreating as fast as their vehicles would go. Allied infantry, artillery and tanks were pursuing just as quickly. The scene was one of chaos and turmoil. Soon, the American troops were to cross the Rhine into the heartland of Germany and come upon incredible scenes that neither the fighting men nor the world's conscience were ready to accept.

Many servicemen came across camps marked "Dachau." Like a spider's web the camps spread out from the main camp, less than 15 miles from Munich. The sub-camps of Dachau numbered 240. Some were large, some very small, but all were under the administration of the main camp that had come into being in 1933. The main camp was the only one in the entire complex that maintained *gas chambers* and *ovens*. Many of the old time GIs, made legitimate errors in their stories about Dachau. Others found that if they contacted certain groups, they could achieve monetary gain by telling stories about the liberation of Dachau, stories that had no basis in fact.

Two of the most notorious of this group were Paul Parks and Leon Bass. Both went on lecture tours and spoke of their roles in the liberation of concentration camps. Paul Parks was so successful in his oratory that he was awarded a Liberation Medal by the International Division of Bnai Brith, a major Jewish organization in the United States. This, in spite of the fact that they were aware of the controversy concerning the claims made by Paul Parks.

In November, 1991, an official report emerged that revealed the truth about which military groups were responsible for the liberation of the main Dachau Concentration Camp. An Inspector General's Report had taken place immediately after the liberation of the camp, and a report issued in June, 1945. Nevertheless, for 46 years, whether by design or misfiling errors, the Inspector General's Report had remained hidden.

Until this report emerged from the military archives in

Washington, many false claims by various organizations had been made, and were unchallenged. Strangely, even after the report was declassified and available to the public, more false claims continued to be made by those historians and authors who were not thorough enough or knowledgeable enough to check the Pentagon and Archive records.

Outraged by the audacity and number of men seeking glory and honor who were totally undeserving of either, a group of angry veterans organized into fraud hunters. Many of the impostors claimed to have been Navy Seals or Prisoners of War. Using email and the internet, the Fraud Hunters have been able to expose thousands of impostors. The Chief of Naval Operations, Adm. Jeremy Boorda, killed himself after being accused of wearing decorations he had not earned. Then, in 1998, a book was written entitled "Stolen Valor." Written by B.C. Burkett, the book exposed some 1,800 false stories told by businessmen and political aspirants. One of these was Wes Cooley, a Republican congressman from Oregon, who was forced out of office in disgrace after it was disclosed that his claims of serving in the Army Special Forces were false. In addition, Navy Seals have exposed some 7,000 phonies and maintain a Wall of Shame on the internet with 650 names posted.

Fraud Hunters and legitimate veterans' groups attempt to humiliate impostors who are apparently prisoners of their own fantasies. In his book Burkett says, "I'm convinced some of them could pass a polygraph test. They often know more about the battle, they study it and work at it much harder than the guy who was there. Because the guy who was there only remembers six feet on either side."

On May 12, 2000, President Clinton awarded the highest military honor, the Medal of Honor, to 21 Japanese Americans. They were decorated for heroic acts performed during World War II when they were in the 100th Infantry Battalion/442nd

Regimental Combat Team.

That unit was among the most highly decorated of its size in military history. The 100th was composed of mostly Japanese American National Guardsmen from Hawaii. When the 442nd Regimental Combat Team was organized in 1943, the two units were merged. After 1944, the combined unit was referred to as the 442nd Regimental Combat Team.

Great confusion arose when a part of the 442nd was detached from the larger group and transferred from Italy to Germany. This unit, known for its speed and accuracy in laying down artillery fire on the enemy, was known as the 522nd Field Artillery Battalion. At various times they served with the 1st, 3rd, 7th and 9th Armies in Germany; they were in great demand and in almost constant movement in Germany territory.

Members of the 522nd liberated several sub-camps of Dachau as they headed south towards Austria, where Hitler was expected to make his last stand. On their way, they encountered and liberated the notorious Kaufering Group of death camps near the Lech River. The 522nd, however, was not near the main Dachau camp when it was liberated on April 29, 1945.

Together with the men of the 100th, and the 442nd, the 522nd shared the motto, "Go for broke."

For their courage and effectiveness, these Japanese American units were honored with:

- 18,000 individual decorations

- 9,486 Purple Hearts

- 7 Presidential Unit Citations
       (the nation's highest award for combat units)

- And an astonishing 21 Medals of Honor

Senator Daniel Inouye, honored guest of the 522nd field artillery battalion at the opening of the Japanese-American Museum, Los Angeles, 1995.

The author with two veterans of the 522nd, george Oiye and Sous Ito. In the lower right, Larry Lubitsky of Mexico City. As a teenage survivor of Dachau he became the guide and interpreter for the 522nd and remained with the unit until the end of the war. Located after a fifty year search, he was reunited with the men of the 522nd at their reunion in 1995.

Willie & Joe

There were 16 million Americans who served their country during World War II. Every one of them was familiar with Bill Mauldin, the GI who captured the thoughts and emotions of the average guy who found himself in uniform in a foreign land and who wanted nothing more than to get the job done and go home. Mauldin put those thoughts and emotions in cartoon form and brought tears of humor to millions of average Joe's from Anzio to Iwo Jima. He was a high school dropout who went on to win a Pulitzer Prize by war's end.

After basic training as a rifleman, Bill Mauldin was assigned to Company K, 180th Infantry Regiment, 45th Infantry (Thunderbird) Division. On July 10, 1943 he went in with the first assault wave of the Invasion of Sicily.

As a cartoonist for the "45th Division News" and "*Stars and Stripes*" in Italy, Mauldin developed his most famous two cartoon characters, Willie & Joe, two combat hardened GIs who were invariably muddy and exhausted by extended infantry combat, but whose spirits were never broken. Willie & Joe were average American GIs who were bored by inaction, complained about Army food, complained about living in water-filled ditches, complained about trudging up mountains, complained about marching through valleys loaded down with equipment, rifle and backpack, complained about digging foxholes for non-caring officers, complained about being thousands of miles away from family and friends, but most of all complained about receiving senseless orders from Headquarters. Willie & Joe were loved by the GIs at the front and by the families back home.

Not everyone agreed with Bill Mauldin's point of view. General Patton tried to get Mauldin court-martialed for making fun of officers in his cartoons, but Eisenhower overruled Patton's sensitivities. Willie and Joe continued in their conversations and observations, trying to make sense of the military bureaucracy while retaining their humor and humanity.

Finally, in 1945, General Patton wrote a letter to "*Stars and Stripes*" threatening to ban the paper in the Third Army if it did not stop carrying "Mauldin's scurrilous attempts to undermine military discipline." Believing that such an action of censorship would undermine GI morale, General Eisenhower overrode Patton's threat. Ike, in hopes of reconciling their differences, set up a private meeting between Patton & Mauldin. They met in March, 1945. Patton led off with a lecture on the dangers of producing "anti-officer cartoons." Mauldin responded that GIs had legitimate grievances that the Army needed to address. At meeting's end, neither party felt that anything had been accomplished.

However, later that same year, 1945, Bill Mauldin was awarded the Pulitzer Prize for Editorial Cartooning. The award read, "For distinguished service as a cartoonist, as exemplified by the cartoon entitled 'Fresh, spirited American troops, flushed with victory, are bringing in thousands of hungry, ragged, battle-weary prisoners.'" Looking at the cartoon, it was impossible to tell the victorious Americans from their battle-weary prisoners. Mauldin was 23 when he won the prize. Bill saw the war through the eyes of an average GI. Many an American saw himself and his buddies in the faces and actions of Willie and Joe. The cartoons Mauldin created made army life more bearable.

Thirteen years later, during the Cold War, Mauldin won his second Pulitzer Prize for a cartoon. Two prisoners in a Russian prison camp were getting acquainted with each other. One says to the other, "I won the Nobel Prize for Literature. What was your crime?"

One of Mauldin's best civilian cartoons was created after President Kennedy was killed. This showed Abraham Lincoln at the Lincoln Memorial. Lincoln's head was bent. His hands covered his face.

The hospital room in Southern California was filled with letters, emails and messages of all kinds from veterans all over the world. They wanted Bill to know how much he meant to them when things were very black and he was able to put a little spark in their eyes as they thumbed through "Stars and Stripes" eagerly looking for their friends, Willie and Joe.

Bill Mauldin died January 22, 2003. He was buried in Arlington National Cemetery.

Book Three

"All that is necessary for the triumph of evil is that good
men do nothing."

Edmund Burke

The White Rose

The guillotine came down swiftly and sharply as the student's head fell into the dirt. Raised for a second time, the blade again came down sharply, this time separating a young girl's head from her body. Her head rolled into the dirt alongside the boy's head. On that cold and dreary February afternoon, two members of the White Rose gave up their lives for their political beliefs, which opposed those of Adolf Hitler and his Nazi party. Chopping off their heads was Hitler's way of setting an example for any other German who might harbor ideas that were in any way different from Nazi ideology.

Hans Scholl had been a medical student in Munich. His sister, Sophie, studied biology and philosophy. During one summer in 1942, they joined a group of other students who were mutually interested in music, art and philosophy. They also were violently against the ideas and philosophy of Hitler's Third Reich, and vowed to act upon their beliefs. Hoping to spread their ideals and bring about the downfall of the government, the White Rose group wrote and distributed "Leaflets of The White Rose." The leaflets criticized Germans who did not act upon their beliefs and suggested passive ways to resist the war. Using a hand operated duplicating machine, the leaflets were mailed from Bavaria as well as distributed at colleges and universities all over Germany. Every action of the White Rose group was fraught with danger. Buying too many stamps at one time or place could tip off the Gestapo that an unusual activity was taking place. Recruiting new members, usually students or faculty, to join the resisters, could lead to the death of the entire group involved in White Rose activities.

The most dangerous efforts took place in February, 1943. Slogans were printed on houses located on a main thoroughfare in Munich. Using tar and paint, the students drew crossed out swastikas and wrote slogans such as "Freedom" and "Down with Hitler." Luckily the police and Gestapo were unable to find any White Rose suspects.

On the 18th of February, 1943, Hans and Sophie Scholl dropped a bunch of leaflets from the third floor of the University in Munich to the inner courtyard below. A handy-man gazed up as the leaflets floated down, catching sight of Hans and Sophie. The Gestapo captured the brother and sister with copies of the Seventh Leaflet of the Resistance in their possession. Four days later, on February 22, 1943, the top justice Hitler's People's Court was summoned from Berlin to Munich to conduct the trial of the White Rose students. The trial began at 9:00am and ended at 1:00pm. By 5:00pm on the afternoon of February 22, 1943, the heads of Sophie and Hans Scholl lay in the dirt of the Munich prison courtyard.

One week later, the parents of Sophie and Hans Scholl received a letter from the German government. Inside was a bill demanding 600 Reichmarks for the wear and tear on the guillo-tine used in executing their son and daughter.

Hans and Sophie Scholl who were guillotined for opposing Nazi ideology.

Make Me Mute

Upon entering the first German concentration camps, American troops were horrified by what they saw. The GIs were embarrassed to stare at the shapes and forms in front of them. They were ashamed for themselves and they felt shame for all mankind. They had not been prepared to see human beings deprived of all human dignity, starved to the point of not being able to stand or crawl, and worst of all, deprived of hope. Prisoners referred to this stage of degradation as "musselmen," the last stage of life before death when hope leaves the mind and one's eyes lose their spark.

Many a GI cracked under the strain of trying to absorb the sights that drifted, as if in a nightmare, before his eyes. Reporters, in talking to hundreds of soldiers heard the same expression from everyone. "We were never prepared for anything like this."

Anxious to send home news about the camps, reporters interviewed German citizens in towns all around the notorious cities where the camps were located. The main Dachau Concentration Camp was located less than a mile from the nearest civilian housing in the city of Dachau.

Many of the townspeople performed functions in the camp and the camp personnel spent their free time in the town's taverns, restaurants and bistros boasting about the powers they possessed over the prisoners.

Nevertheless, not one reporter could find a civilian who

would admit that he or she was aware of what went on in the nearby camp. They would admit only to hearing rumors of persons being subjected to harsh living conditions in the camps, but nothing further. Everyone had heard of a friend, neighbor or relative being picked up during the midnight hours and being hauled off to a camp, often never to be heard from again, but how or why that happened they did not know, did not want to know or even question.

Criticism of the government or words of discontent about anything having to do with Hitler or his henchmen could lead to a knock on the door and imprisonment. If someone coveted a new apartment, a few words whispered to a Gestapo stooge was enough to have the legitimate owner "taken away." If one held a subordinate job in a factory or other workplace and was displeased with a superior, it was a simple matter to spread a story of his criticism of the methods of National Socialism. In short order, the supervisor would be removed to a "protective custody" compound for additional training and education. The empty apartment could now be taken over by the Gestapo stooge and his family, and the supervisor's position could be given to someone more sympathetic to the disgruntled worker.

In Bavaria, not daring to speak out became the way of life. Resistance to authority, with very rare exception, was silenced. The daily religious prayer during the Hitler regime was replaced with:

Dear God, make me mute...so I don't get sent to Dachau.

The Clergy

The large number of priests sent to Dachau referred to themselves as "Nummermenschen." They were men with no names, only numbers on their uniforms. Soon, their captors would order them out of their barracks and send them to their ultimate destination, the chimneys of the crematorium. There they would escape their tortured existence at the hands of the Nazis, and their ashes would finally come to rest on the fields of the farm land which surrounded the camp.

As the remaining prisoners said their last good-bys, they vowed that, if by some miracle they should be able to survive, they would tell about what had taken place at Dachau. They vowed to tell the world about what had happened to them as Hitler tried to wipe all traces of religion from Europe.

Outside the gates of Dachau, fog permeated the area for much of the time. The Nazis did everything in their power to see that everything that took place within Dachau was likewise shrouded by fog. Those who were fortunate enough, in the early days, to leave the camp were warned that anything told about their experiences would mean immediate re-arrest, not only for the prisoner, but for his family as well. This fear, plus the fact that conditions changed from year to year in the camp, meant that very little concerning the number of inmates or deaths in the camps could be verified later.

In 1945, a poem by Pastor Martin Niemoller was inscribed over a symbolic box of ashes at the entrance to the camp. The memorial states that 238,756 individuals passed through the gates of Dachau during the years of its existence, 1933-1945. Of this number, which did not include Russian prisoners of war, some 30,000 had been exterminated. Great differences and uncertainties exist about the numbers involved due to the secretive atmosphere instituted by the Nazis and the fact that, in the last weeks before liberation, they attempted to destroy as many records as possible concerning the atrocities committed within the camp. Many Germans preferred to deny or minimize the atrocities, saying they were due to allied wartime propaganda. Surviving priests preferred to say, "We will forgive, but not forget."

Although most people in Germany took little notice, a story appeared in the Munich papers on March 21, 1933. It announced that on the following day, March 22nd, the first concentration camp would be opened, in Dachau. The camp would accommodate 5,000 people and would help to restore calm to the country. The opening of the Dachau Concentration Camp would be in the best interest of Germany. The announcement was signed by Heinrich Himmler, Commissioner of Police of the city of Munich.

The concentration camp of Dachau was located about 10 miles northwest of Munich. The main part of the camp had served as a munitions factory during World War I. Located on swampy land, the camp was always damp and foggy. It can truly be said that Dachau was built on an area of wasteland. Originally built to house 5,000, by the end of the war the daily prisoner count exceeded 30,000. There were 30 numbered barracks. Number 15 became known as the barrack where the most severe punishment was administered. The prisoners in Number 15 were mostly Jews, but there were also others who had tried to escape or who had violated camp regulations.

Seven machine gun watchtowers surrounded the camp. An electrified barbed wire fence was erected on the outer side of a

10 foot area called the "Neutral Zone" which went all around the camp area. It was strictly forbidden for prisoners to enter this zone. Additionally, on the west side of the compound a deep moat had been dug which was filled with water. This moat was within the perimeter of the camp. Immediately outside the prisoner area was the fast flowing Amper River.

At the northwest corner of the prisoner compound was a gate leading to a path which most prisoners were totally unaware of. This path led to the crematorium and gas chambers originally housed in a wooden barrack. Polish Catholic priests were later forced to rebuild the crematorium as a stone building. Located very close to the prisoner compound, it was surrounded by a small forest of trees, making it completely invisible to the prisoners in the camp. However, everyone in the camp was aware of its existence from the smell of the burning corpses that permeated the area. In 1942, the Catholic priests were assigned to begin construction of the gas chambers of Dachau. This building was constantly sabotaged and was not completed until 1945. Prior to its completion, those unfortunates designated for gassing were sent to the gassing facility in Linz, Austria.

The assignment of the clergy to build the gas chambers and crematorium was intended to inflict the severest punishment possible. Prior to implementing this new concept for breaking the will of the clergymen, they had worked at the degrading job of cleaning the brothels that operated in the camp. One brothel was in the Deer Park area and was reserved specifically for the use of SS men, while the other was used by kapos and other prisoners, who were given special privileges from time to time.

In addition to cleaning the brothel areas, members of the clergy were forced to remove their caps while saying loudly, "Heil Hitler!" Two posts were erected, 20 paces apart. On each post, an SS cap was placed. The clergymen had to walk from one post to the other, taking off their prisoner hats and saying, "Heil Hitler," every time they approached one of the posts. This procedure lasted anywhere from one to three hours daily, depending on the mood of the captors. Breaking the will of the clergymen by forcing them to polish SS boots, clean the brothel areas or "Heil Hitler" every 20 paces was meant to make their minds accept the fact that they were "nothing," not a name or a person of religion or anything else but numbers who could be forced to do anything their captors wanted.

Trenton State Prison in New Jersey once established an experimental program for teenagers who were in trouble. They were brought to the prison and turned over to prisoners who were serving life sentences. The prisoners volunteered for the program hoping to show the teenagers what they faced if they didn't turn away from a life of crime. At one point, they took all shoes away from the teenagers. The youngsters were devastated when asked to give up their shoes. They felt personally violated. The program, called "Scared Straight," was an overwhelming success.

At Dachau, the prisoners gave up their clothes, their worldly possessions, their names and their identities. They became numbers, nothing more. The Germans attempted and, in most cases, succeeded in breaking their wills. Indignities imposed on the unfortunate prisoners were meant to destroy the human mind and the will to live. It is not surprising that many prisoners threw themselves on the electrified fences or committed suicide in a variety of other ways rather than go on living as little more than animals.

Although the author of this poem is unknown, the words are most often attributed to Pastor Martin Niemoller, written after his release from Dachau in April, 1945. There are many different versions of the poem.

First they came for the Communists,
and I didn't speak up, because I wasn't a Communist.
Then they came for the Jews,
and I didn't speak up, because I wasn't a Jew.
Then they came for the Catholics,
and I didn't speak up, because I was a Protestant.
Then they came for me,
and by that time, there was no one left to speak up for me.

Niemoller, a U-boat Captain in World War I, was an early follower of Hitler and Nazi ideology. However, prior to 1933 when the Nazis officially came into power, Niemoeller had become a Lutheran pastor, forming the Pastor's Emergency League to protect Lutheran pastors from the police and Nazi instigated mobs. Eventually his protests landed him in Dachau where the Nazis kept him in solitary for four years in an attempt to break his will.

After the war, Niemoller became an advocate for those Germans who felt that Germany should accept collective guilt for the suffering Germany had caused the entire world during World War II.

The Uprising

Two days before the liberation of Dachau, German anti-Nazi patriots in the town of Dachau staged an ill-fated revolt. Led by Ruprecht Gerngross, groups of undercover partisans seized the radio station and Town Hall in Dachau. Hoping other groups would join in the fight, the patriots used the station name "Freiheit Action Bavaria," which they shortened to "BAV." BAV then announced the revolt to all Germans, inviting them to join in. They called the revolt a "Putsch." Observers had informed the leaders that a small unit of SS guarded the city. Cutting off incoming roads and manning the bridges leading into Dachau, the anti-Nazis also hoped to block all railway lines leading to Dachau in order to prevent reinforcements from entering the area.

The "Putsch" groups were all very small, usually no more than five members each, with no one knowing who the members of the other groups were. Only Ruprecht Gerngross knew all the members involved. Many of the members were told to join the Nazi Party for their own protection and as a conduit for receiving vital intelligence information.

In the afternoon of the 27th of April, the code word "Pheasant Hunt" was broadcast over "BAV." The groups hoped to induce the many foreign workers in the Dachau-Munich area to join the revolt. Most of the factory workers in this area were from France. They refused to join in. Nevertheless, by nightfall, many freedom action fighter groups had joined the revolt. The Munich police station was captured as were many other strategic points in the city.

The Putsch intelligence, however, did not know about a strong SS contingent that had been brought into Munich shortly before the revolt began. Using heavy artillery, SS troops engaged the small groups and within two days killed most of the BAV fighters. Still, the leaders of the freedom fighters were willing to risk their lives to show the world that not all Germans were Nazis. Finally, all those who were captured were hung.

On April 30, 1945, General Patch's Seventh Army marched into Munich. They met very little resistance. In effect, this was the end of World War II for General Patch and his men.

Misfits

Born 8 years before the beginning of World War I to a working class family, Egon Zill grew up during the chaos that overwhelmed Germany immediately after the war. Leaving school after completing his elementary education, he bounced around from one unskilled job to another until he joined the Nazi Party. In its infancy, the Party had signed up only 534 members before Egon Zill received his party card and number.

In the beer halls of Munich he mixed in well with other unemployed, psychological misfits who were seeking friendship and social acceptance. Although of small stature, Zill felt at ease among the rogues, desperados and other social misfits who were Hitler's followers in the early days of the Party. All "losers," they felt secure and unchallenged in each other's company. Egon Zill, perhaps because of his size, tended to be more brutal and sadistic on those occasions when his group was called upon to break up opposing political group meetings or beat up some Communists or Social Democrats. Nazi Party officials took notice of how brutal Zill could be.

In November, 1938, the phenomenon known as Kristallnacht erupted "spontaneously" all over Germany. Well organized and orchestrated by Nazi storm troopers, the horror of mass burning, killing, beatings and arrests spread as if by magic from town to town and city to city. Thousands of Jewish businesses, homes and synagogues were torched and thousands of Jews killed by the SS and their former neighbors. Thousands more were sent off to concentration camps.

The Jewish community of Germany was blamed for this "spontaneous outbreak" and was presented with a bill of 1 billion marks for the damages done to the Fatherland.

From Kristallnacht to September, 1939, it was still possible for concentration camp inmates to buy their way out of the concentration camp system in some manner. After the war with Poland began, the gates of the camps were closed forever. The only way out, prisoners were told, was through the chimney...as smoke.

Egon Zill, by now a member of the Death's Head formation was the Commandant of the Dachau Concentration Camp in 1941. Having received his Death's Head unit training in Dachau, he was familiar with all the terrors the camp had to offer its inmates. Egon Zill became one of the most sadistic commandants in the history of concentration camps. Not only did he devise new and organized methods of torture for the unfortunate prisoners, he took joy in taking part in the punishment personally, or else watching from the sidelines as the prisoners died at the hands of equally sadistic guards. Zill thrived on watching men beaten, drowned, hung, and broken until their bodies were unrecognizable masses of bone and skin. A tag attached to their toes listed an identification number so they could be properly recorded in the record books as having died from a heart attack or some other medical ailment.

It was Zill who initiated the table where a prisoner was tied by his upper body with legs and feet hanging over the edge of the table. Another prisoner would strike the prone prisoner with bullwhips that had been soaked in a solution that would burn mercilessly as the thongs cut into the prisoner's body. The one being punished would have to count the number of lashes as they came down. If they lost count or hesitated, the count would go back to "one."

Egon Zill would watch with joy as prisoners were hung with

their hands tied behind their backs until their arms were torn from their sockets. Not able to work after this type of torture, they were never seen again.

Egon Zill had his dogs trained to react to the raising of his arm. On special amusement days, Zill would have a table of food placed in front of the starving prisoners who stood at attention. Should a prisoner relax his body, the dogs would react automatically. As time went by and Zill became impatient, he raised his arm signaling the dogs into action. They attacked the genital areas of the prisoners until they were dead. At this point the bored commandant would leave the scene.

There was one bunker at Dachau reserved for the most severe tortures. Prisoners were kept in solitary confinement. The tortures inflicted on the prisoners were so cruel they were kept secret even from the regular SS guards.

Having the prisoners sing anti-Semitic songs as they dug pits to be filled with stones, only to have the stones dug up and used to fill other pits, was a common pastime for the guards. At other times, they would bind the prisoners' hands and feet and have them crawl on the ground grunting like pigs. As the prisoners approached the pigsty, food was put out for their meal to be eaten among the pigs. The SS men stood watching as the bound prisoners fought with the pigs for the food. This type of torture was used with Jews, priests, Jehovah's Witnesses and Poles.

New and special tortures were devised daily for the Catholic priests. Sometimes, if they were lucky, they would be assigned to clean the dog kennels or the horse stables. On those occasions, they could sometimes get some of the leftover food which meant another day of survival. Being assigned to the pigsty was almost sure death; many of the prisoners never returned. Their bodies remained where they had been drowned in the pig swill as the SS guards looked on.

Like many of the other camps, Dachau had its mandatory sign at the entranceway, "Arbeit Macht Frei." Work Sets You Free. Egon Zill had other signs strategically placed for the prisoners to read. One said patriotically "Alles Fur den Endsleg." All for Final Victory. On the roof of the administration building where all prisoners could see the slogan every time they lined up for roll call a sign declared: "There is one road to freedom. Its milestones are obedience, zeal, honesty, order, cleanliness, temperance, truth, sense of sacrifice, and love for the Fatherland." The prisoners were required to memorize these lines which had to be repeated on demand. Failure to repeat the words on the sign, word for word with cap in hand, meant immediate death for the unfortunate soul.

When the war ended Egon Zill was able to evade capture until 1950. Put on trial in a Munich courtroom he was sentenced to life imprisonment for his crimes. This sentence was later appealed with the life sentence reduced to 15 years in jail. Zill died in the town of Dachau in 1974 within walking distance of the ovens and gas chamber where he had once been the camp commandant.

Commandants of Dachau

1. SS Standartenfuhrer Hilmar Wackerle (Killed by the Russians)

2. SS Gruppenfuhrer Theodor Eicke (Killed by the Russians)

3. SS Oberfuhrer Heinrich Deubel (Not prosecuted)

4. SS Hauptsturmfuhrer Egon Zill (Died after serving 15 year prison term)

5. SS Standartenfuhrer Hermann Baranowski (Died of old age)

6. SS Oberfuhrer Hans Loritz (Committed suicide)

7. SS Hauptsturmfuhrer Alexander Piorkowski (Executed by the Allies)

8. SS Obersturmbannfuhrer Martin Weiss (Executed by the Allies)

9. SS Hauptsturmfuhrer Eduard Weiter (Committed suicide)

Fantasies

The first words he remembered hearing were "SCHNELL" and "RAUS" – "quickly" and "out." He didn't know how old he was then – maybe one and half or two years old. He heard the older boys in the group talking about mothers and fathers, but he didn't know what the words meant. The others all had names, but when they spoke to him, they only pointed with a finger or said, "you do this or you do that." He never thought about the fact that he didn't have a name. He didn't think much about anything. There was no one to teach him otherwise, so he assumed this was the way things were.

When he was 4 years old, an older boy called Thino offered him a piece of bread. By then he had learned to be wary of older people. He knew about the tricks the guards played on unsuspecting youngsters and he knew about the horrible punishments they handed out when they were displeased. He knew that he was safest sitting by himself and not mixing with others who might trick him or steal his piece of bread or drinking cup, or even worse, his shoes. He knew how to snarl and bare his teeth and kick out at youngsters who came near him. He learned by hard experience that these methods were not to be used with older people. When they approached, his eyes would dart from side to side, like those of a trapped animal – but he would not strike at them.

Since he was never taught anything, his limited vocabulary was a mixture of guttural sounds and random words in German, Polish, Russian and Yiddish. He learned the Yiddish from some of the women who lived in the brothel. For some unexplained reason, he was sent to clean there together with the Catholic priests who were always given that particular duty. The women sometimes saved a sweet for him and sometimes even stroked his head and patted him on the arm. The first time this happened, he felt warm inside, but did not know why.

One day Vera asked him what he did during roll call when the German guards handed out punishments. He didn't know what to answer. He looked at her mutely. She hugged him to her bosom and said, "little one, you must learn to fantasize – to dream – to see beautiful scenes in your mind. You must look straight ahead but not see the terrible things the guards are doing to us. You must remember what is happening, and most important of all – you must live!" Seeing puzzlement in his eyes, she went on, "Before I came to the camp, I lived with my mother and father and 3 sisters. I was a ballerina. I danced to the most beautiful music. My life was filled with love and beauty. Now, in this place of horror, when we are forced to watch beatings, torture or hangings, I think in my mind of the beautiful ballets and I picture myself dancing – dancing to beautiful music as my eyes look out on the terrible punishments the Germans force us to witness. We must look at them without seeing, and you, little one, must do the same. My mother, father and sisters are all gone now. I will soon be gone. You must live!" There was no time for further explanation. The boy never saw Vera again.

By the time he was seven, a strong bond had been established between the boy and Thino. The older boy knew how to organize things and would now and then share extra pieces of bread and, sometimes, even a potato with the smaller boy. One time Thino was able to "organize" to get an orange – something the younger boy had never seen before. He bit down on the pieces and let the sweet juice run down into his throat. He never knew things could be so good.

The day after one of the boys received a terrible beating from a guard, the boy asked Thino about what Vera had told him. Thino held the younger boy by the shoulders as he looked into his eyes. "You must live. You must survive to tell. If you do not learn to dream, to fantasize, you will not be able to survive. I speak with many of the men I work with outside the camp. Each has his own fantasy. The mathematician thinks of problems and solutions. The architect dreams of building huge buildings. The musician composes beautiful pieces of music in his mind. The chess player creates new moves and plays games over and over. The artist paints beautiful, bright pictures of happy scenes."

"Each one is forced to watch as a friend, a comrade, is being beaten, tortured or hung, but he doesn't see the terrible tragedy. His mind would break if he wasn't able to fly away in his dream. He looks but he does not see and, you, little brother, must learn to do the same. Others have taught me how to survive. You must now learn from me. You must live!"

The boy felt a warmth inside his body when Thino called him little brother, and he thought deeply about the ballet dancer and the musician and the chess player.

The day they hung Thino from his thumbs, the boy was lined up at attention with all the other boys in the camp. Their eyes were focused straight ahead at the proceedings, but they saw nothing. One boy dreamed of making new and wonderful toys for children. Another dreamed of playing in a huge play yard where children were laughing and smiling and screaming and running and falling down – all the time shouting with happiness.

The little boy, who was not seven, dreamed of building a bridge – a huge bridge – a bridge that stretched from Dachau to America. On the bridge were hundreds and hundreds and hundreds of people in zebra striped uniforms. All were walking and singing their way to freedom. The boy was on the bridge, too. Hand in hand he walked with Thino on one side and Vera on the other as they approached the shores of America. These two older people were the only ones he could remember who had shown him kindness. They would go to America together. This was his fantasy.

The day after Thino's death, the boy was awakened with a start. At the foot of his bunk were Thino's boots. Stuffed in one boot, a tiny scrap of paper stuck out. In a childish scrawl some-one had written, "Little brother, we will live!"

The author and Yamina Cywenska, a Polish Catholic survivor who danced ballets in her mind when forced to watch Nazi atrocities.

Deception

The camps were all the same; the camps were all different. Dachau, the first camp established, became the prototype for all future camps. Commandants for all the major concentration camps were trained at Dachau. Those who showed how brutal, how sadistic, how murderous they could be were rewarded with a camp of their own where they could implement their particular brand of brutality. Like the captain of a ship at sea, the commandant of a camp became the ultimate authority. Within the flexible guidelines developed at Dachau, his thoughts, words and actions became the law in his camp. There were no exceptions. Beatings, torture and hangings took place regularly in every camp. The degree depended on the mood of the guards on any particular day.

But, who was to be in command of the first of these brutal organizations?   Where could such a sociopath be found? Heinrich Himmler, head of the Gestapo, knew the perfect candidate. A man he had personally committed to an insane asylum. A man his SS superiors had labeled "a dangerous lunatic" shortly before he was placed in a psychiatric clinic. This was the man Himmler appointed to be the commandant of the first concentration camp in Germany, Dachau.

Theodor Eicke started out at Dachau by hanging anyone he branded as "agitator." This definition included anyone who collected true or false information about the camp and tried to get it to the outside world. Instituting a regime of torture, beatings and hangings against individuals sent to the camp for "protective custody," Eicke's reputation quickly spread throughout

Germany. His underlings became known as Death's Head detachments. His methods were considered so successful by those in authority that his position was elevated to that of Inspector of Concentration Camps. Only those members of Death's Head squads whose methods were as brutal as Eicke's could ever hope to advance.

Eicke's methods became the normal routine of all concentration camps until the final weeks of the war. Before the allied armies arrived, individual commandants had taken precautions to cover up the atrocities they had ordered and supervised. In their final moments of control, the Germans tried to burn and destroy as many of the camp records as possible. In this, they were only partially successful. Prisoner-workers, anxious to provide authoritative records of what had taken place, hid and buried many of the records they had been ordered to destroy.

At the Mauthausen Camp, prisoners hid a set of books in which deaths at the camp had been meticulously recorded. Each book had inscribed on its cover "Totenbuch Mauthausen" (Death Book). The books contained 35, 318 entries, covering a 5-year period. Prisoners of war were not listed. The entries for March 19, 1945 contained 203 names. Every name listed showed "heart attack" as being the cause of death and, miraculously, each prisoner had died in alphabetical order. The first name being Ackerman, and the last on the list for that day being Zynger.

Russian prisoners of war were not entered in the death books. Forced to work under the worst conditions imaginable, the Soviets were starved, beaten, tortured and coerced into doing the most inhuman kinds of work. Their deaths mounted daily. In one group of 7,000 at the Mauthausen Camp, only 30 survived after a three month period.

In the Dachau death books, the names of prisoners who

died in transit were not recorded. Nor were the names of Russian prisoners who were killed, deemed not worthy of entry in the death books.

The concentration camps located in Germany, at their very worst. never matched the camps that Reichsfuehrer Himmler set up to deal with the "undesirables" in Poland. Home to more than 3 million people who were Jewish, Himmler set in motion the means to exterminate the entire Jewish population not only of Poland but of all of Europe as well. Shipments of Jews arrived daily from France, Belgium, Holland, Germany, Greece, Italy, Hungary and the Soviet Union.

Most Russian Jews were killed by Special Task Force troops (Einsatzgruppen), soldiers specially trained to round up huge numbers of helpless people who were then marched into wooded areas where they were shot individually in the back of the neck and then buried in huge communal pits. Others were shipped to the extermination camps in Poland where they were gassed, after being judged unable to perform the labor necessary to build roads and fortifications. The concentration camps in Poland consisted of relocation centers, labor camps, slave labor concentration camps, and the ultimate answer to the final solution, extermination camps.

Auschwitz, Maidanek and Stutthof were combination concentration-extermination centers. Four other camps were established in Poland in order to carry out the mass murder of all European Jews. These were Belzek, Sorbibor, Treblinka and Chelmno.

The extermination centers used diabolical methods to create an impression among the arriving prisoners that they would be housed in a new area and retrained to work at jobs that were necessary to sustain the German government until the war ended. Everything possible was done to create the illusion of a resettlement area and a new way of life. Post cards were distributed to be sent to loved-ones at home. The prisoners were encouraged to tell their relatives how good things would be in the future. Then, all clothes and shoes were collected to be disinfected. They were told their clothes would be redistributed after they had showered and been deloused. They were told this was necessary to prevent illness and epidemics. Quietly assured, the prisoners were then led an area marked "shower room." Twenty minutes later, their bodies were removed by specially selected prisoners who burned the bodies in huge ovens or over large pits crisscrossed with railway ties. The bodies were laid out like logs stacked over a barbeque pit. Women, whose bodies contained more fat, were placed at the top of the pile so that their fat could drip on to the lower bodies, thus making the fire burn more efficiently. The German engineer who devised this system of efficiency was given a medal by his government for services rendered above and beyond the call of duty.

However, even at top efficiency, the ovens could not keep up with the inflow of human fuel that was gathered from the far corners of the Nazi empire. The ovens burned until the last moments before allied troops entered the individual camps. In many of the camps, the ovens were still warm as the GIs entered the crematorium area. As they opened the doors of the giant ovens, an unbelievable sight met their eyes.

Eighteen and nineteen year old combat veterans had never seen anything like women's and children's bodies being purposefully burned in ovens. Some of the soldiers were unable to control their emotions. Spreading like wildfire, a collective frenzy developed. Who had done these terrible deeds? They must be found and made to pay for their crimes...NOW! The frenzy spread. The hunt for the perpetrators was on.

Inside the Compound

The trash detail was taken over by an SS guard who was cooperating with the prisoners. This created an opportunity for the SS guard and the trash detail prisoners to escape. The group left the camp at 5:00pm on April 26th. Two days later Karl Reimer, one of the prisoners, made contact with an American officer of the 157th in Pfaffenhofen, a town 20 miles north of Dachau, which had already been overrun by the advancing 45th Division of the 7th Army. After Reimer explained the urgency of the situation, the American officer said that immediate help would be sent to the camp.

Almost at the same time, several other escaped prisoners contacted some German former prisoners who were living in the town of Dachau. This group of dedicated Germans took over the radio station in Dachau and on the 28th of April broadcast an appeal from "Bavarian Freedom Action." This alerted other freed former prisoners as well as other escapees who joined together in taking over the Town Hall of Dachau. SS troops in the town of Dachau attacked the Town Hall, killing or capturing everyone involved in the anti-Nazi group, including several veterans of the Spanish Civil War who had been held prisoner in Dachau.

The shooting at the Town Hall stopped the evacuations from the camp. The SS appointed older German home guard units to take over the guard duties at the camp. By then, most of the SS men had disappeared from the area.

By late afternoon of the 28th of April, the Prisoner

Committee was in effective control of the camp. They issued two instructions to the inmates. The first, to fill all receptacles with water, should the Germans blow up the buildings, as was rumored. The second order was for discipline to be maintained at all costs and to wait for further instructions from the Committee. The remaining German guards in the camp were interested only in making friendly gestures to the inmates hoping this would be enough to keep them alive when the Americans finally arrived.

At 11:00pm, on the 28th of April, the members of the International Committee met in Block 24. Representing 12 different countries, the 15 members discussed the status of their group, how long the remaining food in the camp would last and what the medical situation was. Major O'Leary, a Canadian, was voted the Commander of the International Committee. In truth, O'Leary was a Belgian doctor named Albert Guerisse. The atmosphere and security in Dachau, as in all other camps, made it necessary for many Allied prisoners to assume fake identities since German informers infiltrated all the international groups, hoping to get some extra food in trade for secrets passed on to the German administrators. Guerisse, in fact, was a much wanted intelligence officer and undoubtedly would have been put to instant death had his true identity been known. The only American prisoner at the time of liberation, Lt. Rene J. Giraud, assumed the rank of Major for the same reason. Rank meant authority, which put him on equal footing with the Russian, French and Belgian officers who were the decision makers. It was only during the Inspector General investigation, which took place after liberation, that Rene J. Giraud's true rank became known.

Deciding which language to use when passing instructions to the prisoners or even in the committees' discussions became the first major obstacle to be overcome. The French insisted French was the language of diplomacy, and therefore should be used in all discussions as well as announcements to the prisoners. It was pointed out to the French that not all committee members spoke or understood French, and that it would be impractical to conduct committee meetings in a language not understood by everyone. The French remained adamant. They threatened to walk out. With their very lives at stake, the French still wanted to talk about diplomacy. The agreed on compromise specified that meetings would be held in German but notices to the 32,000 prisoners would be sent out in many different languages. The French were not happy, but reluctantly agreed.

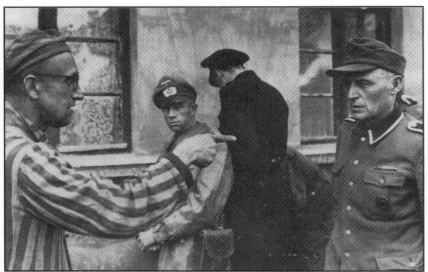

A prisoner confronts a guard after liberation.

Why? Why?

Part I

A group of older men visited the Office of Military History in Washington, D.C. in 1993. All the men were veterans who had been in World War II in Germany. The men, all in their seventies and eighties, were intrigued by a black and white map of Europe that hung in the Director's office. The map was a German military map that indicated the locations of concentration camps all over Europe. Dated 1945, the map reflected the location of 5,000 camps. The visitors pointed to the areas of Europe they had gone through during their military service. Most of the men had been liberators of Buchenwald or Dachau or one of the many sub-camps. (Dachau alone had 240 sub-camps which led to much confusion post war when many different military units claimed they had liberated Dachau.)

Within two months after Hitler assumed total power in Germany, the first concentration camp, Dachau, was put into service. From its inception in March 1933, Dachau was destined to become the prototype for terror and death for all other concentration camps that were to follow over the next twelve years. Dachau became the testing ground for the most brutal, sadistic, maniacal forms of torture, deprivation, starvation, humiliation and death ever to be devised by the human mind. The limits of these unspeakable and unthinkable horrors knew no bounds. Within a short time, the mere mention of the name "Dachau" put fear and terror into the hearts and minds of the people of Europe.

It was here in Dachau that Hitler, his henchmen and the SS Deaths Head leaders devised the means and methods for turning doctors, lawyers, politicians, teachers, journalists, babies, mothers, daughters, fathers and sons into inhuman, unseeing, unthinking animals of a type hitherto unknown to man.

In the spring of 1945 it was clear that an Allied victory was imminent.   To Hitler, however, the number one priority remained the extermination of European Jews. He gave orders for all prisoners to be moved from concentration camps about to be liberated by Americans. They were to be sent to Dachau, deep in the heart of German controlled Bavaria. From the east, from the west, from north and from the south, the death trains all headed for Dachau, destined to be among the last of the death camps to be liberated by the Allied forces. Inward, ever inward, deeper into the heart of Bavaria. 12 miles northwest of Munich, Dachau's ovens continued to burn. From the ovens of Dachau, ashes showered down on Bavaria, the birthplace of Nazism.

In this laboratory of death, American GIs were to see with their own eyes what Hitler and his followers had spewed forth on planet earth. This would be an experience that was not wartime propaganda or something thought up by a psychological warfare team. This was factual – Americans seeing with their own eyes the outcome of hatred and persecution. Bodies, some still alive, of Gypsies, Slavs, Russians and Jews, the human beings the Nazis called "vermin." In Dachau they saw Protestant and Catholic clergymen suffering and dying from degradation and dehumanization. They were the remnants of all those who offered resistance or had not agreed with the insane machinations of Adolf Hitler. In Dachau, the American GI learned many things about World War II he hadn't understood before.

Of the sixteen million men and women in the Armed

Forces, three and a half million served in Europe. This story could have happened to any one of them. It did in fact happen to infantrymen of the 42nd and 45th Divisions of General Alexander Patch's 7th Army. Average American boys, many of them only 18 years old. They came from Pennsylvania, New York, Colorado, Oklahoma, Texas, Illinois, California and almost every other state in the union. They were youngsters when they arrived in Dachau. They left as men. Their lives would never be the same again.

Part II

The war was rapidly winding down. No one knew it at the time, but within two weeks peace would be declared and all the killing would be over and done with. A few short months ago when GIs from different outfits would pass each other on the road they would call out, "END THE WAR IN FORTY FOUR." That was when their officers had assured the men that the war would be over by Christmas. The greeting had now changed to, "STAY ALIVE IN FORTY FIVE!!" Now that the Germans were in full-fledged retreat it was not unusual for the infantry troops to advance forty or fifty miles a day. They utilized any type of transportation available in their race towards Bavaria, in southern Germany. General Patton, pushing his Third Army to its maximum effort, was competing with General Patch's 45th and 42nd Divisions of the Seventh Army in their efforts to be the first to reach Hitler's stronghold. Capturing Hitler would insure immortality for the group lucky enough to reach Hitler's Eagles Nest first.

Racing towards Munich, the 3rd Battalion, 157th Infantry Regiment of the 45th Division was stopped in its tracks, not by the Germans, but by a radio message from Headquarters diverting the Battalion to a place called Dachau, some 12 miles northwest of Munich. The message advised the Battalion

Commander, Lieutenant Colonel Felix Sparks, to take control of the area, seal it off, allowing no one to enter or leave the area until the arrival of an International Committee. The men of I Company of the 157th Infantry Regiment accomplished their mission. For the rest of their lives they would be proud to be liberators, but would remain haunted by the memories of that hell on earth called Dachau.

One month earlier, the 45th Division had entered Germany. They had fought the German army in Sicily, Anzio, up the boot of Italy, invaded France and at last were fighting on German soil. Then, at Aschaffenburg, they were held up for more than a week by some of the most brutal fighting of the entire war. Lieutenant Colonel Sparks was told that the Aschaffenburg area had been cleared by Patton's tanks. He was told nothing about Task Force Baum.

Less than 24 hours before the 45th Division had been assigned the Aschaffenburg area, Task Force Baum had been sent on a mission impossible deep behind the German lines. At the specific request of General George S. Patton, the Task Force headed towards Hammelburg, a prisoner of war camp, 60 miles beyond the Americans' furthest penetration of German territory. Although Patton had originally requested 3,000 men for the operation, his request had been turned down by his superior, General Omar Bradley. When authorization for a 300 man Task Force was received, the group immediately took off with Captain Abraham Baum as its commanding officer. Neither General Bradley nor Captain Baum had been told that Patton's son-in-law was one of the prisoners in the camp at Hammelburg.

Miraculously the task force reached Hammelburg. After freeing some of the officers as well as enlisted men held in a separate enclosure Baum had not known about before the raid, Task force Baum attempted the return trip to Aschaffenburg.

The entire Task Force was decimated. All of its members were killed, wounded or taken prisoner. Patton's son-in-law was wounded and remained in the Prisoner of War (POW) Camp. Less than a week later, Patch's 7th Army freed all the American POWs.

With the fighting at Aschaffenburg behind them, the 45th Division continued in its rout of the retreating Germans. As they approached Dachau, a sweet but terrible smell permeated the air. One of the men said it smelled like the Chicago stockyards. Another said it reminded him of a jute factory. Their Commanding Officer, Sparks, told them to avoid the front gates and come in from the rear. As they emerged from the woods they came upon a long line of railroad freight cars. Someone asked, "What's a freight train doing here?"

Part III

The train's cars were filled with what looked like stacked cordwood. Closer inspection proved the cordwood to be human bodies with bones, arms and legs sticking out in every direction, 39 railway cars filled with the bodies of dead skeleton like figures that used to be men, women and children. 2,300 bodies with only one still able to move and moan for help. On top of one pile lay a young girl with her eyes wide open as if looking up at God and asking, "Why?" The GI who came across the little girl would see her face in his mind every night for the next 60 years until he was mercifully able to fall asleep. Even as an old man he was unable to answer her innocent question.

The entrance to Dachau, with the huge sign "ARBEIT MACHT FREI" (Work Will Make You Free), deceptively beckoned the GIs towards the buildings. At the railway cars GIs were running from one car to the other and shouting and screaming at the top of their lungs. Inhuman sounds were com-

ing from the GIs. Some were kneeling. Some were bent over
and retching. Some seemed to be crying. Most were just staring straight ahead, wide-eyed with horror and disbelief. Guys
were running and pointing in all directions.

Suddenly, a huge shout arose from among the railway cars.
An 18-year-old walked over to see what the commotion was
about. As he neared the cars, he involuntarily dropped his rifle,
which for the past 9 months had become an extension of his
body. Even when he slept, his hands never left his rifle. He did-
n't stop to pick the piece up; his eyes were glued to the railway
car. His mouth was open, but he couldn't breathe. An overwhelming stench covered the whole area. He found himself
moving forward as if in a nightmare. He heard himself saying,
"No, it can't be, it can't be. Please, God, make it be just a dream.
Dear God, make it just a dream. Please, don't let it be for real."

Up ahead, the shouting grew louder and louder. GIs were
climbing into one of the railway cars. Maybe it's just these few
cars that are like this. Maybe the others are different. Jesus, I
hope they're different. Maybe that's why they're shouting so
much. He was breathing with great difficulty and his eyes automatically peered into each car as he passed, silently praying that
the horror would stop. But, they were all the same. Packed as
solid as could be with human bodies, arms, legs pointed in all
directions. Some were naked, some in torn, striped remnants of
cloth. All looking like skeletons with bones sticking out from
every part of the body. Some cars had only women, some children.   But most were crammed full of bodies that had once
been men.

The shouting grew louder and louder. One of the bodies in
the next car had moved. One of the skeletons had somehow
survived. It was still alive!

The battle hardened, rough, tough infantrymen handled
that body with the tenderness of a young mother holding her

newborn baby for the first time. With tears streaming down their faces, they gently passed the survivor from man to man. "Medic! Medic! We need help!"

One German SS officer stood in the shadows of a nearby building, observing the frantic efforts of the GIs. He whispered to himself in perfect English, "Nothing will help, assholes. There's no way you can keep that piece of garbage alive." One GI heard the German's comment. Suddenly, a shot rang out; it was impossible to tell from where. The German officer, impeccably dressed in shiny boots and a well-pressed uniform, slumped to the ground.

Part IV

Before Hitler, before concentration camps existed, the small town of Dachau had been known as a quiet artists' community. It boasted a castle and a 1,200 year history of peace and tranquility. Then, in 1933, the Nazis established the Dachau camp. Built to hold 5,000 "undesirable elements," considered to be enemies of the Reich, the camp was operated by the SS and Gestapo. In the beginning, the prisoner population was made up of political opponents, clergymen, Jews, homosexuals and common criminals. Dachau was not set up as an extermination center. It would take the Germans ten years to develop their infamous "Final Solution" and to find the man capable of implementing it.

German industrialists worked for ten years to refine their processes for killing in volume. The German military machine devised punishment camps, slave labor camps, medical experimentation camps and finally, the most horrible concept ever thought of by human minds, the extermination camps. These camps were so inhumane that the Germans established them in Poland and the Ukraine using, for the most part, willing native overseers. This was done so that the German population could be far removed from the fiendish events that took place there. Dachau, however, was the prototype for many of the innovations that the other concentration camps later adopted.

The character and make up of the prisoner population changed many times during the 12 years of the camp's existence. Different Commandants imposed their own rules and regulations as to who would be registered as an inmate and who would not. Russian prisoners of war were eliminated without recording their names and numbers. Some were shot in the back of the head; some were used as running targets for the SS to practice their shooting abilities; some were made to stand outside their barracks stripped naked with vicious guard dogs surrounding them. Doused with cold water, they would stand at attention in the freezing cold of winter nights until their frozen bodies were removed in the morning. Those that moved from their designated spot were killed by the dogs. No names or records were kept of these unfortunates.

Under the "Disciplinary and Penal Code" issued by the first Commandant, Eicke, prisoners could be hanged for any infringement of the camp rules, which included everything imaginable. Guards were able to kill prisoners whenever the urge came over them. By 1940, dead bodies became a problem. It was solved by the installation of the first crematorium.

For the SS and Gestapo agents assigned to Dachau, life was good. They lived in a country club atmosphere with many trees and flowers, comfortable living quarters, a swimming pool, tennis courts and plenty of space for their children to play. They were a short drive from Munich, the third largest city in Germany, with many beer halls and other places of entertainment. It was a deceptive picture.

In the prisoner compound, separated from the SS living quarters by trees, bushes, a moat and an electrified fence,

30,000 slave laborers existed. Only death could release these tormented souls from the tortures and deprivations which were their daily way of life.

Smoke from the crematorium at Dachau never stopped, until they ran out of fuel with which to feed the ovens. The daily ritual of watching fellow inmates being flogged, hanged at the stake or executed by a pistol shot to the back of the head did not cause the other prisoners to flinch. They had seen and experienced even worse, if that can be imagined. They had grown incapable of reacting to the norm.

The prisoners had developed a defense mechanism of turning off their minds to the events in front of them. Those that were not able to turn off their minds, ran into electrified fences that surrounded the prisoner compound. Their burnt bodies were then thrown into the water-filled moat that was next to the confinement area. This practice of throwing bodies into the moat went on for a long time until the townspeople complained that their underground water system was becoming contaminated. Since the townspeople provided many of the goods and services for the camp, the administration complied with the request to stop throwing the bodies into the moat. From then on, the bodies went up in ashes, as did the other prisoners who died at Dachau.

Some prisoners were provided with special services, and even fed special foods. Two German medical specialists were in charge of that section of the camp. To some extent, they tried to keep their special prisoners alive. In the "experimental station," Dr. Rascher and Professor Schilling carried on their various bio-chemical experiments. Prisoners were injected with serum containing malaria or typhus germs in order to study how the body reacted. In most of their experiments, the patients were not given painkillers of any kind, in order to observe the body's reactions and resistance. Prisoners were frozen and then thawed out, using the most unconventional methods imaginable in trying to revive them. Prisoners were held underwater until their lungs burst in order to see how long the body could survive without oxygen. Prisoners were submitted to high altitude tests so doctors could determine how high a pilot could fly before blacking out. There was virtually no experiment the medical profession would turn down. They had millions of prisoners. A single sheet of writing paper was worth more than a prisoner's life. Anesthesia cost money, therefore, it was not used. The prisoner would soon die anyway. No special precautions were necessary.

The guards at the camp adopted the same attitude as the medical specialists. Not for the "advancement of science," but for their own amusement. Every day after lunch, they would pick thirty prisoners at random to be taken to an area where there was an open latrine. Chairs would be there for the guards to sit on. At a given signal, ten of the prisoners would kneel next to the open latrine. The other twenty prisoners would lie down, one on each side of the kneeling prisoners. At the next signal, the kneeling prisoners would grab the heads of the ones lying down, a head in each hand, forcing the heads into the slime and filth of the latrine. The guards would bet on which pair of legs would stop kicking first. Then, with great laughter, they would bet on which prisoner would last the longest. Finally, when all the legs had stopped kicking, they would shoot the kneeling prisoners in the back of their heads, kick their bodies into the open latrine and head back to their prisoner compound. Tomorrow would be another day. Life could be good.

The guard who had learned this form of entertainment at Buchenwald claimed that the women guards were the first to play this wonderful game. Ya, life could be good. After the day's entertainment, a meal consisting of chicken and knockwurst, accompanied by some good German beer, was consumed. And then, back to work with the Untermenchen, "the inferiors."

Part V

The young GI took a long, slow drink from his canteen. He sat down on the ground with his back leaning against a concrete building. He took some long, deep breaths, and then decided to go on. Nothing that he would ever have to face again in this world could be as horrible as what he had just seen, he told himself fearfully. "Right?" he whispered hesitantly.

As he turned the corner of the building he had been sitting against, he began to sweat and throw up violently. Tears were coming from his eyes in torrents. He retched uncontrollably. All around him, other GIs were bent over, suffering the same symptoms. There were bodies all over the place. An attempt had been made to stack them in piles, but that job had never been completed. There were thousands of them. Lying in every direction. Some with black and white-type clothing, others totally naked. Legs and arms pointing in every direction. The smell in the area was incredible. The stacks of bodies were perhaps 4 feet tall. From a distance, one would think they were piles of logs.

He moved dumbly through the bodies toward dirt mounds with huge pits behind them. The pits stretched endlessly. They were filled with still more grotesque, naked, staring bodies. Thrown in randomly, many of the bodies ended up facing straight up with their eye sockets staring at those who came close enough to the edge of the pit to look in. The skeletal faces seemed to be saying, "Look, look. See what they have done here at Dachau. Don't let them lie. Don't let them say it never happened. They will try. Don't let us lie here in our final indignity in vain. Don't betray our memory. Go into the buildings,

GI. Go into the buildings and you will learn why dying was so easy for us. See what the German Reich has done, and make them pay for their crimes. Don't betray our memory."

The young soldier dazedly followed other GIs into the buildings of Dachau. He saw the large shower room, properly marked. He saw the rooms where people undressed and were given soap and a towel. He saw the huge doors that would close and seal the fate forever of those who had gone into the room, thinking they were going to take a shower. He saw the peepholes the SS had prepared for visitors who would line up to see the spectacle. He saw the showerheads from which no water could ever flow. He saw the canisters, Zyklon B gas, developed after much experimentation by the great German Industrial complex. The gas was perfected. Guaranteed. The scientist who developed it was given a medal. The gas would do its deadly job in a few minutes. There would be no survivors. Guaranteed.

Clean up and disposal of the bodies was no problem. Other prisoners knew their assignments. Wash and clean out the shower room mess, transport the bodies to the next step in the process, the ovens. Prisoners stood waiting with huge tongs and crowbars. The bodies were pushed and pulled until they were in the right places in the double door ovens. The huge flames turned the flesh into ashes in minutes. The ovens did not discriminate. They took Poles, Russians, Jews, Catholics, Protestants, Gypsies, homosexuals, deformed, demented, French, Italians, Czechs, Greeks and even Germans who refused to fight for Hitler. The ovens kept burning until the fuel ran out. That's when they dug the pits. The prisoners shoved the bodies in as fast as they could work, all the time knowing that when the job was done, it would be their turn to join their brethren on top of the pile.

The sound of the big guns was coming closer and closer to

Dachau. The SS was prepared to leave the camp before the Americans arrived. They didn't want to be captured anywhere near the camp or in an SS uniform. A token force was left to guard the camp with instructions that the prisoners be fed soup for lunch the next day. It was a matter of importance that the prisoners be fed before the camp would be liberated. The SS left, taking thousands of prisoners with them on a forced march headed south. "Feed the prisoners the soup."

The Americans came too quickly. The soup, which had been poisoned, had not been served. An SS officer with shiny boots, who claimed he had arrived only two days before the Americans came, was the one who surrendered the camp to the American officer. More than 30,000 prisoners were still alive on that last day. Many of them, having lived for that glorious moment, died in the days and weeks that followed.

The young GI tried to make some sense out of the insanity. The war was almost over. Except for isolated incidents, there was very little opposition to the American troops. Why did they keep up this insane killing in the camps? Why keep slaughtering these poor, unfortunate souls? There had to be a reason, or, at least a word for this mass insanity. But, the GI could not think of it. All he could say to himself over and over again was, "Why? Why?"

The camps kept their killing machines running until the last seconds before being overrun by the British, the Russians, the French, Canadians and the Americans. The Germans tried to destroy the evidence of their massive crimes against humanity, but at this at least, they were unsuccessful.

In the end, after many trials, some individuals were hanged as War Criminals. Among those were the SS officers who had been the commandants of the larger concentration camps. However, by 1951 not many people were interested in punishing German war criminals. The High Commissioner for

Germany, John J. McCloy, had commuted the sentences of almost all those sentenced to be hanged. Shortly thereafter, all prisoners were released.

Sixty years later, an estimated 50,000 SS members or their widows are still receiving pension checks from the German government. Under the German Federal War Victims Act, $400 million per year is currently being paid out in pensions to former war criminals. All members of the SS during World War II, by definition, were classified as war criminals.

The death train in Dachau.

Viewing bodies in the death train.

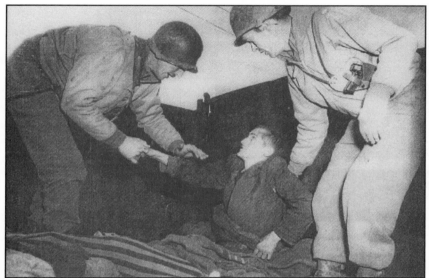

Col. Don Downard, 42nd infantry division, rescuing the only survivor of the death train at Dachau.

Main entrance to Dachau.

*Women
concentration
camp guards.*

*Prisoners in
barracks bunks
on liberation day.*

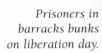

*A woman and her three
grandchildren on their
way to the gas chamber.*

This deceptive building housed the crematorium.

Ovens in the Dachau Crematorium.

The Coal Yard Wall

Part I

In the main camp of the Dachau complex an order was issued on April 23, at 1pm, to "immediately evacuate all Jews without exception." An exact count of how many Jews were in the camp on that date is not known, but 2,000 Jews responded and were lined up on the parade ground. During the night, 60 of this group died. At 8am the next day the group of Jews were forced on a Death March with ex-German prisoners as guards. These "guards" were more brutal to the unfortunate prisoners than the Wehrmacht soldiers had been.

As this Death March headed south towards Austria the SS still in the camp were burning papers, prisoners' lists and card files. Some prisoners were assigned to help with the sorting and burning. This gave the prisoners the opportunity to preserve and bury many of the lists and card files pertaining to the history of Dachau. The SS was also busy plundering Red Cross packages, which had been stored in warehouses. At the same time, prisoners who were important to the resistance were hidden in the hospital block with substitute names and the identity numbers of prisoners who had died within the past few days.

The chaos was such that by then the SS had no idea who belonged and who had been marched out or who had died. Prisoners working in SS offices heard and copied messages being received from Berlin. One such message directed to SS Lt. Gen. Pohl from Heinrich Himmler and then relayed to the

Commandant in Dachau stated that, "The surrender of the camp is absolutely out of the question. The camp is to be evacuated immediately. No prisoners must be allowed to fall into the hands of the enemy alive." The International Prisoners' Committee (IPC) knew what the message meant and reacted immediately.

On the 26th, the Germans ordered everyone in the camp into the roll-call area ready to march. The committee sent out word that this assembly was not to take place; following the order would mean certain death for the prisoners. The IPC committee ordered all prisoners to remove from their shirts the badges indicating their nationalities.

The inmate population of the main camp and nearby sub-camps amounted to 67,000 prisoners. Polish prisoners predominated with 15,000, followed by Russians, 13,500; Hungarians 12,000; Germans, 6,000; Frenchmen, 6,000 and approximately 2000 Jews. By stalling as much as possible, it was thought many people could be saved. Tensions rose to the breaking point. Chaos reigned supreme. Something different was going on within every group in every corner of the Dachau complex.

In the camp itself the atmosphere changed hourly from dark pessimism to extreme optimism. The committee was determined to save as many of the prisoners as possible. They implemented measures for internal security hoping to keep the camp in the hands of responsible members and to prevent provocations of any kind by unorganized groups. In the event that the SS attempted a massacre, the Committee planned to call for an all out confrontation and implement their most secret plans for a general breakout.

When an American Infantry Company goes into combat mode, every man is assigned a specific duty. What may look like bedlam to an outsider, in reality is a well-organized, coordinated attack by a group of men trained and ready to perform their individual specialties. The chaos taking place in the prisoner compound of Dachau, however, was absolute and total turmoil. For the prisoners, survival was the key word and anything that could be done to insre survival was being done.

The first Americans who entered the main Dachau prison compound were devastated. Having no idea what to expect, the sights that met their eyes as they viewed the condition of the skeleton-like bodies before them pushed them beyond the limits of what a human mind could rationally accept. They cracked.

One GI was able to handle the sights relatively well until he spotted a young girl of perhaps four or five. She was holding her mother's hand tightly. Every bone on their bodies was visible with tightly pulled skin showing their state of starvation. As the prisoners looked at the American soldiers marching past the little girl whispered a question to her mother. The GI asked a prisoner nearby what the girl had said. "She is asking the mother, yes, if now that the Americans have saved them, yes, if now she will be allowed to cry." The GI lifted the little girl in his arms. He hugged and squeezed her frail little body as her tears mixed with those running down his face.

Within hours of liberation, Dachau resembled a scene from the Tower of Babel. Hundreds of American troops from the 42nd and 45th Divisions tried to bring about some semblance of order. English as well as German, Russian, Greek, Polish, Dutch, Spanish, French and an assortment of Slavic languages could be heard coming from the different groups of prisoners.

One individual recognized an opportunity to escape punishment for the obvious war crimes that had taken place at Dachau. In the turmoil, a German SS lieutenant surrendered the concentration camp to Brigadier General Henning Linden. of the 42nd Infantry Division. The lieutenant, identified for more than 54 years as Heinrich Wickert, told the Americans that he had just arrived at the camp and had taken charge of the surrender arrangements with Victor Maurer of the International Committee of the Red Cross (I.C.R.C.). For 54 years historians tried unsuccessfully to uncover information relating to Heinrich Wickert. It was an impossible task. Wickert's background remained a total mystery.

Arthur Lee of Aurora, Illinois had been a sergeant major in the 42nd Infantry Division during World War II. Tracing the chronological events that took place during the liberation of Dachau became a passion with the former sergeant major. In December 1991, he became one of the first historians to uncover the missing Inspector General's Report that surfaced 46 years after it was "lost." Tracking the background of the man erroneously identified in the International Red Cross report as Wickert took Arthur Lee 6 years.

Utilizing every tracking service available, including those of the German Army in Berlin and Munich, Lee finally solved the mystery. The man identified as Wickert in the Red Cross Report was really Heinrich Wicker, a lieutenant in the notorious SS Death's Head units assigned to concentration camps. By telling the Americans he had just arrived in Dachau two days before liberation, he hoped to escape the responsibility for the atrocities that had taken place in Dachau at the hands of the SS.

What finally happened to Heinrich Wicker is still a mystery but his identity is now a certainty. Fifty books refer to his false name, all taking their lead from the first I.C.R.C. report written by Victor Maurer in 1945. By definition, all members of Hitler's elite SS squads were classified by the Allied Forces as war criminals. Heinrich Wicker graduated from the ranks of Hitler's Youth Groups and then enlisted in 1937 in the SS-Totenkopfver Band. He supervised atrocities committed in Berlin-Oranienburg, Natzweler-Struthof as well as in Dachau He was a war criminal.

Part II

As the Germans surrendered, orders were given to troops to assemble the regular German soldiers in one area while placing the Death's Head SS men in the hospital coal yard. Several riflemen, a B.A.R. man, (Browning automatic rifle) and a machine gun team were assigned to guard these SS men. As the machine gunner began to assemble his equipment, there was a visible movement at the far end of the wall where the SS men had been told to stand. It is not known what caused the 58 men to start moving forward.

Suddenly a shout was heard. "Fire." Pandemonium broke out. As shots rang out the entire line of SS men dropped to the ground. Witnesses then stated they saw a running figure enter the area emptying a .45 calibre pistol into the air while shouting for the shooting to stop. Four prisoners remained standing while the others, most of whom were feigning death, remained on the ground. When the shooting subsided, the prisoners arose. Seventeen lay where they fell.

Unknown to any of the participants, a movie film as well as still pictures were being taken of the shooting at the wall by an army photographic combat team. The films were flown to England that evening where high ranking officers digested their meaning.

Eisenhower's communique for April 29, 1945 stated, "Our forces liberated and mopped up the infamous concentration camp at Dachau. Approximately 30,000 prisoners were liberated; 300 SS camp guards were quickly neutralized."

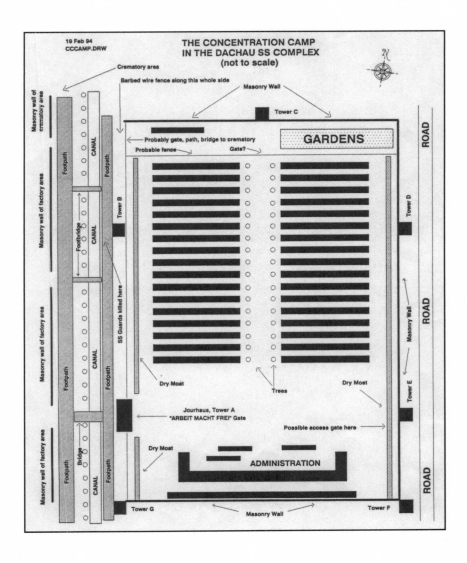

19 Feb 94
CCCAMP.DRW

Crematory area

Barbed wire fence along this whole side

Masonry Wall

Masonry wall of crematory area

Footpath

CANAL

Footpath

Tower C

Probably gate, path, bridge to crematory

Probable fence

Gate?

GARDENS

ROAD

Masonry wall of factory area

Footbridge

CANAL

Tower B

Tower D

SS Guards killed here

Masonry wall of factory area

Footpath

CANAL

Footpath

Masonry Wall

Dry Moat

Dry Moat

Tower E

Trees

Jourhaus, Tower A
"ARBEIT MACHT FREI" Gate

Possible access gate here

ROAD

Masonry wall of factory area

Footpath

Bridge

CANAL

Footpath

Dry Moat

ADMINISTRATION

Tower G

Masonry Wall

Tower F

ROAD

A series of four signal corps photos showing Lt. Colonel Felix E. Sparks stopping the shooting of German guards at the coal yard wall.

U.S. CITIZENS INCARCERATED AT THE DACHAU CONCENTRATION CAMP BETWEEN 1940 AND 1945.-

NAME	U.S. BORN	FOREIGN BORN	POW	JEW	DATE OF ARRIVAL	MOVED TO ANOTHER KL OR AK*	DIED AT KLD*	LIBERATED AT KLD*
Alif, Rudolf		X			Jan 45			X
Berkovitz, Eugen		X		X	Oct 44			X
Dziegiet, Eugenius	X				May 40			
Engel, Nikolaus		X		X	Oct 44		X	
Fleisher, Josef	?			X	Aug 44	X		
Friteh, Karl		X			May 40	X		
Günsberger, Eugen		X		X	Oct 44	X		
Günzberger, Desider		X		X	Oct 44		X	
Guiraud, René	X		X		Sep 44			X
Klein, Ignac	X			X	Jan 45			X
Kronowit, Zoltan		X		X	Oct 44	X		
Kunos, Benő	X			X	Jan 45		X	
Lesnik, Karl		X			Jun 44	X		
Martinot, Pierre		X	X		Jul 44	X		
Michalski, Jan	X				Apr 40	X		
Michalski, Konrad	X		X		Apr 45		X	
Osos, Paul	X				Jul 44	X		
Pasternak, Thomas		X		X	Oct 44		X	
Pasternak, Tivadan		X		X	Oct 44		X	
Pasternak, Wilhelm		X		X	Oct 44		X	
Prine, Hugo		X		X	Aug 44	X		
Rosenberger, David		X		X	Oct 44	X		
Roskos, Johann		X			Apr 45			X
Sargarow, Alexander		X			Nov 44			X
Schlamm, György		X			Jan 45			X
Spanier, Jonny	X			X	Nov 44		X	
Spira, Arthur		X			Jan 45		X	
Steiner, Ernő		X		X	Jan 45		X	
Vlcek, Aurel		X		X	Jan 45	X		
TOTAL(S)	8 + 1 ?	20	3	16		12	10	7

NOTES : (*) KL, AK and KLD are the acronyms for "Konzentrationslager" (Concentration Camp), "Aussenkommando" (Subcamp) and "Konzentrationslager Dachau".

René Jean-Anare Guiraud was a First Lieutenant who was born in Chicago on October 5, 1920, retired from the Service on May 31, 1952 with the grade of Major and died on January 29, 1970.

Pierre M. Martinot was a Captain who was born in Lunéville (France) on August 19, 1903 and he was liberated at Allach, a subcamp of KL Dachau. He retired on disability on December 27, 1945 and died on October 5, 1986.

Konrad Michalski was born in Chicago on June 23, 1919 and his records at the Dachau Memorial show only that he was a "Kriegsgefangener" (Prisoner of War).

Josef Fleisher's records show that he was born in Chicago on August 18, 1912, however, the name of that city is followed by a question mark.

Prepared by Pierre C.T. Verheye
Buchenwald Political Prisoner No.   February 22, 1997

Prepared by Pierre C.T. Verheye, Buchenwald Political Prisoner.

Fixed Bayonets

During basic training, a long time ago, the men had been taught bayonet fighting. Never once in real combat had they ever been given an order to "Fix Bayonets." Now, deep in Bavaria, Germany, with the war in its last stages, they were given the order. In bewilderment the men fell in with fixed bayonets and waited with disbelief for what was to come.

The Dachau Concentration Camp had been liberated on Sunday. The next day the inmates of the camp staged a parade that was to be followed by a religious ceremony. No one knew where the flags came from, but every national group had a flag of its own which they carried proudly as they marched before the observing American troops. Colonel George S. Stevens, the famous Hollywood producer was filming the former prisoners as they marched by laughing and gesturing while shouting words of comradeship to their American liberators.

Off to one side Stevens noticed a group of prisoners who were even more bedraggled than the marchers. They looked like living skeletons. He asked who they were and was told, "Oh they are only the Jews." Stevens approached the group and started asking questions.

"We are not allowed to march with the other survivors because we have no flag. Nor do we have a country to go back to. We are told that we are different. We have only our religion," the spokesman told Stevens. Stevens felt a great compassion, but had no immediate answers for the people without a flag or a country to return to. When the conversation was over, he headed straight for the office of the American Commander of the camp. Within a few minutes an orderly was sent to deliver a message to the isolated group of Jewish survivors. They were all to gather the next day at the appelplatz (assembly area) to hold a religious service that would be filmed by Stevens and his photographic crew.

The next morning, Stevens and his crew arrived and set up their equipment. Not one Jewish survivor was there to meet him. Furious, Stevens went looking for the men he had spoken with the previous afternoon. He was directed to the horse stables where he found a group of some 200 men praying. When asked why they were holding their services in the horse stables rather than on the parade grounds where the photographers were waiting, the spokesman for the group told Stevens that the Polish prisoners had forbidden the Jews from having a religious service on the parade grounds. The Jews had been told that the stables could be used for their ceremonies. Since the Poles numbered 8,000 versus the Jewish number of 200, the Jews decided to hold their service in the stable area as ordered. Stevens was speechless. "Who the hell is running this camp?" he asked in exasperation. Once again he patiently explained to the spokesman that he would like the group to hold their religious service on the parade grounds and that the photographers would take pictures of the ceremonies. Stevens went on to explain that these arrangements had been cleared with the American Commander. On leaving the group Stevens made another trip to the Commander's office.

The next day a company of United States Infantry marched onto the parade grounds of the Dachau Concentration Camp. Each soldier had a bayonet affixed to his rifle. Closely behind the soldiers, trying to keep up with the military pace, came 200 Jewish stragglers, survivors of Hitler's Holocaust. As the soldiers peeled off at specified intervals, they came to parade rest facing thousands of other survivors who looked on in astonishment from the perimeter of the parade grounds.

The Jewish group, clustered together at the center of the field, began their religious ceremony as Colonel George S. Stevens and his film crew recorded the event. The soldiers on guard stared straight ahead as the bayonet blades glistened in the morning sunlight. As the wailing of ancient chants drifted above the parade ground, thousands of survivors stood around the perimeter wondering why tears were coming from the eyes of the young Americans who stood erect, guarding the small group of Jews as they poured out their hearts to their God.

Retribution.

Survey of Internees at Dachau Concentration Camp
By Nationalities at Liberation - 29 April 1945

German Nationals ....(including 6 women) 1,173
Belgians...848
Danes 1
British 8
Estonians 11
French 3,918
Greeks..195
Italians..2,184
Croats...103
Serbs 79
Slovenes...2,907
Latianis 27
Lithuianians 39
Alsace Lorraines 36
Luxembourgers...133
Dutch 558
Norwegians...79
Poles..(including 96 women) 9,082
Rumanians 50
Russians ....(including 9 women) 4,258
Slovaks 44
Albanians 30
Americans..6
Maltese 1
Arabians 1
Armenians 2
Finns..1
Iraqs 1
Irans 1
Turks 3
Spaniards 194
Exiles 21
Czechs 1,632
Hungarians ....(including 34 women) 670
Bulgarians..8
Portugese 4
Swiss 2
Austrians..253
Annex-Germans 2
Sudetens 3
Jews..(including 225 women) 2,539
Total 31,432

The Forced Deck

The other men all called him Ace. He always had a deck of cards in his hands, and whenever a replacement came into the outfit he always greeted the new man with a, "Hi how are you? Where are you from? Pick a card-any card. Go ahead. Don't be bashful, pick a card."

The new man, feeling unsure of himself, and not wanting to offend anyone, would pick a card from the middle of the deck after giving it a thorough shuffle.

"Ace of Diamonds," the hustler would announce with a flourish. The new man would be properly amazed at this performance of skill and would heap all kinds of praise on Ace for his obvious display of skill. The old timers in the group laughed in good spirit for they had all been through the drill and each one could have come up with the same correct guess. Everyone knew Ace's forced deck of card trick, an ordinary looking deck of playing cards in a sealed box. Any newcomer would be convinced that Ace was a true performer, only to find out much later that all 52 cards in the deck were the ace of diamonds. It was impossible to pick anything other than the ace of diamonds. Everyone always had a good laugh over the looks of surprise when an ace of diamonds was turned up, and it was always the right card.

"Ace" was one of the first riflemen into the hellhole at Dachau. He retched along with his fellow squad members and gasped for a breath of fresh air just as everyone else did. His inner organs felt like they were being torn apart as he viewed the survivors and the unbelievable condition of their bodies. As the survivors reached out to touch the liberators on the hand, foot or any piece of GI clothing or equipment, a few who had memorized some English greeting whispered, "Hello soldier. What is your name?"

Tears streamed from the faces of the American youngsters as they searched their pockets frantically for some item of value to give to the wildly outstretched hands – candy bars, cigarettes, gum. "Why don't I have anything I can give to these poor people?" Slips of paper, dirty filthy, yellow stained paper, were thrust at the GIs, and with pleading eyes the survivors begged the Americans to contact the name on the paper to tell them that a brother, cousin or uncle was still alive. There was precious little paper to go around, and then suddenly, as if by magic, little cards appeared; the survivors were able to write their relatives' names on a clean, white surface. A giant roar went up from the surging crowd in the middle of which stood Ace, handing out cards to the cheering mob, and on each card one could clearly see an Ace of Diamonds.

In that instant, Ace became a hero. He pulled deck after deck from hidden pockets which he threw to other nearby GIs so that they too could hand out the Aces to the grateful survivors. Many in the mob begged the GIs to write their name and their outfit on the little card so that they would always be remembered as the first liberators into the notorious concentration camp of Dachau. A blinking eye from a survivor signaled heartfelt thanks to the GIs as they handed back the playing cards with their names and outfit inscribed. As the prisoners gratefully accepted the prized possession, an unspoken feeling of friendship passed between the two individuals. Words were not uttered, but the look that passed between them would be remembered for many years to come.

Ace never played the guessing game with his cards after that eventful day in Dachau. It was no longer fun.

Grateful survivors ask GIs to write their names and outfits.

The Gray Ghosts

By the middle of April 1945, the Germans were retreating with such speed it was almost impossible for the Americans to keep up with them. The orders from Eisenhower were to pursue with every means possible, giving the enemy no opportunity to regroup. With victory in sight, the feeling that the war was in the last stage strengthened the American GIs as they used every type of transportation imaginable to rout the retreating Germans.

In the concentration camps located in Bavaria, the sound of artillery fire could be plainly heard. Arrangements were quickly made to evacuate some of the prisoners for a march south towards the Austrian border. The German guards called the roll of the marchers - Jews, Russians and Slavs. In the midst of great confusion and chaos, the groups lined up in columns of fives, left the prisoner compound of Dachau and headed south, their final destination a total secret. The prisoners were frequently ordered into the ditches at the side of the road as Allied planes swooped low, dropping bombs and strafing at what the Allied pilots thought were retreating German troops. At one point during an air raid, the Jewish prisoners saw a direct hit on a locomotive. Belching smoke and steam, the huge machine reared up and blew apart. The prisoners stood up and cheered, totally unmindful of the danger they exposed themselves to. They knew they were watching the destruction of the Nazi war machine and they could not deny themselves the joy they felt.

When the air raid ended, the few remaining German guards ordered the prisoners to begin marching again. Any unfortunates who could not go on were shot on the spot. Giant shepherd dogs and Dobermans ran alongside the prisoners, snapping and biting as they struggled to keep up. As the weakest ones fell, the dogs lunged for their throats, finally putting them out of their misery.

In spite of the shootings and killings by the dogs, the column of Gray Ghosts never grew smaller. More Jews, Russians, Ukrainians and Slavs joined the long line. Suddenly, the line came to a halt. At the head of the line, a white truck could be seen with red crosses on the huge white body of the vehicle. The prisoners crowded around the truck as the guards stood to one side, watching the prisoners struggling with each other, trying to get some bread that was being handed out of the truck to the dying marchers. The scene was bizarre with thousands of gray, ghost-like prisoners on their final death march being given time to consume some bread thrown to them by the Red Cross workers. The bread would give them the strength they needed to continue their march to death. This group of gray ghosts had no idea that similar scenes were taking place all over Bavaria as Red Cross trucks came upon the groups marching five or eight across, heading in all different directions.

Chaos reigned supreme. Rumors were repeated up and down the lines that prisoners would be used to build fortifications in the area where the Nazis would make their last stand. No one stopped to ask why some lines of prisoners were going north, while others went south or west. The truth was, no one knew where they were headed, only that it had to be in a direction away from the advancing Russian troops. The Germans knew about the horrors inflicted on the Russian people by German troops. The Russians also knew what the Germans had done. They had no use for future war crime trials; they meted out justice on the spot without wasting time on tribunals. The marchers continued on in any direction away from the Russian soldiers.

As the artillery sounds grew louder and louder, the long line of prisoners was directed down into a ravine. The German guards remained on watch at the top of the ravine as darkness fell.

At first light the next morning, some of the stronger prisoners climbed to the top of the ravine where the German guards had been when night fell. This morning brought them the most surprising and shocking news of their lives. The German guards had gone. Disappeared. In the distance, a jeep was approaching with four smallish men dressed in khaki uniforms. Surprisingly, they appeared to be Asian. As they grew closer and closer, the prisoners heard the unmistakable language the soldiers were speaking; it was English!!!

The American soldiers hugged the gray, ghostlike figures, offering them cigarettes and chocolates. "We are Americans. It is over. You are all free!" The line of gray ghosts fell to their knees with bodies heaving. They wanted to cry, to thank these strange looking Americans for their freedom , but, only strangled, guttural sounds came from the prisoners. Some were wracked with guilt. "Why me?" "Why were 60 members of my family burnt in the ovens while I survived - why me?" "And, what will happen now? Tomorrow at roll call, what will I do? How will I react to the freedom the Americans are giving us? What will I do tomorrow? Where will I go? Where will I sleep? Will the Americans feed us? These Asian Americans are leaving for Berchtesgaaden; what will happen to us when they leave? Will the Germans come back? What will be?"

The sign at the side of the road said "Waakirchen." By the next day, there were swarms of tanks and jeeps and thousands of American soldiers, all wanting to touch and help and feed the prisoners in their awning-like uniforms. The Americans wanted to give and give and give, but all the prisoners wanted was some soup and bread so that their bodies could be brought to the point where, once more, they could accept food like normal human beings. The prisoners wanted to touch the American angels. They couldn't express their feelings toward their rescuers, but their eyes said it all. Watching as the wretched survivors realized that they were free, that their ordeal was over, the GIs vowed never to forget. NEVER!

To Bear Witness

Bradley had to divert his eyes. Eisenhower felt ill. Patton went quickly behind a building and threw up. Three of the greatest generals America had ever produced were reacting to their first encounter with a German concentration camp.

Eisenhower immediately cabled President Roosevelt that he wanted a delegation of newspaper and magazine editors to come to Germany immediately to record for the American people and for posterity what the Allied forces had discovered in Hitler's Germany. Within days, the group was on its way. A similar group of Congressmen and Senators, made up of equal numbers of Republicans and Democrats, was also selected to bear witness to the German atrocities. Eisenhower stated specifically that he wanted this unimpeachable witnessing so that it could not be said in the future that these atrocities never happened.

They came, and they saw. The editors and publishers represented the following publications:

New York Times

Detroit Free Press

Los Angeles Times

Chicago Sun

Saturday Evening Post

Reader's Digest

Washington Star

New Orleans Times

St. Louis Post Dispatch

Minneapolis Star Journal

Kansas City Star

American Magazine

Scripps Howard

Houston Chronicle

Colliers

The greatest names in American publishing bore witness to the Nazi horrors. They saw and they wrote and they took pictures and movies of the survivors of the Nazi terror.

The Congressmen and Senators came as well. On May 15, 1945, just one week after the unconditional surrender of Germany to the Allied Forces, before a joint house, the Committee reported to their colleagues what they had witnessed in Germany.

Senators		Representatives	
KY.	Alben W. Barkley	TX.	Ewing Thompson
GA.	Walter F. George	SC.	James P. Richards
UT.	Elbert D. Thomas	CA.	Ed V. Izac
IL.	C. Wayland Brooks	OH.	John M. Vorys
NB.	Kenneth s. Wheery	OR.	James W. Mott
MA.	Leverett Saltonstall	MO.	Dewey Short

Camps inpected
Buchenwald
Nordhausen
Dachau

79th CONGRESS 1st Session	SENATE	DOCUMENT No. 47

ATROCITIES AND OTHER CONDITIONS IN CONCENTRATION CAMPS IN GERMANY

REPORT

OF THE

COMMITTEE REQUESTED BY
GEN. DWIGHT D. EISENHOWER THROUGH THE
CHIEF OF STAFF, GEN. GEORGE C. MARSHALL

TO THE

CONGRESS OF THE UNITED STATES

RELATIVE TO

ATROCITIES AND OTHER CONDITIONS IN
CONCENTRATION CAMPS IN GERMANY

PRESENTED BY MR. BARKLEY

MAY 15 (legislative day, APRIL 16), 1945.—Referred to the
Committee on Foreign Relations and ordered to be printed

UNITED STATES
GOVERNMENT PRINTING OFFICE
WASHINGTON : 1945

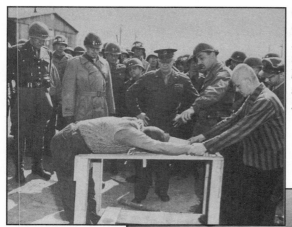

Generals George Patton, Omar Bradley and Dwight Eisenhower at the first camp liberated by Americans. A survivor demonstrates an SS torture method.

Members of the congressional party investigating German atrocities inspect the gas chamber at the infamous Dachau prison camp.

American editors view rows of corpses at Dachau.

General Sparks Remembers

"The confusion about the units which liberated Dachau and the ensuing events which happened there will never be entirely clear. Even those who were there on the first day cannot remember with clarity the sequence and times of the various events which took place on liberation day. The traumatic shock of the scenes and events of the first day was simply overwhelming. However, I will attempt to identify the units and time sequences in the narrative that follows. This narrative is based upon my own memory and upon exhaustive research of all records that are available to me.

A day or so after the fall of Nuremburg, I was designated as a task force commander, with the mission of moving with all possible speed to Munich. The task force consisted of my own infantry battalion (3rd Battalion), the entire 191st Tank Battalion, Battery C of the 158th Field Artillery and an engineer company. With the organic infantry battalion weapons, the artillery battery, and the over fifty tanks of the tank battalion, we had a formidable array of firepower. We were able to smash through the sporadic German resistance with ease, although the many blown bridges caused some problems.

By the late evening of April 28, we were less than thirty miles from Munich. Shortly after midnight, I received the regimental attack order for the next day. I was ordered to resume the attack at 0730 the next morning, with the mission of entering Munich. The order stated that, if my task force encountered any delay because of German opposition, the following first and second battalions of our regiment would continue the attack into Munich by bypassing the resistance area.   I was also informed that the concentration camp near the city of Dachau would be in my attack area, but my orders did not include the taking of the camp.

At 0730 on the morning of April 29, the task force resumed the attack with companies L and K and the tank battalion as the assault force.   The attack zone assigned to Company L was through the city of Dachau but did not include the concentration camp, a short distance outside the city.   Company I was designated as the reserve unit, with the mission of mopping up any resistance bypassed by the assault forces.

About an hour after the attack began, I received a regimental radio message directing me to capture the Dachau concentration camp.   I then located the Company I commander and assigned this mission to him, advising him that I would stay with his company.   However, I did not wish to commit Company I until Company L had cleared the city of Dachau.   While there was only spotty resistance in the city, the Germans had destroyed almost all of the many bridges in and outside of the city.   The progress of our tanks was therefore greatly slowed.

There is absolutely no agreement as to the hour of that day when Company I entered the concentration camp.   My recollection is that it was around the noon hour.   Others believe that it was earlier than that or several hours later.   A problem with any journal recording of the time is that I did not have my radio with me.   As there was a masonry wall to climb getting into the camp, I left my radio and operator outside the camp, along with my jeep and driver.   In the normal course of events, I would have received a radio message from Company I advising me of the camp entry.   However, since I was already there, there was no point in such a message.   There was therefore a considerable delay before any radio message was sent back to higher headquarters.

The horror and shock to all of us who first entered Dachau is beyond description. We were simply overwhelmed by the enormity of the bestial crimes that had been perpetrated against fellow human beings. However, within an hour or so, I was able to restore some semblance of discipline and to establish a method of communication with the some thirty thousand prisoners, some of whom were dying almost hourly. Thousands were already dead when we arrived.

In the order to secure the camp that I had received, I was also informed that our first battalion would take over after the camp was secured, in order that my task force could continue the attack into Munich. After things became fairly quiet within the camp, and my radio operator had joined me, I sent a message to the regimental commander requesting that the first battalion relieve Company I. This was probably the first message that I sent after entering the camp. A return radio message informed me that a unit of the first battalion was on its way.

Sometime later that afternoon, Company C arrived and established various security posts. I then started moving Company I out of the camp in order to resume the attack into Munich with a full task force. Before I could again assemble the task force, I received an order that the tank battalion, less one company was to be relieved of attachment to my task force. The 180th Infantry was encountering strong resistance in its sector, and the tanks were needed there. Sometime later, I received another order informing me that our first battalion would lead the attack into Munich the next day and that I was to relieve Company C at the concentration camp. I then dispatched Company L to relieve Company C. This relief was completed by about 10:00pm that night.

The foregoing narrative includes all of the rifle companies that were in the Dachau concentration camp on the day of liberation, those being companies C, I and L. With these rifle companies were attachments from companies D and M, along with the forward observer parties from the 158th Field Artillery. Small elements of other units were also there, namely a small patrol from the regimental I&R Platoon that was with company I, and some personnel from the first and third battalion head-quarters. There were some troops from the 42nd Infantry Division somewhere in the vicinity. Earlier that morning, Company I had reported that they were being fired upon by troops of the 42nd Division. This information was relayed to regimental headquarters with a request that the 42nd Division be informed that we were both on the same side.

On the morning of April 30, our first battalion resumed the attack towards Munich. The second battalion was also launched in that direction. Shortly after the attack began, the first battalion came upon and occupied another concentration camp. It was a slave labor camp and contained about eight thousand prisoners. In order that the first battalion could con-tinue its attack with the complete battalion, I was then ordered to relieve the first battalion company at this second camp. I assigned this mission to Company K, where they were to remain for the next several days.

During the morning of that day, I assembled Company I in the city of Dachau, leaving Company L at the Dachau concen-tration camp. At about 6:00pm that evening, Company L was relieved at the camp by the 601st Artillery Battalion from the 15th Corps. My battalion then moved into Munich, minus company K."

—⋙—⋙—⋙—⋙—⋙—

The report submitted by General Sparks accurately reflects the chaos and confusion that existed in both the Dachau

Concentration Camp and in military headquarters. Unclear orders were given to company and battalion commanders. Orders received one hour were sometimes superceded by completely opposite orders less than an hour later. The normal state of confusion in a military operation was made even worse by the inhuman conditions discovered in Dachau. Until the late evening hours, on April 29, 1945, the military situation remained unclear. One day later, troops were able to continue their attack on Munich as military government and hospital personnel arrived to help the Dachau survivors.

The shooting at the coal yard wall.

The Inspector General's Report

Classified as secret by the Army in 1945, the report entitled "Investigation of Alleged Mistreatment of German Guards at Dachau," administered by Lt. Col. Joseph M. Whitaker, came to be known simply as the I.G. Report.

Dachau was liberated on April 29, 1945. The investigation began less than one week later on May 3, 1945 and went on until May 18th. Questioning took place in Pullach and Munich, Germany. Twenty-three officers and enlisted men of the 45th Infantry Division were questioned by the Inspector General. Nine officers and enlisted men of the 42nd Infantry Division were questioned as well. Two surviving prisoners of the Camp were also questioned .

General Haislip, who evaluated the findings of the investigation before they were submitted to General George S. Patton for final disposition, recommended that the entire matter be reinvestigated. General Haislip stated there had been too many deficiencies in the investigation.

General Patton, in ruling on this suggestion, burned all papers relating to the report. He then commended the men of the 45th Infantry Division on their fighting abilities, ending the matter by telling the men to "go back to work."

In 1986 Howard A. Buechner wrote a book titled "The Hour of the Avenger." The book, written by the first American doctor on the scene, purported to tell the story and chronology of what happened on April 29, 1945 when the first troops entered

Dachau. The doctor's book, written 40 years after the incident took place was in many ways in direct conflict with facts as outlined in the Inspector General's Report written in 1945.

The doctor, unaware that a copy of the I.G. Report would surface in 1991 in the National Archives in Washington, D.C., was very creative in setting out the chronology of events that took place in the concentration camp on Liberation Day. To cover up the fact that he took liberties with many facts, Buechner, on page 5 of "The Avenger" states, "stories about Dachau are so varied that no one will ever know exactly what happened on the day of liberation." This undoubtedly was the reason the doctor neglected to mention that he was cited in the I.G. Report for dereliction of duty with the recommendation that he be court-martialed for his actions on the day of liberation.

Buechner's inaccuracies and arbitrary use of figures in citing the untrue story about the total liquidation of all SS troops found in Dachau was eagerly accepted by Revisionist organizations and exploited to meet their own distorted stories of Dachau. However, in a report published by the Dachau International Committee it is clearly stated that 160 German prisoners were utilized in cleaning up the camp in the days following liberation.

Among other false stories in "The Avenger" are descriptions of Native American Indians taking vengeance and justice into their own hands. Stories of a machine gun being set up by Lt. Busheyhead and of scalpings committed by the Native Americans spread rapidly among all the troops, with exaggerated descriptions of men of the 157th Regiment going berserk, committing every possible type of atrocity imaginable against the helpless SS troops. Even the act of a liberated prisoner was attributed to the GIs. This survivor wanted an SS ring that was on the finger of its dead owner. Unable to loosen the ring, the survivor cut off the dead man's finger to retrieve the ring.

Everything and anything written about Dachau took on new significance after the I.G. Report emerged from the National Archives. The material in Dr. Buechner's book was seen as pure fabrication when compared to his sworn testimony given to the Inspector General in Munich, Germany on May 5, 1945. (I.G. Report, questions 363 to 374). Almost anyone could have memory lapses after 40 or 50 years. However, the I.G. Report, which contained the exact words of the participants could not be disbelieved or disputed. In the years since Buechner's book was published many other books on Dachau followed using Buechner's useless information as a factual source. Thus, the false information has been spread far and wide by unsuspecting authors who neglected to utilize the declassified Inspector General's Report which contains sworn testimony and certainly deserves more credence than the machinations of Howard A. Buechner.

Lt. Col. Felix Sparks, away from the shooting which took place at the wall, responded to the sounds of the shooting. Instantly becoming aware of what was happening as he ran to the scene, he fired his .45 pistol into the air while shouting for all firing to cease. He emptied his .45 before the shooting finally stopped. However, his explanation of what had taken place at the wall was not believed by the military authorities. With the war over, Sparks left the Army, eventually becoming a Supreme Court Judge in Colorado. For 50 years, Sparks lived under the shadow of the incident at the wall on April 29, 1945. In the early '90's four photos of the shooting at the wall emerged. These pictures completely vindicated Sparks' version of the happening at the wall. Shortly after the emergence of the four photos Sparks retired as the Commanding General of the Colorado Army National Guard.

Quietly but effectively, a group of military historians worked for years tracking the events that had taken place at Dachau on the Day of Liberation.   Coming from varied military organizations, this group had only one goal - to uncover the truth about what had happened at Dachau on that fatal day.   Curtis Whiteway of the 99th Infantry Division had taken part in the liberation of 8 different concentration camps, among which were some of the Dachau sub-camps.   Art Lee, a former Sergeant Major in the 42nd Infantry Division and Sol Feingold, an infantryman in the 42nd were extremely helpful and cooperative in sharing their extensive information with the other members of the group. Lt. Col. Hugh Foster (Ret.), who lives in Carlisle, PA where military archives are domiciled, found reams of material about the liberation and generously shared his findings with other members of the group. James Strong, whose father-in-law was one of the liberating troops, made a documentary film in 1990, "The Day of Liberation of KZ Dachau" in which 10 liberators told their stories of what they remembered about the day of liberation. Al Panebianco, Steve Resheff, Jim Bird, General Russ Weiskircher (Ret.), all former members of the 45th Infantry Division, were all very helpful in giving first-hand accounts of their war-time experiences in Germany. Henry Kaufman, also a member of the 45th Division, was a prisoner of war and contributed his experiences at the hands of the Germans as well.

Where Buechner got the figure of 560 killed in Dachau on the 29th of April 1945 is anyone's guess. However there is no doubt that this figure met the needs and approval of Revisionists and Deniers who continue to use the picture at the wall with the accompanying caption stating that this massacre in Dachau was the worst atrocity committed during World War II. The Inspector General's Report stated that the total number of SS men killed in the prisoner compound in Dachau on April 29, 1945 was somewhere between 50 and 60.

Leitenberg

There is a graveyard on a grassy, low hill in Dachau. When American GIs liberated the camp, they found the bodies of 7,500 prisoners; they were from almost every country in Europe. SS guards had fled in panic without cremating this evidence of their atrocities.

The outraged Americans required Dachau townspeople to transport the bodies to their final burial place. There, they were buried in long lines of mass graves. There are no individual graves in Leitenberg.

Leitenberg is a desolate place. When it snows and the wind is blowing, one can look out across the rooftops and see the chimneys of the crematorium at the camp. One shivers, not so much from the cold, as from the memories of what these poor, unfortunate souls lived through during their last days on earth.

Looking down from the top of the hill one sees the roofs of the pretty homes that are so common in Dachau. In the distance is the camp. Now there is a vast, grassy area that looks like a military parade ground. This is the area that was covered with 30 wooden barracks. Originally built to house 200 prisoners in each barrack, as many as 1,600 were crammed into each building as the war ended. The over-crowded conditions led to all kinds of diseases that ravaged Dachau in April, 1945.

The seven guard towers in the prisoner compound stand just as they did then, with machine guns pointed at the prisoners as they did the various jobs assigned to them. At times, one would crack under the strain and attempt to climb the wire fence surrounding the area. The prisoner would be electrocuted immediately.

The Italian government built a small but beautiful monastery at the top of the hill in Leitenberg. Rarely visited, the building stands in lonely vigil guarding the graves which attest to the truth of what happened at Dachau. Those who attempt to rewrite history, deny that this genocide occurred. These revisionists and deniers never mention Leitenberg. For good reason.

Signpost indicating mass graves at Leitenberg Cemetery, Dachau.

Law and Order

Although the two men had several things in common, their destinies never brought them face-to-face. One was Henry Senger, a 19-year-old kid from Brooklyn, the other, William Denson, the son of a Baptist preacher from Alabama. They were both Americans, both in the Army, and both in Germany in 1945.

The 19 year old was in the 292nd Field Artillery Observation Battalion. The observer's job was to locate enemy positions by the flash and sound coming from their gun nozzles and to direct American artillery fire and aircraft to the enemy location. By April of 1945, the Germans were retreating so fast they had no time to set up artillery and were more interested in surrendering than fighting. The 292nd was sent in to Munich to help the Military Police round up German soldiers who wanted to surrender.

One day, while on "round up" duty, American GIs standing near a checkpoint were approached by two emaciated living skeletons. To the kid from Brooklyn, the clothes the two slaves were wearing were like the awnings that used to cover storefronts during the hot weather in Brooklyn. They were canvas awnings with black and white stripes, just like the clothes the two emaciated figures were wearing. With heated words and gestures, one of the slaves was trying to tell the GIs something. Pointing, gesturing and jumping up and down, he was shouting at the GIs. One of the Americans knew enough German to understand what the slave was trying to tell them.

Quickly crossing the street, the GI pointed his rifle at two men trying to make themselves unnoticeable by looking into a storefront window. Protesting, the two prisoners said they were innocent of any crime. They wanted to know why they were being held at gunpoint. The GI told them to start marching. The older of the two prisoners said that he would not be taken prisoner by anyone but an officer of his equal rank. The rifle butt soon convinced the two Germans to stand against a wall, feet spread apart, with hands on the wall so they could be properly frisked.

When no weapons were found, they started marching towards the MP post. The officer in charge refused to accept the prisoners, stating that he was interested only in military personnel, not civilians. The young GI prodded his prisoners forward, finally coming to a Counter Intelligence Corps position. The guard on duty told the GI that the C.I.C. could not accept these men because they were military prisoners and the C.I.C. dealt only with civilians. At this point, the GI changed the position of his rifle and politely asked to see the Commanding Officer. Within minutes, the situation was clarified with the C.O. commending the kid from Brooklyn, saying that these two prisoners were on a War Criminals' Black List.

> "You've brought in the Commander of the Dachau Concentration Camp and his adjutant. Congratulations, soldier."

The war ended a week later. Within weeks articles began appearing about a coming war crimes trial that would take place in Dachau. Forty former SS officers and men were being charged with war crimes at the first trial to take place in Germany. As the young GI from Brooklyn read the story, his eyes stopped at the next line. The case was entitled "Martin Gottfried Weiss and 39 others at Dachau." The name jumped out at the teenager. Martin Gottfried Weiss was the German prisoner he had turned over to the C.I.C. officer. Instinct alone had made him trust the accusations of the two survivors. Instinct alone had made him continue on when the MPs refused to accept the prisoners, and instinct alone was responsible for his refusal to be turned down by the C.I.C. guard. The GI swallowed hard as he vowed to attend the trial of Martin Gottfried Weiss and the 39 other war criminals.

William Denson was teaching law at West Point in 1945 when he received orders to report for duty at Dachau. Denson had been picked by the Army to be the lead prosecutor in the first war crimes trial to take place in Germany.

When Denson got to Germany, he admitted to the other prosecutors that he knew very little about the Nazi system or any of the crimes that they were being accused of. He had come to Germany with a completely open mind. In the beginning he found the stories of the survivors hard to believe. He dutifully took notes about their testimony but found the accounts of the atrocities committed by the SS Deaths Head Squads to be beyond anything the human mind could comprehend. As the stories continued unabatedly from citizens of Russia and Poland and Greece and Czechoslovakia and France and Belgium and Norway, the attorney's ideas and opinions changed drastically. By the time he was ready to enter the courtroom in Dachau, there was literally nothing the Nazis could have done that he wouldn't believe.

In the first Dachau Trial, the proceedings against "Martin Gottfried Weiss and 39 others at Dachau" ended on December 13, 1945. The trial had lasted one month. All forty were found guilty on the grounds that they had been active in the camp where the crimes took place, thus participating in the "common design." Weiss was sentenced to death by hanging, along with 35 others. (Hanging is the most degrading method of death for a German.) Eight death sentences were later commuted to life imprisonment.   The remaining 28, including Weiss and his adjutant, were executed on the 28th and 29th of May, 1946 at Landsburg prison.

In a final irony, they were put to death within view of the cell where Hitler had been imprisoned in 1925. There, Hitler had written "Mein Kampf," his plans for the glorious future of Germany.

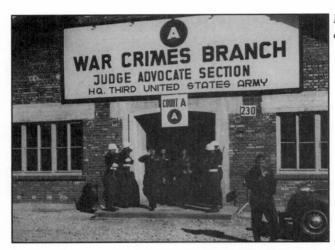

Military tribunal at Dachau.

Concentration camp guards on trial in Dachau.

The Werewolves

By the end of 1944 it was quite evident to anyone who was willing to face the facts that the outcome of the war in Europe was a virtual certainty. Only Hitler, his youth organization and a few Nazi party fanatics still hoped for a miracle that could turn the tide in the Nazis' favor. It was at this point that the Werewolves Organization was formed; its purpose was to create havoc among the Allies and to sabotage any facilities still intact in Germany to prevent them from falling into the hands of the conquerors. Their final goal was to organize an underground resistance movement in order to prepare for the resurgence of the Nazi Party under the 4th Reich.

Acts of sabotage and assassination against the American Occupation Forces continued sporadically during the first two years of occupation. These acts against the French and the Russians were quickly curtailed by immediately executing the perpetrators. In the American Zone, most notably in Bavaria, the Werewolves would stretch wires across a road to decapitate unsuspecting GIs who were in the habit of riding with their jeeps' windshield turned down. After several deaths, the jeeps were fitted with steel bars which protected the soldiers from this trap. Spreading oil on the roads at night caused many accidents for the Americans, but both these tactics caused only minimal obstacles to the occupying forces.

By the end of 1945, all survivors had been moved to hospitals or displaced persons camps. The Dachau Prisoners Compound was then used as a German SS Prisoner of War Camp where 15,000 hard-core SS men were housed in the quarters previously used by concentration camp survivors. German speaking undercover men of the American Office of Strategic Services were sent in to mix with the SS prisoners to discover the extent of the Werewolf Organization. The blood type of all SS men had been tattooed under their left armpits. With capture imminent, the SS men tried to remove all traces of the telltale tattoos, using acid or burning cigarettes. However, ugly scars remained. It was therefore necessary for the American infiltrators to create similar scars on their bodies.

The undercover agents found that there were some 5,000 members of the Werewolf Organization and, except for isolated instances of sabotage, murder and harassment, they were of no great danger to the reforms being imposed on Germany by the Occupation Forces. The Werewolf Organization eventually failed as its die-hard membership drifted into other, more successful endeavors including "rat lines" established to help Nazis escape to South America and the Middle East.

Among the American OSS officers who infiltrated the Dachau prisoner of war camp was John Weitz who uncovered key information about the Werewolf Organization. In civilian life, Weitz became a world-renowned clothing designer as well as a champion racecar driver.

Book Four

"There is nothing new in the world except the history you do not know."

Harry S. Truman

The Kid from Tennessee

The men in the Hammelburg Prisoner of War camp had little to be happy about except when thinking of escape or liberation, when receiving mail from home, or opening the occasional Red Cross package filled with goodies. For the most part the men knew nothing of the messages, cameras, radio parts, maps, saws and other escape equipment hidden within certain items in the packages. They had no idea that a baseball could contain a radio or that a deck of ordinary playing cards could become a map of Germany showing the best escape routes as well as safe houses along the way. They would have been surprised to find that a common shaving brush contained a compass that could make the difference between life or death to an escapee.

The men were unaware that one particular officer in the camp bore the designation "X" and that this security officer sent messages out of the camp and received secret messages advising which packages contained escape equipment. "X" designated who would attempt an escape and when. A few fellow officers were aware of "X's" identity.

The men were totally surprised when an unexpected Red Cross shipment arrived. In addition to the regular food packages, the shipment contained a dozen musical instruments. The trumpets, clarinets and saxophones were quickly spoken for. A huge bass tuba lay in the middle of the barracks with no one making a move to adopt the forlorn instrument. Quietly, the boy from Tennessee approached the tuba and ran his hands over the endless curving brass leading to the large opening at the top. Volunteering to take care of the tuba, Parsons and two of his friends hauled the huge instrument away amidst a lot of laughter and crude jokes from the other GIs.

Over the next few days Parsons was observed talking quietly to some of the medical personnel. Inquisitive eyes observed the elderly German guards bringing what looked like rubber tubing and metal clamps to Parsons' bunk. He smiled and laughed with glee as he carefully accepted the assorted items. No one ever heard a note of music come out of that bass tuba. Some of the guys thought the tuba's appearance had gone through a change, but they couldn't quite explain how.

A week later the secret was out. The best Tennessee brass moonshine still in the European Theatre of Operations was churning out more booze than the boys in the barracks knew what to do with. The German guards, who had supplied the rubber tubing, got their share and the medical boys, who had supplied the alcohol, got theirs as well. Parsons and his friends became the most popular musicians in the barracks. No one ever laughed at him again, and many a GI seemed to be bowing with respect as he filled his canteen with the Tennessee moonshine that came pouring out of the "C" key of the big bass tuba at Hammelburg.

Berga

When the war ended in Europe the men often found themselves with time on their hands. Discussions would break out on almost any topic and that's how the whole dog tag bit started. One man asked when and where GIs started wearing identity tags; another spoke of the changes that had taken place since World War I. When someone mentioned that in World War I the GIs wore bracelets on their wrists, the inevitable "Bushwah" comment came forth. When another mentioned that he had seen dog tags from World War II with guys' home addresses stamped on the tags, again the "Bushwah" word was heard.

Each looked at his own dog tag. Stamped in the lower right corner was "C" for Catholic, "P" for Protestant and "H" for Hebrew.

In one prisoner of war camp, GIs with "H" on their dog tags who had been captured during the first days of the Battle of the Bulge, were separated and placed in segregated barracks. One day at Roll Call all Jewish GIs were told to step forward. The Germans had received orders to send a contingent of Jewish soldiers to a particular camp for special treatment. Three hundred and fifty-two men were called for. Only 80 men with "H" on their dog tags were found. The Germans picked others who looked Jewish or had Jewish sounding names or were troublemakers of one kind or another. No one knew where the group was being sent or what to expect. All they knew was that 352 men were separated from their fellow GIs.

Their destination was not another Prisoner of War camp;

they found themselves in an SS concentration camp called Berga Am Elster. The experiences the Americans went through there were so unthinkable, so unspeakable that for more than 50 years most of the survivors repressed all memories of what had taken place in the slave labor camp. Seventy of the 352 Americans died before the camp was liberated in April, 1945. This 20 percent death rate was the highest for any group of Americans in captivity in Europe.

When the survivors told their officers about their horrendous experiences, they were officially told by the Pentagon that Germans never placed American GIs in concentration camps. This in spite of the fact that the survivors were barely alive at liberation and looked like survivors of the Bataan Death March. The average survivor had lost 50 or more pounds while at Berga. The men were told that if they continued to tell these outlandish tales they would be placed in mental institutions.

For more than 40 years the men kept quiet. The American government continued to deny their stories. This disbelief by their fellow Americans added major stress to already damaged lives.

Fear of being locked up in a mental institution, labeled a "psycho," was deterrent enough to enforce the GIs silence until 1995, 50 years after the war ended. It was then that the Pentagon did a complete turnaround, admitting that everything the GIs had said was true. It was then that the German government admitted that Berga did exist and that the survivors had been telling the truth.

The experiences of Americans imprisoned in the Berga concentration camp were the subject of a court trial. Hugo Princz (who was not a GI) and 10 other American civilians who had been similarly confined, humiliated and tortured brought a class action suit against the German government and were awarded $2.1 million. Finally, a precedent had been set that GIs who had been victimized so long ago could be compensated. More than

800 applications were submitted by the deadline date.

Unfortunately the agreement stated that only those still living could apply for compensation. This meant that their families could not apply after a survivor's death. One of the men who had contacted the attorney, William Marks, died before the case was settled. However, because he had filed before his death, his wife received a fixed sum from the German government based on the time he had spent at Berga and the injuries he received there. Under the Settlement Agreement the men received $10,000 for each month in the concentration camp plus unspecified amounts for injuries sustained while at Berga.

For those who, for their own purposes, claim GIs were never in Berga, the following is a copy of the US Army Security Certificate which was released by the archives after the first settlement with the German government was agreed to.

Please note: The war in Europe ended May 7, 1945; the war in the Pacific continued until August 14, 1956. The first item in the Security Certificate on the next page was intended to protect American soldiers who were still in Japanese captivity at that time.

—w— —w— —w— —w— —w—

RESTRICTED

HEADQUARTERS

EUROPEAN THEATRE OF OPERATIONS

MIS-X Detachment

Military Intelligence Service

APO 887

SECURITY CERTIFICATE

For

Ex-Prisoners of War

1. Some activities of American Prisoners of war within German prison camps must remain secret not only for the duration of the war against the present enemies of the United States but in peace-time as well. The interests of American prisoners of war in Japanese camps require maintenance of the strictest security on the activities of American prisoners of war in German camps. The interests of American prisoners in the event of future wars, moreover, demand that the secrets of this war be rigorously safeguarded.

2. I therefore understand that under Army Regulations and the laws of the United States, during my military service and later, as a civilian, I may not reveal, discuss, publish or otherwise disclose to unauthorized persons information on escape from enemy prison camps or evasion in enemy occupied territory, clandestine organizations among prisoners of war, any means of outwitting captors or of promoting intelligence activities within prison camps.

3. The authorship of articles or stories on these subjects is specifically forbidden and military personnel are warned that they will be held strictly accountable for the communi-

cation of such information to other persons who may sub-
sequently publish or disclose such material.

4. I understand that any information suggested by the above
    mentioned categories is SECRET and must not be commu-
    nicated to anyone other than the agency designated by AC
    of S, G-2, War Department, or the corresponding organiza-
    tion in overseas theaters of operations.

Name (print) _____Signed _____
Rank _____ASN _____Dated_____
Unit _____Witness_____

194-215

The following account of life at Berga was written by Norm
Fellman of the 45th Division.

RESTRICTED
Testimony of Norm Fellman
"We Have Already Been to Hell -
Memories from Berga!"

I believe it was Winfield Rosenberg, Berga Survivor, who,
when asked by a reporter if he thought he was going to heaven
when he died, replied he was sure he would because he had
already been to hell!

My memories of that place are a mixture; blurry in spots,
altogether too clean & sharp in others. Please forgive if the following appears disjointed but it's the way they are recalled and

the dots will connect after a fashion.

The order came down at Stalag 9B for all Jews to step forward; I made the decision & did so. My memory of the segregated barracks is fuzzy. I draw a blank when trying to recall the days & nights on that packed boxcar ride to Berga. The memory of marching into Berga is sharp, the high wire compounds on both sides of the road, the guard towers with their machine gun muzzles tracking our progress; clear as hell! There was a mass of humanity pressed against the wire observing our entrance. Those emaciated, pajama clad figures with huge eyes devoid of expression watched us in total silence. The eyes haunt me.

Then it started; twelve hour shifts in the mines, daily beatings, the ongoing starvation diet, body lice and the intense cold. Always the cold!

As all of the above took effect, the dying began to mount. Our SS guards stacked the bodies alongside what was our "chow line." We stood a few feet from the frozen bodies of our comrades without any conscious feeling. They might as well have been sticks of wood. Realizing how low a human could sink causes me great guilt. I had become numb. Another time, while seeking relief from dysentery-induced gas, distorting my gut over a tub near the barracks, the head non com (Metz) stopped near me and indicated that I was to return to the barracks. I refused, saying that I was in no condition to do that. He drew his Lugar and placed the muzzle end on my forehead. Here again, completely devoid of any feeling, I told him to go ahead & shoot, I wasn't going. He stared at me for a minute, holstered his pistol and left. I just didn't care either way!

When I arrived in Berga there were thoughts of when I would be liberated. The workload increased, the lack of food plus the treatment wore me down & the outlook began to change. First it was live through the week, then the day, the hour & finally the next 10 minutes.

After the blasts in the tunnels we were forced back in the mines to clear the fallen rock. Straining to load the rock into gondolas, choking on the clouds of powdered rock dust, we could never work fast or hard enough to suit the guards. They all carried rubber hoses, which were used at any or no provocation. We lost 40 men in the mines.

One morning we fell in and started our march to the mines and never got there. We wound up on our final death march. The guards, desperately anxious to avoid the Russians, had us wandering on the roads. I don't know how many died on the march. We had been broken into smaller groups and were scattered. The figure heard is a 20% loss from the original number of 352 men. Survivors for the most part lost 50% of their body weight and were all close to death at liberation.

I will always be grateful to the pilot of that hospital DC3 who did a 180 each side of the beautiful Lady Liberty as we flew into New York Harbor.

WE WERE HOME!

Norm Fellman

The information in this chapter came from two survivors of Berga, Winfield Rosenberg and Norman Fellman and the PBS film titled "Berga."

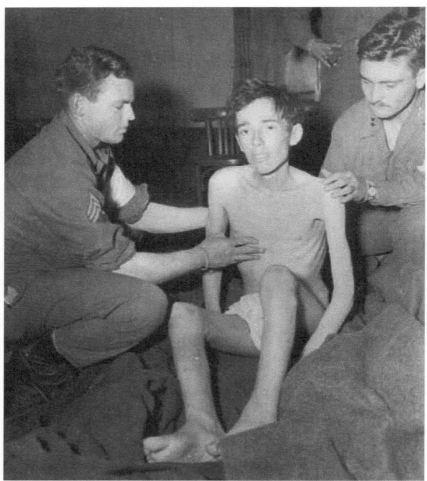

Pfc. James Watkins, 20, an American soldier survivor of Berga.

Best Damned Outfit

Made up of men from Oklahoma, Arizona, New Mexico and Colorado, the 45th Infantry Division, whose emblem in World War II was the thunderbird, was praised for its fighting abilities, not only by its American commanders, but by enemy officers as well. Several German commanders referred to the 45th Division as one of the finest fighting forces they had ever encountered. But it was General Alexander Patch, Commander of the 7th Army in World War II, who admiringly wrote of the men of the 45th Infantry Division, "The best damned outfit in the U.S. Army."

In 1940, when it became more and more evident that the United States would sooner or later enter the war against Hitler, President Roosevelt activated the 45th Infantry Division. The 45th Infantry Division had been a National Guard unit since 1923. It became one of the first American divisions to see action in Africa. Before the war ended, the unit had been in 511 days of combat. Bill Mauldin, a member of the 45th, achieved worldwide fame depicting the lives of Willie and Joe, two infantry soldiers, as they made their way through Africa, Sicily, Italy, France, Belgium and Germany.

German soldiers referred to the men of the 45th as "The Falcon Division." However, the men of the 45th wore their shoulder patch, the thunderbird, with great pride. They all knew the mythology of their symbol, and that the thunderbird was the bearer of unlimited happiness.

Ernie Pyle, the most famous World War II correspondent,

spent much time crouched in a foxhole as he followed the path of the 45th through Europe. While writing of the horrors of war, he praised the courage of the men of the 45th. Pyle brought alive to the folks back home the stories of their fighting sons, many of whom wore the patch of the famous Thunderbirds.

On April 18, 1945, Pyle was killed in action on the island of Ie Shima, in the Pacific. A simple marker states:

At this Spot
The
77th Infantry Division
Lost a Buddy
Ernie Pyle
18, April, 1945

The Writer

In the days after the war ended, GIs were given time off to visit friends in other outfits, to go sightseeing or to just lounge around until their point count was reached so they could head for home. Many went searching for European souvenirs to send home as memorabilia.

In Munich, there were huge concrete kiosks where all kinds of notices and notes were posted. Many were from displaced persons looking for information about loved ones. Some were from Germans looking to sell what they considered to be items of value. Some were from GIs looking to barter for Leica cameras, binoculars, silverware, Bavarian china or other items not easily found in the states.

It was at just this type of kiosk that a displaced person approached a GI who was scanning the notices of items for sale. The man asked if he could help the GI by reading the notes written in German. The GI accepted the offer and then invited the gentleman for a cup of coffee. Within a short time, a friendship was established.

The elderly gentleman had been a prisoner in the Dachau Concentration Camp. He had been a newspaper reporter and, although a Swiss national, was imprisoned by the Gestapo for writing articles which ridiculed the Nazi regime. Imprisoned for two years, he was finally liberated by the Americans.

The young GI met with the Swiss reporter many times, always in a restaurant where the youngster was able to buy the

older man a good meal. The GI tried to give the older man food
and money, but the offers were always politely refused. It was
obvious that the old man's pride would not allow him to accept
the gifts from the young American.

One day, the GI came up with a novel idea. He asked the
older man if he would write about his experiences as a prisoner in some of the camps where he had been held. The younger
man asked if he would accept payment for the stories exactly
the same as if he were writing for a newspaper. The old man
eagerly agreed. This was "work" he knew and loved. He
arranged for a translator and typist and immediately went to
"work". He was paid for his stories on a word for word basis.

The following are excerpts from stories written in 1946 by
Albert Steinitz, the Swiss newspaperman. They have never
appeared in print before. They are being published exactly as
written without changes of any kind.

—₥— —₥— —₥— —₥— —₥—

*"Since a week already the work outside the camp was dis-
continued. the woodcutters didn't go out anymore, and the part-
ly bombed factory in which thousands of prisoners had toiled
under the strict supervision of armed government officials lay
deserted. No food supplies were delievered to the camp anymore.
the guards on duty were dobbled, and when allied aircrafts were
reported even trippled.*

*Everything as so unusual as it never had been before. One
cold be chooked by the atmosphere itself. No disturbence however, could be noticed at the Stormtrooper's headquater. Our bread
ration which was extremely small since a long time already was
cut down again. The barracks were overcrowded and medical
facilities and care early unobtainable, and as an inavitable con-
sequence, the death rate increased with such a rapidity that the*

six furnices in thecrematorium which had a capacity to handle 576 corpses a day prooved inadequate. Orders were isued and with the help of explosives deep holes were blown into the earth (outside the inclosure) and filled with thousands of human bodies, which were relieved from thier pains and sorrows.

Everyone of the prisoners pretended to be completely indifferent as of what his fate is going to be. The fact however was that eberyone of us was asking and answereing quetions for himself, questions like that: "Will I survive it, or won't I?" Or our mind would go like this "If I die doesn't matterr, but before I die I would love to see these men punished who Killed my dear onces, conquered and destroyed my country, violeted my religion and did so many many evil things."Some of us made promises like this " I'll help to build a new world and try not to be selfish anymore and live alongside my fellowmen just as I do now with my fellow presoner, if I only manage to survive it."

As often as we looked up to the sky and saw the vast flying formations of the U.S and British air forces we got disgusted and called them names, we couldn't understand every unimportent place around us was blown to pieces and the quarters of our oppressors weren't touched at all.

On the 8th of April the loudspeaker announced that all the jewish prisoners had to appear on the assembly field ready for evacuation. This was the first order which was obeyed reluctently, after the diappearence of 4000 jewish prisoners the Russians were summoned to appear and many other nation in the same manner. The "Lagerkommandatur" managed it so far to reduce the number of inmates from 64000 to 21000. At the same time rumors were spread about that the 3rd U.S. army was within thirty miles from our camp. No one dared to believe but everyone hoped it would be true. In the same night the echo of the advancing self-propelled artellery could be heard very distinctly. The Prominent prisoners held a secret meeting in some sewer. We got word form the secret board to do our utmost in passiv resistence, and not to appear on the assembly field the next morning when summoned by loudspeaker. WE also tore our numbers and national identifications from our clothes. The same night it was *announced that the guards would shoot on everyone on sight between dusk and dawn. (Which they did). The next morning when the loudspeaker summoned various nationalities to get ready for evacuation no one obeyed. After several useless threats guards entered the camp armed with bazookas and killing many. The evakuation were discontinued. At the i0th it was ordered that all the records of the camp have to be used as fuel for the crematorium. (Only parts of them were destroyed.) WE had a secret defence meeting the same day, we obtained information that the Stormtrooper's division "Dillwanger" was expected every minute with orders to kill every prisoner alive and to burn their bodies by flame throwers. We were ready for action, some firearms which were smugled inside the camp previously were distrbuted. It was our luck that the division "Dillwanger" didn't reach our camp that day, otherwise Iam sure nothing of the whole matter would ever be mentioned. The other morning we noticed (This was the IIth and final day as prisoners,) we noticed that the artillery fire had ceased, a fact that increased the general tension, because nobody of us could explain it. The general rumor was, the American's in this part of the front were defeated and had to withdraw their troops for a great distance in order not get cutt off. At 4 haevy allied planes bombed one of the closely located industriel cities. We heard the din of the exploding bombs echo in the mountains. This sound filled our hearts with glee and haelped us to forget our grief at least temporarily.*

No sooner had the sun come out however, when the hated voice in the loudspeaker resounded in the camp, demanding for this group of us which was supposed to do the cleaning in side the compound. These men were ordered to clean the main assembly field immediately, on which the letters "S.O.S." had been laid out (in briquetts , stolen for this purpose from the yard of the crematorium) under the protection of the darkness of the night. Hoping to attract the attention of allied recconaissance planes. This order was several times sharply repeated, but never carried out not even at the threat that drastic action would be taken.

Around IIo:clock we saw columns of stormtroopers marching downhill from their barracks the path alongside the fence and disappearing in the woods. They carried in addition to their usual firearms, handgranades, bazookas, flamethrowers and heavy mashine guns, all of them were outfitted with "Panzerfaust" the famous anty tank weappon.

We couldn't think of anything else but that we are going to be doomed and soon. Everyone was employed thinking for himself of what is going to happen. Someone brought up the slogan "EITHER-OR" which meant that we shouldn't let them sloughter us like sheeps but should fight with all means available against the guards. We said for our selves that it is our only way out, it made us feel somewhat better and many regained courage, tore the planks out of their bunks hoping to use them as clubs if nessesary. Whatever we had done for our defence everyone knew that the chances were ninety - nine out of a hundret negative for us. (I realized later that if order from the headquarters would have been given given to kill us we wouldn't have had no chance at all either to escape or to survive, not even one of us).

At noontime only the guards on the towers were left all the others had left their stations and had disappeared in the woods.

By then the silence was interrupted by the noise that seemed to come from the noise of many airplanes, but none could be seen except for a single L-5. The noise however grew louder and louder and we supposed it to be low flying bombers invisible on account of the forests. After a while the noise was so distinct coming out from the valley that we all looked in that direction. --What we encountered startled us to death, greenly painted tanks appearing out of the forest right on the foot of the hill on which our camp was located and many of them, coming out faster and faster starting to climb up to us.

The desperation among us was great, nevertheless we obeyed orders to disperse given by the prisners who were appointed as officer by the secret board of defence.

As soon as the tanks reached the foot of the hill they turned right and left and by so doing made a semicircle and sorrounded us. A terrible shooting started all around us, the tanks' guns fired unceasingly,---but not against us, they fired against those stormtroopers who lay flat on their bellies discharging anty tank weappons and defending their bodies by throwing flames against the tanks. Shortly after this only rifle and machine gun fire was to be heard which continued for about half an hour, after this one of the tanks appeared right on the main entrance of the camp. It posted itself there letting noone in and no one out. A great white star presented on its gunturret. It was an American tank.

Here I stop relating , there is nothing more that I can tell you everything else you know from the reports of war correspondents which related it to you much better then I can do it. But they and you forgot it like everything else, but I can't forget it and never will it was a very great day for me, I dare say the greatest. And I celebrate and will celebrate the IIth of April."

The Chaplain

Part I

The Protestant Chaplain sighed deeply as he wrote his long and detailed letters from Bavaria to his wife back home. He put in all the details, wanting to leave nothing out. The Chaplain was one of the first American officers into Dachau. As a man he was totally overcome by what he saw. As a man of God, he was devastated.

"Margaret," he wrote, "I must explain my inner feelings to you on a day by day basis because in my heart I know that 50 years from now there will be people who will say this never happened. They will say the reports are exaggerated or that they were embellished for propaganda purposes. I am writing to you now to give living testimony to the horrors and devastating scenes I am witnessing day after day in the Dachau Concentration Camp in Bavaria. I don't know what reasons they will dream up to say that what I am witnessing never happened, but I know they will arise. For their own purposes, they will try to tell future generations that the Germans were a clean and orderly people who could never participate in such gruesome atrocities. They will say the Germans were educated, cultured and law abiding people incapable of inflicting monstrous crimes upon other peoples."

The Chaplain's wife, who received a letter from her husband on a daily basis, lovingly saved every letter. Sixty years later the letters were reopened. Coincidently, archives in Moscow,

Washington, D.C. and Berlin were opened for the first time since World War II. The Chaplain's description matched the reports from the archives almost word for word.

Historians are amazed at how perceptive the chaplain was. Revisionist organizations, with patriotic sounding names, have been trying desperately to whitewash German actions in World War II. By doing so, they hope to lay the groundwork for a revival of Nazi ideology and, ultimately, a Fourth Reich. Their insane idea of ruling the world has never died.

Part II

The war ended. Fifty years passed. Almost as if the Chaplain had the ability to see fifty years into the future, his vision turned out to be true. Revisionists and deniers, backed by huge sums of money from Germany and the Middle East, began their assault on the minds of Americans, particularly vulnerable high school and college students.

Launching an insidious campaign in school publications, revisionists attempted to deny Germany's use of gas and extermination facilities. Directed from Visalia, California by Bradley Smith, ads began to appear in college newspapers. Discounting any evidence universally accepted by historians, scholars and judicial experts, deniers bombarded new generations of students with half-truths and venomous lies about the Holocaust. This in spite of the fact that extermination camps and the Holocaust in general were among the most heavily documented events in the history of the world.

Quoting the first amendment of the constitution, Bradley tried to place these deceptive advertisements in University papers all across America. He was partially successful in attempting to whitewash the crimes of the Third Reich. Some newspapers printed the ads reluctantly but accompanied them with historical evidence pointing out the falsehoods stated in the ads. Other newspapers acknowledged the first amendment but stated it did not obligate any newspaper to print false and misleading information. Unfortunately, some editors were intimidated and printed the ads as submitted without comment. The University of Southern California, Yale, Harvard, Brown and the University of Pennsylvania were among the group of educational institutions which refused to run the revisionist lies. Coincidentally, a Superior Judge in California, Judge Thomas T. Johnson in ruling on a Holocaust related case stated, "the Holocaust is not reasonably subject to dispute."

Many legitimate historians were deeply concerned by the attempts not only to diminish and deny Nazi guilt, but by attempts to demean and place blame on the victims themselves. Shouting, "the Holocaust is a hoax," branding the witnesses, historians, jurists and liberators as liars, Bradley and his followers disregard all factual historical evidence saying it is all "propaganda."

Shortly after WWII ended Dwight D. Eisenhower, the Supreme Allied Commander in Europe, published a book about his thoughts and experiences. Eisenhower said, "...the same day I saw my first horror camp. It was near the town of Gotha. I have never felt able to describe my emotional reaction when I first came face to face with Nazi brutality and ruthless disregard of every shred of decency. Up to that time I had known about it only generally or through secondary sources. I am certain, however, that I have never at any time experienced an equal sense of shock. I visited every nook and cranny of the camp because I felt it my duty to be in a position from then on to testify at first hand about these things *in case there ever grew up at home the belief or assumption that 'the stories of Nazi brutality were just propaganda.'"*

Dwight D Eisenhower

Crusade in Europe, published 1948

Haskell

His official papers spelled out his name as Haskelovich, but from his first day in service, he was known to everyone as Haskell. During his 16 weeks of Infantry Basic Training in the states, he showed no special talents of any kind. But once overseas, his abilities were recognized immediately. It was only then that he became known to everyone as "Haskell the Rascal."

Getting men overseas is one thing. Seeing that the men have the proper equipment, clothing, food and everyday needs is another. Rarely did it ever happen that the proper mixture of men and supplies met the needs of the men in the field. There was always a shortage of something the men needed or wanted which the army was unable to satisfy. Haskell became the company, then battalion, and finally regimental organizer.

In civilian life, an organizer was a person who put things together, like organizing a meeting or a party or a public event of some kind. In the military, the term had a completely different meaning. In the army, one known as an organizer was simply a procurer, someone who took over where the quartermaster corps left off. The organizer could arrange to get anything a unit needed without going through official channels or legitimate protocol. When given a mission, the organizer would blink his eyes as a sign of acceptance, and announce to one and all, "I will arrange it." After his first "mission impossible," Haskell proudly became known as "Haskell the Rascal" to the other members of his unit. Whatever was needed, Haskell could be depended to supply it.

Organizing equipment, whether it was for a jeep or truck or military supplies of any kind, became ordinary. However, when it came to special items, or dealing with the French army or civilians, Haskell really excelled. His ability to reach out to the highest levels insured the men of the unit that they would have the necessary equipment to carry out their missions.

When the war ended on May 8, 1945, many of the infantry troops found themselves in a waiting situation with not too much to keep them occupied. They toured around a bit, went sightseeing, whiling away the time as they waited to be returned to the states. Some took college courses, hoping to make up for time that had been lost fighting a war. They took classes at the Sorbonne in Paris, at Oxford or Eaton in England and at some of the well known universities in Glasgow, Scotland. Some got involved with buying and selling mementos of all kinds, particularly those having to do with the German army. Haskell did none of these things. He kept biding his time, waiting for the right opportunity.

On one such day of lounging around the barracks, someone commented on a story in *Stars and Stripes* about 1,000 jeeps sitting at a pier in Le Havre, waiting to be shipped back to the states. There were also the latest model Pershing M28 tanks with their huge 90MM guns. How often the men in their lighter Sherman tanks, which had been no match for the German Tiger and Panther tanks during combat, had prayed for an American tank that would equal the German armament. Now that the action was over, there were hundreds of brand new Pershing tanks sitting at the pier in Le Havre waiting to be reshipped stateside. However, it was the mention of the 1,000 jeeps that most aroused Haskell's attention. This was something worthy of investigation that could lead to some challenging possibilities. Haskell clipped the story from the paper and began his investigation.

In the weeks that followed, Haskell paid several personal visits to higher echelon personnel in both the American and French armies. This was followed by a series of phone calls to the U.S., France and Germany.

Within a month, a new story appeared in *Stars and Stripes* concerning the 1,000 jeeps still at the port of Le Havre. It had been decided by the "powers that be" to hold an auction for the sale of the 1,000 jeeps. The story went on to say that only American nationals could bid at the sale and that it was an all or nothing sale, meaning the bid would be for the total sale of the 1,000 jeeps, and nothing less. The story meant nothing to the thousands of GIs waiting to ship home. Haskell's eyes glittered as he looked out towards the future. To him, the story had great meaning. This was the opportunity he had been looking for.

Most Americans who even thought of bidding for the 1,000 jeeps were put off by the expense the government would charge to ship the jeeps back to the states. Haskell never gave it a thought as he filled out the bid sheet, throwing away the paper that explained the shipping procedure.

The day after the successful bid was announced, the newspapers carried a big story about the 1,000 American jeeps and a celebration that would take place on that Friday, sponsored by the mayor of Le Havre. All school children would be released from school early so that they could attend.

With bands playing and balloons flying, several French government officials stood up, one after another, making speeches. None of the Americans there that day knew what was being said. And, none of the townspeople seemed to be listening. Some how or other, Haskell had managed to get a seat up on the stage with the French dignitaries. When the mayor of Le Havre finished his speech, he sat down next to Haskell. Then, a French general made a short speech and, after saluting Haskell, the General shook Haskell's hand warmly. At this point, one of the school kids asked the American GI sitting next to him who the man was sitting next to Monsieur Haskell. As the afternoon wore on, it became clear what was going on. Somehow or other, the French government was now the proud owner of the 1,000 American jeeps which Haskell had purchased from the American government.

The French government was happy with their 1,000 American jeeps. The American government was relieved of the burden of reshipping the jeeps to the states. The French school children were happy to have a day off from school. And, Haskell went back to the states with a bank roll that enabled him to become the largest automobile wholesaler on the East Coast. To this day, no one has been able to figure out the details of how he pulled off his greatest coup of the war. In admiration, the men of his unit would wink to each other as they whispered, "Well, Haskell scored again."

Woman of Valor

The American Colonel met the woman while on a trip to Norway in 1990, forty-five years after World War II had ended. Her name was Dagny Loe. In a soft voice she told the American Colonel why she wanted to find the soldier who had been in the 42nd Division. Sorrowfully she spoke of the execution by the Germans of the seven fishermen from her village who had been active in resisting the German conquerors. She did not mention the fact that her husband was one of the seven killed that terrible day.

Russia's survival in the dark days of 1943 was due to the ability of American merchant ships to plod their way through the Nazi submarine packs waiting in the frozen waters of Norway's North Cape. The convoys suffered tremendous losses as they made their way through toward Russia's vital year round port of Murmansk. If the ships were unable to get through with the much-needed supplies, Russia would not be able to survive Hitler's armies.

The convoy losses continued to grow. Convoys made up of forty or more ships would often be reduced to four or five before they arrived at the port of Murmansk. It was at this perilous stage of the war that the resistance fighters in Norway organized to alert the Russians about the locations of the German wolf packs. Russian radio contacted British bomb crews who were then able to eliminate the underwater menace.

For more than a year Norwegian resistance fighters moved from cave to cave, avoiding German intelligence forces searching for their radio location. In July of 1943, acting on a tip from a local Quisling, a notorious collaborator, the seven Norwegian fishermen were arrested and sentenced to be executed. Dagny Loe, the 30-year-old wife of the resistance leader was also taken into custody. Her seven oldest children were distributed to foster homes in all parts of Norway, but she was allowed to take her infant daughter, 3 months old, to her jail cell.

On the day of execution, the seven fishermen were forced to dig their own communal grave. As they slowly dug, a voice called out, "Take care of the children." Standing in her cell, Dagny knew these were the last words she would ever hear from her husband. The German captain called out to the partisans, "Hurry up, I have more important things to do today." One of the condemned men answered back that they were in no hurry to die. The angry German Captain spit down at the unfortunate men. Before the German could take one step back, the resistance leader swung his spade in a wide arc at the captain's neck. The head separated from the sinking body as it flew off in another direction. The German soldiers quickly killed the seven partisans as they stood in their half dug grave.

The next day Dagny Loe's identity papers were marked with the N/N label as she was sentenced to 15 years of hard labor. The N/N signified that she was a nacht und nebel, (night and fog) prisoner. From that moment on she ceased to exist as a person in the world of the German prison system. Eventually, she would simply disappear as the fog in the night. When she was moved from her first prison to another across one of Norway's many waterways, her baby was placed in a box on deck of a small boat while she was chained below deck. The next morning she was handed the frozen body of her baby who had spent the night in a box of fish on the upper deck.

Dagny was transferred to prisons in Norway, Finland, Poland and finally after a death march, to a prison in southern

Germany. The dreaded N/N designation went along with her; the jailers knew that eventually when she was to be disposed of, she would leave her final prison as smoke going up the chimney. The only personal item she was able to take with her as she was shipped from prison to prison was a small handkerchief on which she stitched the names of the locations where she had been. Her final destination was Aichach, a women's prison in Germany where her fellow cellmates were women from Belgium, France and Norway. Forced to make parts for the German electronics industry, the women labored day after twelve-hour day with no news of the outside world or any clue as to their eventual fate.

In a state of near death from malnutrition, the prisoners were unable to notice that on one Sunday the guards failed to open their cell doors at the designated time. Lying in filth and in a state of confusion, they listened as strange outside noises entered the prison compound. Tanks, halftracks and heavy artillery pieces were moving outside the prison walls in the early hours of April 29, 1945. In a state of delirium they lay in their bunks the entire day, too weak to even stand up to peek through the tiny cell windows. Despondent, uncaring, unthinking, unseeing they lay in their filth and waited.

The following day a tearful young American soldier opened Dagny's cell door. On her day of liberation she weighed 81 pounds. Incoherent, she was to spend the next two months in a Red Cross hospital regaining her senses and strength. On returning to Norway her first concern was to begin a search for her seven children. The search was made even more difficult because the retreating Germans followed a policy of scorched earth destroying every structure and all the records in Dagny's village. When finally located, Dagny found she was unable to support all her children by what she earned as a dressmaker. Several of the children remained in foster homes but were continually in contact with their natural mother. Dagny never remarried and continued to live in her native village.

The young American soldier who had brought Dagny back to the world of the living remained a blank spot in her mind. Whenever she came in contact with an American she would show her handkerchief and tell what she remembered about World War II. She hoped that somehow she would be able to make contact with the soldier so that she could properly thank him for saving her life. Every boy and girl in Norway learned of her heroism when in 1992 the King and Queen of Norway visited Dagny at her home to pay tribute to her. However the real honor Dagny was looking for was to meet her American liberator. This lifelong goal continued to evade her.

After hearing Dagny's story, the American Colonel returned to his home in Minnesota determined to help this tiny Norwegian heroine. The Colonel contacted a group of military historians who specialized in American military operations in Bavaria. Within two days the sergeant who had opened Dagny's cell was located. He recalled that on the 29th of April 1945 a huge convoy of the 42nd Infantry Division was on the road leading south towards Munich. As the convoy ground to yet another halt, the impatient sergeant told his jeep driver to turn down a side road in order to find an alternative route to Munich. Five miles down the side road, they came upon what looked like an abandoned prison complex.

Inside they found one very overweight old German guard and four floors of locked prison cells. As the sergeant questioned the guard, three other GIs went from cell to cell unlocking doors. Shocked at the condition of the women prisoners inside the cells, the Americans ran from floor to floor. Most of the prisoners were in such poor condition that they showed little reaction upon being told that they were free. They were confused about who would tell them what to do next and where to go. When the Sergeant opened Dagny's cell and knelt at her side his radio advised him that the convoy was on the move again. As the Americans raced from the prison they warned the German guard that they would be returning shortly. The guard was told to find some food for the women and that the cell doors were to remain open. He was also told that if anything happened to the women he would be held personally responsible.

At the 1993 Annual Reunion of the 42nd Division held in Salt Lake City, Utah, Colonel David W. Pearson of Minneapolis, Minnesota approached the podium. He told the story of Dagny Loe and how he had instituted the search to find the GI who had personally released her from her personal hell. Then he introduced a tiny, frail Norwegian woman to a wildly cheering group of Rainbow Division veterans. When the sergeant, Chet Krawcydowski, came up on the stage to meet Dagny Loe for the first time since 1945, the entire audience stood up and laughed and clapped and cheered as Dagny and the man she had never forgotten hugged and kissed. There were no dry eyes in the audience that day in Salt Lake City.

When order was finally restored, the Colonel asked the sergeant why nothing had ever shown up in the division records about the women's prison in Aichach. "Well Colonel, we had never received permission to leave the convoy that day. Telling about our detour would have lead to all kinds of reports and maybe even gotten us into real trouble. We just figured it was better to forget the whole incident." Dagny held the old veteran's hand as he spoke. Her lifelong wish had been fulfilled.

The American Dream

Part I

When the Draft began in 1941, after being passed in Congress by one crucial vote, it called for men to be inducted into the Army for one year. After Pearl Harbor, men were inducted for what was patriotically called "The Duration." The first number plucked from a large drum was #158. All men holding #158 went into service immediately; many were not discharged until 5 years later.

First discharged in 1945 were the "High Pointers" who had earned a critical score of 85 points in their service records. The points were calculated according to the Army Adjusted Service Rating Scale.

As stated in "*Stars and Stripes*", May 5, 1945:

POINTS. The Army's plan for the readjustment of enlisted personnel calls for an Adjusted Service Rating Card to be issued to each enlisted man and woman. Point totals will be entered on this card covering each of the following factors:

1) Service Credit. One point for each month of Army service between Sept. 16, 1940, and May 12, 1945.

2) Overseas Credit. One point for each month served overseas between Sept. 16, 1940, and May 12, 1945.

3) Combat Service. Five points for the first and each additional award of the following for service performed between

Sept. 16, 1940, and May 12, 1945.

a) Distinguished Service Cross, Legion of Merit, Silver Star, Distinguished Flying Cross, Soldier's Medal, Bronze Star Medal, Air Medal, Purple Heart and Bronze Service Stars (battle or campaign participation stars worn on theater ribbon.)

b) Credit will also be given to Army enlisted personnel who have been awarded the following decorations by the Navy Department: Navy Cross, Distinguished Service Medal, Legion of Merit, Silver Star, Distinguished Flying Cross, Navy and Marine Corps Medal, Air Medal and Purple Heart Medal.

c) Credit will also be given for those awards and decorations of a foreign country which may be accepted and worn under War Department regulations in effect when the readjustment regulations are placed in operation.

4) Parenthood Credit. 12 points for each child under 18 years of age born before May 12, 1945, up to a limit of three children.

CRITICAL SCORE. The total of the points earned by the individual enlisted man or woman in the above four categories will be considered a total-point score. The score that the individual must have in order to be eligible for separation from the Army will be known as the Critical Score. The War Department will be unable to announce an official Critical Score until approximately six weeks after the readjustment regulations go in operation. There will be one Critical Score for enlisted men in the Army Service Forces and the Army Ground Forces, another for enlisted men in the Army Air Forces and a third one for enlisted women in the WAC (Women's Army Corps).

Until it computes and announces these official Critical Scores, the War Department has set for the purpose of aiding immediate demobilization a temporary, "interim" Critical Score of 85 points for enlisted men of the Service, Ground and Air Forces and 44 points for enlisted women of the WAC. These interim Critical Scores will be replaced by the official Critical Scores within the next two months.

Part II

Upon discharge, an Honorable Service lapel pin was issued to every service member who served honorably in the Armed Forces between September, 1939 and December, 1946. Originally made of plastic because of metal restrictions, the buttons were later made of gold plated brass. The veterans who proudly wore the lapel pins affectionately renamed this proof of service to their country "The Ruptured Duck."

No one can say for sure where the name "Ruptured Duck" came from but one story is that one of the B-25 planes used on the Doolittle raid over Tokyo on April 1, 2942 was named "The Ruptured Duck." The raid did not do much damage to Tokyo but it was the greatest morale booster for the American people up to that point in the war.

Veterans and other Americans faced their future optimistically and hopefully. The changing social and economic scene gave meaning to a new term that came into being at this point in American history, "The American Dream." The G.I. Bill, with its educational, economic and home owning benefits was one of the key elements that enabled millions of Americans to make the American Dream come true.

The Bonus Marchers

It was 1944 and Congress was confronted with the prospect of 16 million service people returning to civilian life in a relatively short time. No one knew when the war would end, but it was obvious that the Allies would be victorious and that the end of hostilities was rapidly approaching. Members of Congress remembered what had happened in Washington in the summer of 1932, when 25,000 World War I veterans had marched on Washington.

To show their gratitude to the four million Americans who served their country in the First World War, Congress had voted in 1924 to pay America's veterans a bonus based at the rate of $1.00 per day for domestic service and $1.25 for each day served overseas in 1918. Called "adjusted service compensation," the bill went before Congress with President Calvin Coolidge declaring that he would utilize his veto power to stop the legislation. Coolidge said, "patriotism which is paid for is not patriotism."

Congress overrode the President's veto. The lawmakers, however, failed to budget for the bonus payments to the veterans. By 1932, in the midst of the worst depression in American history, a group of veterans marched to Washington to demand that Congress make good on the bonus money that had been promised to them.

Led by a delegation from Portland, Oregon, with Walter W. Waters acting as leader of the group, they headed for Washington by freight train, trucks, buses and by foot, picking up supporters all across the country. Dubbed the "Portland Bonus March" by the newspapers, sympathizers helped them all along their way as more and more veterans joined the march. By the time they reached the Capitol their numbers had swelled to 25,000 marchers.

As the veterans approached Washington, the President was advised by his Military Intelligence Agency that the marchers had been infiltrated by Communist agents who were intent on overthrowing the government. Hoover did not take this report seriously. He referred to the march as "a temporary disease."

The Chief of Police in Washington, D.C. was Pelham D. Glassford, a veteran of the war who had great sympathy for the bedraggled group of veterans who were gaunt, hungry, and determined to get the bonus money they desperately needed. Chief Glassford, who had been a general during the war, set aside an area on the outskirts of town where the veterans could camp. Called "Anacostia Flats," the area could be approached only by a drawbridge. The Chief saw to it that lumber, nails and equipment were available for the veterans. He also solicited food from the local merchants who were sympathetic to the veterans, many of whom had come with their wives and children. The need was great and the sympathizers, many of whom were veterans themselves, did what they could.

Banners flew from the tops of many of the tents and shacks erected at Anacostia Flats and other areas of the city. "Bonus or a Job" the banners read as they flew alongside the many American flags that the marchers carried. Military discipline had been imposed from the beginning by Walter W. Waters. His basic rules were "no panhandling, no liquor and no radical talk." Although many of the veterans referred to the government legislation as the "tombstone bonus," meaning many of the veterans would be dead before the money was paid, they followed Waters' instructions implicitly.

With more than 1,000 wives and children in the main "Hooverville Camp," the veterans set up a school and library among the shanties to see to it that the kids' schooling did not suffer. Later, a barbershop was added as well. Sympathetic local people donated whatever they could to the veterans' families. Chief Glassford visited the camp periodically and arranged for volunteer doctors to administer to the needs of the camped-out group. Although unemployment throughout the country was at 25% and many of the local people were veterans themselves and out of work they nevertheless contributed whatever they could. This was often a hardship, but the need was great.

History would show that the Bonus March and all of its ramifications were the final blow dealt to Hoover's reelection campaign. In November 1932, deep in the Depression, one out of four families in the country were destitute and cried out for change. Franklin D. Roosevelt, the governor of New York, saw the writing on the wall.

Roosevelt knew that Hoover was against the concept of paying the bonus at that time. The Republicans opposed payment because they were determined to balance the budget. When the House of Representatives passed the Bonus Bill, the veterans were elated. Two days later, the Senate defeated the Bill and the hopes of the veterans lay smashed in the Washington dust. Some of the Bonus Marchers packed up their meager belongings and headed for home. Others declared they would remain where they were until they received the bonus money.

As June turned into July, Chief Glassford was pressed by the Administration to get rid of the shanties and tents that had been set up in the park areas all across the Capitol. On July 28th, with police and armed troops surrounding the area, tempers reached the breaking point. Bricks began to fly. Suddenly, the sound of shots was heard.

Just prior to the shooting General Douglas MacArthur, who had commanded the 42nd Division in the Great War (World War I) with (then) Major Eisenhower at his side, had taken over control of the troops. The soldiers were ordered to clear the Capitol area of veterans and their housing quarters. George S. Patton, with five tanks and a contingent of men with loaded rifles with fixed bayonets, drove into the crowd of veterans. The infantrymen, wearing gas masks, lobbed tear gas grenades into the assembled veterans. Mounted cavalry troops set fire to the flimsy shanties, sending clouds of smoke into the air around the Capitol building.

As night fell, the troops crossed the bridge leading to the Anacostia Flats veterans' housing area. Within hours, the entire area was in flames, although MacArthur had been given strict orders not to send troops over the drawbridge. In the aftermath, Eisenhower, in writing about MacArthur said, "he was too busy and did not want either himself or his staff bothered by people coming down and pretending to bring orders." The late military historian Stephen Ambrose further quoted Eisenhower saying, "I told that dumb son-of-a-bitch he had no business going down there."

That evening, MacArthur, when questioned by reporters said, "had he let it go another week, I believe the institutions of our government would have been severely threatened." It was at this point that Roosevelt was heard to say to an advisor "This will elect me."

When the shooting and burning came to an end, two veterans' bodies were found in the rubble. The administration branded the two veterans Communists and they were buried without fanfare. A Washington reporter, while searching military records discovered that one of the veterans, Eric Carlson of Chicago, had been a decorated hero overseas. His body was disinterred and reburied in Arlington Cemetery with full military honors. The other veteran was William Huska, but little was known about his background. Three months later, Hoover lost the election. Franklin Delano Roosevelt's prophecy had come true. Roosevelt was now President of the United States.

In 1936 Congress finally passed the "Veterans Cash Now Bill" and the veterans received their long awaited bonus, which came to almost $600 per veteran.

Near the end of World War II, Congress faced the prospect of 16 million returning veterans. Spurred by memories of the 1932 Bonus March, Congress passed the Servicemen's Readjustment Act. The American Legion was indispensable in creating Public Law 387, which veterans promptly dubbed "The GI Bill."

The GI Bill had a revolutionary impact on life in the United States. No longer would only the wealthy and elite be able to afford higher education. College and university enrollments swelled with returning veterans who used the educational benefits of the bill. In addition, low cost V.A. (Veterans' Administration) loans fueled a boom in housing construction. Many new communities were built outside of large cities, in suburbs where land was cheap. This in turn led to the need for more automobiles and extensive highways. All of these benefits, and more, contributed greatly to full employment and the economic booms of the years ahead. The changes in American society created by the GI Bill were remarkable then and are still evident today.

General Eisenhower became a Five Star General and led the Allied troops to ultimate victory in Europe. General George S. Patton achieved worldwide fame as the commander of the victorious Third Army in Europe. General Douglas MacArthur is remembered for his saying, "I shall return," when he was forced to leave Bataan. He later became the victorious Allied commander in the Pacific Theatre. Eric Carlson was laid to rest in

Arlington National Cemetery, Washington, D.C. He was buried with full military honors on August 2, 1932 in grave number 5217, section 18. William Huska, of Chicago, the other veteran killed during the Bonus March, was buried in an unmarked grave within sight of the Capitol.

Living Quarters of the Bonus March families, Washington D.C., July 1932.

The Righteous Ones

Yad Vashem is an organization that was founded with a dual mission. First, it is a memorial to the 6,000,000 Jews (including 1,500,000 children) who were killed in the Holocaust. Second, from the outset it has searched to identify individuals who risked their lives to save other souls during World War II. "Righteous Among the Nations" is the title bestowed on non-Jews who rescued Jewish lives during the Holocaust. Those individuals are flown to Jerusalem where the entire state of Israel pays homage to them. Trees are planted in their names, medals are issued and the Righteous ones and their families are treated as visiting dignitaries.

Captain Stanley Nowinsky was the Civilian Affairs Officer for the American military government in Austria in 1945. A Catholic from Chicago, he had been with the 42nd Division in Dachau on the day the camp was liberated. Of Polish descent, Nowinsky was able to converse with many Polish prisoners rescued by the Americans. He was deeply affected by what he had seen in Dachau. Captain Nowinsky, often acting above and beyond his military orders, aided an estimated 120,000 survivors in their efforts to reach Palestine. In 1973, Nowinsky was flown to Jerusalem by the Israeli government where he was honored by a grateful nation. Many in the cheering crowds were survivors he had helped in their "journey." On the medal given to Nowinsky are the following words: "He who saves a single life is as though he has saved the whole world."

Chiune Sugihara

For four weeks after he was ordered to leave his post by the Japanese government, Chiune Sugihara and his wife remained in Kaunas, Lithuania. The year was 1940. Sugihara was the Japanese Consul-General. With German troops rapidly approaching, the Jews in Lithuania knew they faced certain death if they didn't find a way to escape. Going against the instructions of his government, Sugihara issued hand-written visas that allowed the Jews safe passage out of Lithuania. Current estimates are that 40,000 souls are alive today as a result of the efforts of this rescuer. When asked why he had defied his government's orders, his reply was, "It was the right thing to do."

Varian Fry

Varian Fry saved thousands of artists and scientists who were trapped in France in the early days of World War II. In spite of the orders of the American government, he arranged escape routes for thousands of refugees who faced certain death at the hands of the Germans and their Vichy collaborators.

Age 32, a Harvard graduate and a loner, Varian Fry had been ordered back to the states from his State Department position in France in 1940. When asked about his heroic actions, his answer was, "I stayed because the refugees needed me." Marc Chagall, an artist of unique talents, Jacques Lipchitz, a world famous sculptor and Hannah Arendt, a famous writer, were three of the souls saved by Varian Fry who is honored as a Righteous One Among the Nations.

Curtis Whiteway

Curtis Whiteway was an Infantry Squad Sergeant in the 99th Infantry Division in World War II. Whiteway and his squad were among the first Americans who came upon the "Euthanasia Center" known as Hadamar. This was one of six "Psychiatric Clinics" used by the Nazis for killing children and adults with mental or physical disabilities. Categorized as "lives unworthy of living," these unfortunate souls were designated to be put to death by injection or gassing by the Nazi regime.

Whiteway and his men went on to help in the liberation of six concentration camps in Germany. This Righteous individual has been speaking at churches, schools and universities all over the country, telling of his wartime experiences. In 1983, he was honored in Jerusalem by the Israeli government for his humanitarian efforts.

In 2005, at the 60th Anniversary Dedication Ceremony at the Holocaust Museum in Washington, D.C., Curtis Whiteway lit one of six candles in memory of the six million souls who perished in the Holocaust. Whiteway acts in the belief that "One man can make a difference." Medal number 2869, awarded to Curtis Whiteway, shows two hands grasping a lifeline of twisted barbed wire which seem to reach out from a void. The lifeline, circling the globe, proclaims deeds such as those of the Righteous justify the world's existence and our faith in humanity. Imprinted on the medal is the Talmudic saying: "He who saves a single life is as though he saved the whole world."

Raul Wallenberg

At the age of 32, one man took it upon himself using courage, ingenuity and a great deal of bluff to rescue what was left of Hungarian Jewry from sure death at the hands of the Nazis.

By the time Raul Wallenberg had been appointed Secretary of the Swedish Legation in Hungary, 400,000 Hungarian Jews had been deported to concentration camps in Poland and Germany. Wallenberg vowed to save as many of the 230,000 Jewish souls left in Budapest as he could. Using bribes, threats and bluffs, he created Swedish passes and provided food and blocks of housing projects flying the Swedish flag. As the war was nearing its last stages, his delaying tactics were responsible for saving the lives of thousands of Hungarian Jews.

In January of 1945, Raul Wallenberg was escorted into a car by three Soviet Agents. Nothing more is known about what happened to Wallenberg, other than stories and rumors coming out of Soviet gulags and prisons.

On October 5, 1981 Congress honored Raul Wallenberg by making him an honorary American citizen. This honor had been bestowed previously on only one other individual, Winston Churchill. On the same day Wallenberg became an American citizen, the cornerstone of the U.S. Holocaust Memorial Museum was laid at 100 Wallenberg Place in Washington, D.C.

In 1985 honorary citizenship was granted to Wallenberg by Canada followed by honorary citizenship in the state of Israel in 1986. In addition to these honors, in 2003, the Hungarian government granted honorary citizenship in the name of the city of Budapest in order to preserve the memory of Wallenberg's achievements. It is hoped that such honors will be helpful in educating new generations to the courageous efforts and accomplishments of Raul Wallenberg.

Efforts have been made by the Swedish and American governments to get the Soviets to open their archives regarding Raul Wallenberg, but, thus far, the Soviets have refused all such requests.

Chiune Sugihara

Varian Fry

Curtis Whiteway

Raul Wallenberg

YAD VASHEM - DEPT. FOR THE RIGHTEOUS AMONG THE NATIONS
Righteous Among the Nations - per Country & Ethnic Origin*
January 1, 2005

Poland	5,874
Netherlands**	4,639
France	2,500
Ukraine	2,079
Belgium	1,402
Hungary	658
Lithuania	555
Belarus	537
Slovakia	454
Germany	410
Italy	371
Greece	265
Yugoslavia (Serbia)	119
Czech Republic	115
Russia	116
Croatia	103
Latvia	96
Austria	84
Moldova	69
Albania	63
Romania	51
Switzerland	38
Bosnia	34
Norway	24
Denmark***	19
Bulgaria	17
Great Britain (incl. Scotland)	13
Sweden	10
Macedonia	10
Armenia	10
Slovenia	6
Spain	3
Estonia	3
China	2
Brazil	2
One of each: **Japan, Luxembourg, Portugal, Turkey, USA, Georgia**	6
Total Persons	**20,757**

* These figures are not necessarily an indication of the actual number of Jews saved in each country, but reflect material on rescue operations made available to Yad Vashem.
** Includes two persons originally from Indonesia, but residing in the Netherlands.
*** The Danish Underground requested that all its members who participated in the rescue of the Jewish community, not be listed individually but as one group.

FU-GO

While the boys learned to dig deeper foxholes in France and Germany, their brothers and sisters fighting on Guadalcanal and Iwo Jima learned how to fight against an enemy who would rather die than surrender. Back in the states, kids who were in junior high school when the war started were being sworn in, trained and shipped overseas before they reached their 19th birthdays. All across the United States parents were hanging gold star banners to show that their sons had given their all.

In October and November, 1944, as the Germans were making their final preparations for the upcoming Battle of the Bulge, the Japanese High Command came up with a plan to inundate the United States with bombs carried by unmanned hydrogen air balloons. Called the Fu-Go Project, Japanese military men joined with meteorologists who had been studying the Japanese jet stream, a river of air currents that flows high in the atmosphere. The balloons were attached to baskets that carried high explosive and incendiary bombs. Some bombs were timed to explode at specific set times while others were set to explode on impact.

The initial attempt, the launching of 6,000 balloons, took place in early November 1944 from a site just east of the Japanese island of Honshu. Once the balloons reached the high atmosphere and entered the jet stream, it was estimated it would take 60 hours for them to cross the Pacific Ocean, where their timing devices would unleash the devastating payload on the unsuspecting citizens of the United States.

Being totally uncontrollable, it was not known where the

balloons might land or how destructive their impact might be. After the launch, the Japanese War Lords sat back and waited for reports to come in from the States. California, Oregon and Washington were expected to be the points of greatest devastation. As the Japanese awaited results, 10,000 more balloons were being readied for a second launching.

The Japanese military planned to achieve several results with the FU-GO balloons. Expecting them to land in forested areas, they envisioned forest fires burning all along the west coast of the United States and Canada. These forest fires would not only be devastating to American morale, but would burn down huge timberland areas of the United States. In addition, the Japanese believed that the large numbers of men needed to fight the fires would have to be plucked from military duties to handle the immediate emergency.

The Japanese underestimated American willpower after the attack on Pearl Harbor. When the Fu-Go Project was launched, there were those in the Japanese military who believed the Americans would be so intimidated by this attack from the skies that they would throw up their hands and surrender. Fifty-six years later, in the year 2001, Arab terrorists believed that by attacking the World Trade Center in New York City, they would bring America to its knees. Both were unable to comprehend that emergency situations unify and strengthen Americans.

As the Fu-Go Project was launched in November 1944, America's defense system went into action. When reports began to come in along the West Coast, civilian defense officials decided to take a huge gamble. They imposed a news blackout on any stories involving the Japanese balloons. With the exception of local areas, most Americans never knew about this Japanese attempt to ignite the West Coast forest areas. Due to the news blackout, the Japanese never learned how many balloons actually reached our shores.

Having launched the balloons during the winter months when the jet stream was the strongest, the Japanese did not take into account that U.S. Western forests receive most of their rainfall and snow during those very months, making it extremely difficult for incendiary bombs to ignite forest fires. Although some balloons floated as far east as Michigan, no major fires resulted from the landings.

Fewer than 300 balloons were sighted by American defense forces, although it was felt that some balloons descended in isolated areas and were never recovered. Ironically, one of the balloons landed in a wooded area in Oregon and was responsible for the only civilian deaths on the mainland of the U.S. during World War II.

The wall of silence imposed by the American media resulted in the Japanese calling off their plan to have a second launching of the balloons. On the West Coast of the U.S., news about the danger of the balloons was spread by word of mouth in churches, schools and social organizations. Residents were warned not to touch strange objects and to report their existence to authorities. However, for the most part, people were unaware of the danger the balloons presented.

In the spring of 1945, two days before the war in Europe officially ended, Pastor Archie Mitchell and his wife took five school children on a Sunday picnic and fishing trip to Gearhart Mountain, Oregon. As the pastor parked the car, his wife and five children explored the camping area. Shouting with excitement, the children huddled around a strange object in the bushes. The pastor, who had been warned about dangerous balloons, shouted a warning as he ran, waving his arms, towards the huddled group. The pastor's warning was never heard. Although only one bomb in the cluster exploded, the blast left a crater six feet in diameter and 2 feet deep. All the children and the pastor's wife were killed.

On examining the area, the Army reported that many of the parts of the bomb package were rusted and, that under the balloon, there still remained several inches of snow, indicating how long the balloon had been hidden in the bushes.

As Army, Navy and Civil Defense personnel congregated on the tiny town of Bly to investigate the explosion, statements about the deaths were still subject to the U.S. news blackout. The coroner's first statement was "the cause of death, in my opinion, was from an explosion from an undetermined source."

On May 22nd, the War Department, fearing more civilian casualties, issued a statement acknowledging the bombs and providing information on how to identify and avoid them. Newspapers carried additional warnings to people, especially children, living west of the Mississippi River to be aware of the possible hazards of bombs, and cautioned them about approaching or touching any unfamiliar objects.

On May 31st, the Western Defense Command issued the following statement:

> "You are being informed about these balloons because they are dangerous. Six persons have now been killed. You are now in on the secret. ...Do not be unduly alarmed. Let us all shoulder this very minor load in a way such that our fighting soldiers at the front will be proud of us."

Three years later, the House Judiciary Committee ruled that military authorities had been negligent in failing to warn the public about the balloons, and Congress awarded $20,000 to survivors of the victims.

A monument now stands at the site where the bomb exploded. It is dedicated to the first and last mainland American civilian casualties of World War II.

A Place Called Babi Yar

The operation was called Barbarosa, the German code word for the invasion of the Soviet Union. Although warned by the United States that the invasion would take place, the Russians were taken completely by surprise. Attacking in force on June 22, 1941, the Germans rolled through Russia destroying everything in their path of advance. The Russians adopted a "scorched earth" policy as they retreated, hoping to leave nothing of value for the advancing German armies.

By September 19th, the city of Kiev, capitol of the Ukraine, came under German barrage. While many Kiev residents retreated before the German onslaught, there were Russians who welcomed the German Army thinking they would be freed from the oppressive years under Stalin. Coincidentally, Kiev had a large Jewish population.

Approximately a week after the German occupation, a number of bombs blew up buildings where the Germans were housed. Blaming the Jews for the bombings, the Germans immediately retaliated against all the Jewish inhabitants of Kiev. (Russian archive documents later proved that the explosives were the work of NKVD agents who had been left behind by the Soviet Army to hinder the advancing Germans in any way they could.)

On September 28, 1941, the day the bombings stopped, the Germans posted notices all over Kiev:

"All Jews living in the city of Kiev and its vicinity are to report by 8 o'clock on the morning of Monday, September 29th, 1941, at the corner of Melnikovsky and Dokhturov Streets (near the cemetery). They are to take with them documents, money, valuables, as well as warm clothes, underwear, etc.

Any [Jew] not carrying out this instruction and who is found elsewhere will be shot.

Any civilian entering flats evacuated by [Jews] and stealing property will be shot."

Exactly like the Polish Jews before them, the Jewish citizens of Kiev believed this notice meant they were to be deported. Few among them thought otherwise. At the designated streets the lines started forming early. The unsuspecting citizens of Kiev hoped to get good seats on the trains that would take them to a new location. Tens of thousand of men, women and children waited in long lines unable to see what was taking place far ahead of them.

The people were taken through the Jewish cemetery of Kiev. There they were told to leave all their baggage. Those who questioned this order were told that the Germans were methodical and that there would undoubtedly be special luggage cars on the train.

At this point, machine gun fire could be heard, but still few realized what was happening out of their line of sight.

Then in groups of 10 they were told to move forward. Facing the small groups were two lines of German soldiers 5 feet apart. Holding clubs and sticks, the soldiers motioned the Jews forward, "Schnell, Schnell." Soldiers holding vicious looking dogs were laughing and joking as they struggled to hold the excited dogs on their leashes. As the Jews moved forward down the corridor of shouting soldiers, they were continuously hit with clubs that the soldiers were swinging viciously.   Amid much wailing and crying, the unfortunate ones were ordered to undress. Any that hesitated, even for a few seconds, were hit and kicked by the guards who seemed to be enjoying their sadistic work. The guards who were laughing and shouting and hitting and kicking seemed to be in some kind of drunken rage.

As the prisoners looked around, they realized where they were. Standing in a line, the prisoners overlooked a huge ravine called Babi Yar. The unfortunate ones were very high up on one side of the ravine, standing at its very edge. Looking down into the deep chasm, they saw a sea of bodies and blood. Machine gun bullets tore into the group standing at the edge; as those bodies tumbled down into the steep ravine, another group was gradually lined up to meet the same fate.

33,771 Jews were killed in this way over the two-day period, September 29 and 30, 1941. Methodical to the end this was the number listed on the Einsatzgruppe Operational Situation Report #101.

The next group brought to Babi Yar were Gypsies and mental patients from the Pavlov Psychiatric Hospital who were gassed and then dumped into the ravine on top of the Jewish bodies which had preceded them. Russians who were guilty of hesitating to follow a German order were also buried at Babi Yar as were Russian prisoners of war who were brought to the ravine to be shot.

It is estimated that more than 100,000 souls are buried together at Babi Yar.

The ravine at Babi Yar.

Excerpts from the poem;

Babi Yar

by Yevgeny Yevtushenko

No gravestone stands on Babi Yar;
Only coarse earth heaped roughly on the gash.

On Babi Yar weeds rustle; the tall trees
Like judges loom and threaten...
All screams in silence; I take off my cap
And feel that I am slowly turning gray.
And I too have become a soundless cry
Over the thousands that lie buried here.
I am each old man slaughtered, each child shot.
None of me will forget.

Yevgeny Yevtushenko (1933-   ) is a poet who often dealt with controversial issues. In this poem, Yevtushenko, who is not a Jew, condemned Russian refusal to place a memorial at this mass grave of 100,000 of it's citizens.

As the War Ends

The announcement came simultaneously from Washington, London and Moscow. A representative of the German High Command had signed the unconditional surrender at 1:44am, Monday, May 7, 1945. The war in Europe was over. German land, sea and air forces surrendered to the Allies and Soviets effective 12:01am, Wednesday, May 9, 1945. Immediately after the signing of the surrender documents, all offensive operations were stopped. Allied troops went into defensive positions in order to prevent unnecessary loss of life, which, due to shattered communications, might have occurred at the end of hostilities.

Before the official surrender, piecemeal surrenders of German divisions and even armies had left German troops in action only in Czechoslovakia, where Patton's Third Army was conducting an offensive, and in Norway where Quisling, an infamous Norwegian collaborator, was demanding that German troops resist to the end.

In the autumn of 1944, General Eisenhower had predicted that the Germans would fight their last great battles west of the Rhine. His prediction became reality when Russian forces fighting eastward met up with American forces, effectively cutting Germany in two.

The American Seventh Army lunged southward, capturing Nuremberg and Munich. Eisenhower's aim was to slice into the heart of the threatened "National Redoubt." There, it had been reported, Nazism would make a last stand protected by fanatical SS troops and the natural barrier of the Austrian Alps. At that time, President Roosevelt, who had led the American people both in preparation for the war and during more than four years of fighting, died without seeing final victory.

American forces had confronted German troops for the first time during the invasion of North Africa. This was followed by the invasion of Sicily on July 10, 1943, and then Italy in August. Finally, D-Day, the invasion of the continent took place on June 6, 1944 at Normandy, France.

For the men of the 45th Infantry Division, the war ended where Nazism had started – in Munich. The men of the 45th had been through 511 days of combat. They had been through the concentration camp of Dachau. For any of the replacements who had not been too sure of why the war was being fought, Dachau provided the answer. Having liberated thousands of starving, sick and delirious slaves, there was never another question of what the war was all about.

The Congressional Medal of Honor, the nation's highest honor, was awarded to five men of the 45th Infantry Division. The men so honored accepted their awards in the names of all their comrades – the souls who had fallen in battle and the lucky ones, the men who had lived to see their job completed.

Van T. Barfoot was an infantry Sergeant who for months had been laying his life on the line, exactly the same as thousands of other riflemen who had been living in the mud and slime of Italy, France and Germany. On October 4, 1944, this son of Choctaw Indians stepped into circumstances that were very different from an ordinary day in the life of American infantrymen. On this day, Van T. Barfoot became one of the most honored warriors in American history. For his actions, Van T. Barfoot was awarded the highest honor our country has to offer its heroes – The Congressional Medal of Honor.

"CITATION: For conspicuous gallantry and intrepidity at the risk of life above and beyond the call of duty on 23 May 1944, near Carano, Italy. With his platoon heavily engaged during an assault against forces well entrenched on commanding ground, 2d Lt. Barfoot (then Tech. Sgt.) moved off alone upon the enemy left flank. He crawled to the proximity of 1 machinegun nest and made a direct hit on it with a hand grenade, killing 2 and wounding 3 Germans. He continued along the German defense line to another machinegun emplacement, and with his tommygun killed 2 and captured 3 soldiers. Members of another enemy machinegun crew then abandoned their position and gave themselves up to Sgt. Barfoot. Leaving the prisoners for his support squad to pick up, he proceeded to mop up positions in the immediate area, capturing more prisoners and bringing his total count to 17. Later that day, after he had reorganized his men and consolidated the newly captured ground, the enemy launched a fierce armored counterattack directly at his platoon's positions. Securing a bazooka, Sgt. Barfoot took up an exposed position directly in front of 3 advancing Mark VI tanks. From a distance of 75 yards, his first shot destroyed the track of the leading tank, effectively disabling it, while the other 2 changed direction toward the flank. As the crew of the disabled tank dismounted, Sgt. Barfoot killed 3 of them with his tommygun. He continued onward into enemy terrain and destroyed a recently abandoned German fieldpiece with a demolition charge placed in the breech. While returning to his platoon position, Sgt. Barfoot, though greatly fatigued by his Herculean efforts, assisted 2 of his seriously wounded men 1,700 yards to a position of safety. Sgt. Barfoot's extraordinary heroism, demonstration of magnificent valor, and aggressive determination in the face of pointblank fire are a perpetual inspiration to his fellow soldiers."

When Van T. Barfoot entered the military service from Carthage, Mississippi, he had no idea he would become one of America's most honored heroes. He was given a battlefield commission and became a second lieutenant. When the war ended, Van opted to remain in the Army serving in both Korea and Viet Nam. He retired as a full colonel and is now enjoying retirement life in Ford, Virginia.

Paper Clips

In a little town in Tennessee, not far from Chattanooga, the kids in a small school were studying the Holocaust. There were 475 students in the whole school. There were no Catholics, Jews or Asians, one Latino and 5 blacks. When the teacher told them that 6 million Jews had been killed in the Holocaust, one child asked the teacher, "What does six million mean?" None of the kids in the class had any idea.

While developing a project that would have some meaning for the students, one of the teachers with a Norwegian background told them what it was like to live in Norway under German occupation.   He told them of the Norwegian Underground and the symbol they wore to identify one another. The symbol was a simple paper clip that had been invented in Norway in 1899. Worn on a lapel, the paper clip became a symbol of patriotism and Norwegian resistance to the Germans and to those Norwegians who sided with the Germans.

Motivated by the Resistance Fighters, the students decided to collect paper clips – 6 million paper clips to teach themselves exactly what 6 million of something looked like.

Warming to the project, the students began by writing letters not only to the President of the United States, but to former Presidents as well. Encouraged by the initial response, the students contacted public figures both in the United States and Europe. Several German reporters wrote supportively about the concept and, in a short time, German students began sending their paper clips to add to the collection.

When the *Washington Post* and Tom Brokaw reported on the Whitwell Middle School concept developed in the small town of Whitwell, TN, the paper clip deluge hit monumental proportions. Many packages from Germany were accompanied by letters to the students begging for forgiveness. Some letters and paper clips came from families of relatives who had died in the Holocaust. They thanked the students of Whitwell School for honoring the memory of their loved ones.

As publicity about the project grew, the concept touched the hearts of people far and wide. A group of Holocaust survivors from New York traveled to Tennessee to show solidarity with the students and to tell them about personal experiences. In Germany, citizens searched for a meaningful gift to send to Whitwell, TN. Unbelievably, the German people were able to locate a cattle car used to transport unfortunates to the concentration camps. The railway car was shipped from Germany as a memorial. It now stands outside the Whitwell Middle School; in it are stored millions of paper clips.

As the students collected memorabilia sent from all over the world, they learned of a number much bigger than 6 million. They received letters from families of Gypsies, Slavs, Poles, homosexuals, Jehovah's Witnesses, physically and mentally disabled Germans, and Russian prisoners of war – all of whom perished in concentration camps. This figure of an additional 5 million was added to the 6 million the project began with.

In this small town almost everyone thought alike; they knew little of diversity or the challenge of accepting those who think or act differently. The horrors of the Holocaust and its 11 million victims were far away and unreal.

And then, it started. A child's simple question swelled into a landslide of 35,000 letters of support. Almost everyone in town was drawn into the project. Suddenly, they were connected to people all over the world. Suddenly, they were a part of world history. The memory of the Holocaust was burned into their souls.

A documentary film about this stirring project was made. Appropriately, the name of the film is simply, "Paper Clips."

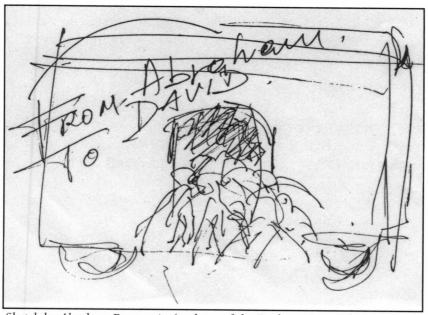

Sketch by Abraham Borenstein (sculptor of the Dachau Memorial Monument), drawn for the author in Dachau, 1995. The sketch is the artist's concept of people being herded into a cattle car for what the Germans euphemistically called "resettlement."

Taps

Among the guys in the squad there was virtually nothing that wasn't spoken about, except for one, religion. Each man prayed or practiced his own rituals, strictly in private. It took them all by surprise, therefore, when one day the kid called Bly asked no one in particular, "You guys know when they started playing Taps at military funerals?" They all kept cleaning their weapons or doing whatever they were doing before the question was asked. Finally, one of the squad asked, "No, when?"

"Well, it goes back to the Civil War. One of those battles where the Union and Confederate armies fought to a standstill over a field in Virginia no one even remembers today. After a bloody battle, both sides retreated to their own sides of the field to give medical attention to their wounded and to plan for the next day's battle. During the nighttime hours, one soldier could be heard moaning in pain. Neither side knew if the wounded man was a Union soldier or a Confederate soldier. No one knows why, but during the night a Union Captain, Robert Ellicombe, took it upon himself to crawl into the field to help the wounded soldier.

It was only when he pulled the young soldier behind the Union lines that it was discovered that he was outfitted in a Confederate uniform. This surprise was quickly followed by the shock of Captain Ellicombe as he looked at the face of the soldier he was holding and discovered that he was staring into the face of his son. The soldier had died from his wounds. Now he lay in the arms of his distraught father.

The boy had been studying music in the South before the war began. The father did not know that his son had enlisted in the Confederate Army. Despite the fact that the boy had been a Confederate soldier, the grieving father requested that his son be given a full military funeral, including a military band. The Union Army agreed to one musician. The Captain chose a bugler and submitted a series of notes that had been found in the pocket of the boy's uniform. The notes the bugler played at the boy's funeral were the haunting tones that we know of as "Taps". The same exact series of notes that we know, are played by a lone bugler at all military funerals."

Bly cleared his throat as he added, "Although their origin is uncertain, the following words were added to the melody:

Day is Done.

Gone the Sun.

From the lakes,

From the hills,

From the sky.

All is well.

Safely rest.

God is nigh."

Not another word was spoken as the men drifted slowly from the area.

Epilogue

When the war ended, Dachau was used as a holding area for the interrogation of SS troops. The search was on for war criminals, the individuals responsible for the deaths of millions who had perished in Germany's concentration camps.

The SS prisoners were kept warm and well fed, but nevertheless they still were in prison. Most of them could not understand why. They knew they had "lost the game;" it was now over and they wanted to go home. But at Dachau and the other camps, the smell of death was still there. The gas chambers, the ovens and the killing machinery were still there. The peepholes, which some thoughtful Nazi had drilled into gas chamber doors so that visiting dignitaries could view human beings clawing the walls in the last throes of life, the peepholes were still there.

The bodies were all gone. Everything in Dachau had been thoroughly cleaned up. The ovens, which had contained human corpses when the first American GIs arrived, were scrubbed, washed and vacuumed until they looked like new.

As the SS prisoners exercised they could look across the parade ground to where the killing center remained just as it had been. The prisoners were aware that the machine used for crushing human bones into fertilizer to be spread on the local farmlands was still there, standing unused. Only the smell, which hung over Dachau like a memory, could not be "cleaned up." The smell would not go away.

The prisoners wanted to go home to their families. Fanatics began planning for the Fourth Reich. Most Germans wanted to forget about the death camps. They wanted to forget about war, but the smell still lingered over Dachau. The memory of millions who perished in the death camps remains. The peephole, now looking in on Germany itself, remains, too.

Appendix

G. I.ˢ FREE 32,000 IN CAMP; FIND 39 CARS OF BODIES

Yank Attack Surprises Dachau Nazis

DACHAU, Germany, April 30 (AP) —The United States 42d and 45th divisions captured the infamous Dachau prison camp today and freed its 32,000 captives.

Two columns of infantry riding tanks, bulldozers, and Long Tom rifles—anything with wheels—rolled down from the northwest and surprised the SS [elite corps] guards in the extermination camp shortly after the lunch hour. Scores of SS men were taken prisoner and dozens slain.

The Americans were quickly joined by trusties working outside the barbed wire enclosure. Poles, Frenchmen, and Russians seized SS weapons and turned them against their captors.

Report Famous Men Moved

Officials said the Nazis recently moved several distinguished inmates, including Marshal Stalin's son, Jacob Djugashvili, captured on the Russian front in 1941; the former Austrian chancellor, Kurt Schuschnigg, and his wife, and Pastor Martin Niemoeller, the German anti-Nazi Protestant leader.

Three princes also were reported moved, among them Frederick Leopold and Xavier de Bourbon de Parme.

One of the prisoners remaining claimed to be the son of Leon Blum, former French premier.

Prisoners who said they had had access to the records and inner workings of the camp said 9,000 internees died of hunger or disease or were shot in the last three months, and that 14,000 more had perished last winter.

Typhus cases were scattered thruout the camp. The water supply of the city was reported contaminated from 6,000 graves on high ground which drains into the Amper river.

A French general was slain last week as he walked toward a truck believing he was to be evacuated, prisoners reported. They said SS guards shot him in the back.

Yank Fury Hits Camp

The G. I.s stormed thru the camp with tornadic fury. Not a stone's throw from a trainload of corpses lay the bleeding bodies of 16 SS men shot as they fled the Yanks.

In the mess hall of the SS barracks food still was cooking in the kitchen. One SS officer was slumped over in a plate of beans, a bullet thru his head. Nearby was a telephone with the receiver down.

Outside the power house were the bodies of two SS men slain by a Czech and a Pole working in the engine room.

Correspondents and infantry men found 39 open type railroad cars on a siding that ran thru the walls of the camp.

At first glance the cars seemed loaded with dirty clothing. Then one saw feet, heads, and bony fingers. More than half the cars were full of bodies, hundreds of bodies.

One Man Still Alive

One man's neck was so small and shrunken it scarcely seemed capable of holding a head, but he was alive. An officer put the man in his jeep and carried him to a hospital, where plasma was keeping him alive.

The best information available was that this trainload of prisoners, mostly Poles, had stood on the tracks several days and most of the prisoners had been starved. Others had been shot thru the head. Clothing had been torn from some and their wasted bodies bore livid bruises. Some had tried to escape; their bodies lay along the tracks five or six steps away. One, shot thru the head, was astride a bicycle.

This spectacle was outside the walls of the camp, along a widely traveled road inside the city of Dachau where Bavarians passed daily.

Civilian Minds on Looting

The civilians were looting an SS warehouse near-by, passing the death train with no more than curious glances at the American soldiers. Children pedalled past the bodies on bicycles and never interrupted their excited chatter. Looted clothing hung from their handlebars.

Seven thousand prisoners of the camp were marched away on foot in the last few days, it was reported.

The main part of the camp, where 32,000 skinny men and women were jammed into wooden barracks, is surrounded by a 15 foot wide moat thru which a torrent of water circulates. Atop a 10 foot fence is electrified barbed wire.

When Lt. Col. Will Cowling of Leavenworth, Kas., slipped the lock in the main gate, there still was no sign of life inside this area. He looked around for a few seconds and then a tremendous human cry rose. A flood of humanity poured across the flat yard, which would hold half a dozen baseball diamonds, and Cowling was all but mobbed.

Hoisted to Their Shoulders

He was hoisted to the shoulders of the seething crowd of Russians, Poles, French, Czechs, and Austrians, cheering the Americans in their native tongues. Soldiers rescued him, but the din kept up.

Flags appeared and waved from the barracks. There was even an American flag, altho only one American was held there. He is a major from Chicago who was captured behind German lines when he was on special assignment for the office of strategic services.

The joyous crowd pressed the weight of thousands of frail bodies against the wire and it gave way at one point. The prisoners rushed out, altho still penned up by the moat. Three tried to climb over the fence, but were burned to death on the top wires, for the current still was on.

Two SS guards fired into the mass from a tower, betraying their presence. American infantrymen instantly riddled the Germans. Their bodies were hurled down into the moat amidst a roar unlike anything ever heard from human throats.

ARMY DIVISIONS

The following United States Army Divisions have been certified by the United States Army Center for Military History as Liberating Divisions:

Division	Camp(s)	Date
1st Infantry	Falkenau a.d. Eger (subcamp of Flossenbürg)	May 7, 1945
2nd Infantry	Leipzig-Hasag (subcamp of Buchenwald) and Spergau	April 14, 1945 April 17, 1945
4th Infantry	Dachau subcamps	April 28–29, 1945
8th Infantry	Wöbbelin (subcamp of Neuengamme)	May 3, 1945
29th Infantry	Dinslaken	April 3, 1945
36th Infantry	Kaufering Camps	April 30, 1945
42nd Infantry	Dachau	April 29, 1945
45th Infantry	Dachau	April 29, 1945
65th Infantry	Flossenbürg subcamp	April 20–21, 1945
69th Infantry	Leipzig-Thekla N42 (subcamp of Buchenwald)	April 19, 1945
71st Infantry	Gunskirchen (subcamp of Mauthausen)	May 5–6, 1945
80th Infantry	Buchenwald and Ebensee (subcamp of Mauthausen)	April 12, 1945 May 4-5, 1945
83rd Infantry	Langenstein	April 11, 1945
84th Infantry	Hannover-Ahlem and Salzwedel (subcamp of Neuengamme)	April 10, 1945 April 14, 1945
89th Infantry	Ohrdruf (subcamp of Buchenwald)	April 4, 1945

List of American Army Divisions honored as liberators of concentration camps.

Division	Camp(s)	Date
90th Infantry	Flossenbürg	April 23, 1945
95th Infantry	Werl (prison and labor camps)	April 2–8, 1945
99th Infantry	Dachau subcamp (vicinity of Mühldorf)	May 3–4, 1945
103d Infantry	Landsberg (subcamp of Dachau)	April 27, 1945
104th Infantry	Dora-Mittelbau	April 11, 1945
3d Armored	Dora-Mittelbau	April 11, 1945
4th Armored	Ohrdruf (subcamp of Buchenwald) and Buchenwald	April 4, 1945 April 11, 1945
6th Armored	Buchenwald	April 11, 1945
8th Armored	Halberstadt-Zwieberge	April 12–17, 1945
9th Armored	Falkenau a.d. Eger (subcamp of Flossenbürg)	May 7, 1945
10th Armored	Landsberg (subcamp of Dachau)	April 27, 1945
11th Armored	Gusen (subcamp of Mauthausen) and Mauthausen	May 5, 1945 May 6, 1945
12th Armored	Landsberg (subcamp of Dachau)	April 27, 1945
14th Armored	Dachau subcamps at Ampfing and Mühldorf	May 2–3, 1945
20th Armored	Dachau	April 29, 1945
82nd Airborne	Wöbbelin (subcamp of Neuengamme)	May 3, 1945

ARMY DIVISIONS (CONTINUED)

9-17-93

DEAR DAVE,

IT's Been OVER 48 yrs. ago. Hope you can put these articles to good use.

with out Its rough writing frontal vision

Thank you for the tape. had a lousy time sleeping that night. Have a good time at the reunion. Return articles when ever possible

Sincerly Yours
John J. Degri

Letter from first GI to enter gates of Dachau.

Unsung GI recalls Dachau

Army Pfc. John Degro, of Newbury, was credited with being the first American soldier to liberate inmates of Hitler's Dachau concentration camp in 1945. This is a 1945 photo of the soldier.

Local man freed inmates

By DORIS O'DONNELL
PLAIN DEALER REPORTER

NEWBURY TOWNSHIP

To the 32,000 inmates of Hitler's Dachau concentration camp, a skinny American private who shot the lock off their deadly prison on April 29, 1945, was their "unknown soldier."

His identity was a mystery until an enterprising retired Army colonel "searched the minds of those who were present that day" and found John J. Degro of Newbury Township in Geauga County.

In 1986, Col. Howard A. Buechner, author of "Dachau, The Hour of the Avenger," cited Degro in his book "as the epitome of the unsung dogface infantryman, who along with countless thousands of his counterparts, were the true heroes of World War II."

Degro "never rose about the rank of private first class. He was simply there when his country called. He did the dirty work and went home when the job was finished, without fame or recognition," wrote Buechner.

SEE GI/6-B

GI

FROM/1-B

On April 29, 1945, Degro was assigned to an eight-man squad to search Dachau. He weighed about 135 pounds, having marched across western France and over the Rhine River to Nuremberg with the 45th Thunderbird Divsion.

Drafted into the Army from his job at Aluminum Co. of America in Cleveland, he was a replacement in the Thunderbirds. The division had started at Anzio in Italy with the 7th Army and joined the 3rd Army with Gen. George Patton.

Degro, who said he had never heard of Dachau before he got to Nuremberg, was the scout.

"We walked toward the tracks, the boxcars, like our cattle cars. I looked inside and saw bodies on top of bodies, waist-deep, stacked like cordwood," he recalled yesterday in Newbury where he lives with his daughter, Marilyn Martell. "The corpses were skin and bones, and human excrement was all around. The stench was awful.

"At that instant, we lost our cool and went sort of nuts," Degro said. "We didn't feel too good. The hospital was at the siding and we ordered everybody out, doctors and patients. Patients were on nice white sheets. We kicked all the Germans into the yard.

"We pressed on to the building and a sergeant ordered me to blow the lock off. I shot it off with my M-1. This was the kid from Woodhill Rd. in Cleveland. Only things I ever shot before the war were groundhogs with a .22," Degro said.

"We went in. There was scream[...] people saying how happy to see Americans. The men — we didn't seen any women — were emaciated," he said. "I remember most the piles and piles of shoes. More than Imelda Marcos has. Here were the gas ovens. I remember the tears, stench and sounds.

"I knew then and there why I was in the Army. I actually came to liberate these people. There were all nationalities," Degro said.

Today, Veterans Day, Degro will attend Mass at his church, St. Helen's in Newbury.

"We can't let people forget, especially future generations. I feel sorry for the Vietnam veterans and their terrible homecoming. They got shot at just like we did. On Veterans Day, I'll be praying for all veterans and their families," said Degro, who is a member of American Legion Post 663 in Newbury.

Degro, who has a combat infantry badge, the Bronze Star and Purple Heart, serves on the Geauga County Veterans' Services Commission.

He and his wife of 48 years, Marta, who died in 1986, raised four daughters. Marta Degro died after they returned from 10 years in Pompano Beach, Fla., and a well-digging business. Back in Geauga County, he built houses.

About eight years ago, Degro and his wife revisited the German battle sites and Dachau.

"When we fought across Germany, we soldiers were out to kill Hitler if we could find him. Revisiting Dachau, we remembered he killed 6 million Jews," he said.

"You never forget. Those scenes at Dachau are impressed on my mind. Sometimes I get up at night and try to erase them, but I can't forget."

JOHN DEGR[...]
looked insid[...]
The corpses
was awful."

John J. Degro, first GI to enter gates of Dachau.

FROM THE ROCKING CHAIR OF
DON DOWNARD

9-26-92

Hello Dave:

Thought I'd just express that I was very excited to hear from someone who had no personal axe to grind.

I'm looking forward to the material you are sending me about "Dachau", one sorta taken a slow move. I do believe that "there is no limit to what a man can do if he doesn't care who gets credit for it."

The info you gave me by telephone is very interesting, especially to learn of the great number of camps there which carried the name Dachau as part of their title

Sincerely

Letter from Lt. Col. Don Downard, 42nd Division, who helped remove the only survivor of the Dachau death train (see page 143).

KZ-Gedenkstätte Dachau Museum-Archiv-Bibliothek

Alte Römerstraße 75   Telefon 08131/1741-1742   8060 Dachau-Ost

August 31,1992
588/92 di-mg

Daer Mr. Israel,

this is to acknowledge with thanks your letter of August 2,1992
together with the included clippings and copies.

Unfortunately I am not able to prove which US miltary unit has been
the first to arrive in Dachau. I send you an article on the liberation
of the camp which I wrote in 1985 and which gave a summary on the
information we have in our archives.

In the meantime the question of Japanese Americans,who also claim to
have been the first to liberate Dachau, has turned up. This summer a
group Japanese American Veterans came to Dachau (only for a very short
visit) and from the talks I had with them, I think that they might have
liberated some of the Dachau subsidiary camps in Bavaria and for them
all the camps were "Dachau". One of them claimed for example that when
they arrived the camp had been completely deserted, whereas in Dachau
were more than 30 000 survivors at the time of the liberation.

We have no information on black sodiers taking part in the liberation.

The story of the massacre has been publicized by groups and magazines
of the extreme right or neo nazi organization. There have been fights
between SS soldiers and US soldiers in the area of Dachau, which had
no connection with the camp.

I send you also copies (unfortunately only in German) of an article I
wrote on neo nazi diffamation and one on the information we have on
the camp crematorium.

We do not have the article by Irwin Steinitz and would be grateful if
you would send us copies.

Sincerela yours.

Barbara Distel

Barbara Distel

*Checking out the facts about the day of liberation. Letter from the curator of
the Dachau Memorial Museum.*

National Archives

Washington, DC 20409

March 4, 1992

Reply to: ML92-1196-rlb

David L. Israel

Dear Mr. Israel:

We have in our custody the historical records of the 522 Field Artillery Battalion. Using these files it is possible to trace the hourly movement of the Battalion during April 1945. The records indicate that they were crossing the Lech River at the time Dachau Concentration Camp was liberated by the 45th and 42nd Infantry Divisions.

Prior to the arrival of the Americans in the Munich area, many of the inmates of Dachau were moved to subcamps in the greater Munich area. It may be one of these subcamps that the 522nd liberated.

You may want to compare the photographs that were taken by the members of the 522nd of the camp they liberated, with photographs known to be of the Dachau main camp. You may also want to check the meterological records for the Munich area. The photographs taken by the 522nd show an area covered in snow.

It would be difficult for you to research this topic in depth without visiting our facility. The records that potentially relate to the liberation of Dachau consist of literally tens of thousands of pages. If, however, you would be interested in tracing the movements of the 522nd during the last week of April 1945, you would be able to do so by ordering copies of fewer than 50 pages of records. Copies are $.25 per page.

The 7th Army Inspector General's investigation of the shooting of German guards by American personnel at the time of the liberation of Dachau is the best account we have been able to find to date regarding that day. This file consists of roughly 70 pages. If you are interested in ordering this or the 522nd's records, let us know and we will gladly provide you ordering information.

Sincerely,

RICHARD L. BOYLAN
Assistant Chief
Suitland Reference Branch (NNRR)
Textual Reference Division

National Archives and Records Administration

Letter from National Archives responding to author's inquiry seeking accurate information about the liberation of Dachau.

"PRESIDENTIAL UNIT CITATION RECIPIENT"

761st Tank Battalion &
Allied Veterans Association

NATIONAL HEADQUARTERS • 617 GOING STREET • PONTIAC, MICHIGAN 48053

LOCAL CHAPTERS
CHICAGO, IL.
CLEVELAND, OH
DETROIT, MI
KANSAS CITY, MO
LONG ISLAND, NY
LOS ANGELES, CA
PHILADELPHIA, PA
PONTIAC, MI
WASHINGTON, D.C.

NATIONA
PHILIP W. LATIN
GLOUCESTER STEPHENS, 1st
JOSEPH O. KAHOE, 2nd
RICHARD R. KEI
HENRY L. MIL
REV. CLARENCE COPEL/
HERMAN TAYI
HAROLD GARY, I

Rt 2, Box 61C
Silsbee, TX 7
Dec 9, 1992

    This letter is being written to confirm what I told you orally in our telephone conversation. At no time, in our history "Come Out Fighting" or in any other publication has the 761st Tank Battalion ever laid claim to the liberation of either Buchenwald or Dachau. If you study our route of march while attached to the 71st Infantry Division you will discover that we came no closer than 40 or 50 miles to either of these camps. It is most unfortunate that this claim was made on national television without most of the membership having been consulted on the matter and we are justifiably unhappy about the situation. Our unit had a good combat record that is well documented and we do not need such errors to appear. You have my permission to send copies of this letter to the members of your unit that were responsible for the actual liberation of Buchenwald.

        Yours sincerely,

        Phil Latimer

        Philip W Latimer
        Lt Col, USAR, Ret
        President

Letter from 761st Tank Battalion clarifying the whereabouts of the unit on April 29, 1945.

JOHN WEITZ

January 19, 1993

Thank you for your generous letter and your fascinating
enclosure. I knew Bill Quinn, of course, and remember being at
his house in Augsburg when Göring was the star attraction. I
was there as an on-the-loose O.S.S. man. I had just completed
some work with the F.A.B. (Freiheits Aktion Bayern).

The number of peace feelers which were floating around between
January 1944 and May 1945 was incredible! I can understand why
the Russians would have wanted to make peace. They had beaten
the Germans and were anxious to lose no further people. Also,
I expect that they were distrustful of the Western Allies, a
mutual condition.

I imagine that Hitler never saw many of the peace offerings
simply because no one had the guts to approach him! Ribbentrop
was one of the few, and he was told to "go away with his
businessman's politics!"

I suppose that all dictators and many senior elected officials
suffer from isolation. No one wants to tell them the truth.

Again, my warmest thinks for writing to me, and I shall keep the
copy you sent to me of the 20th of June 1945 Memorandum to Bill
Quinn. I am hereby de-classifying it since I am now much too
old to hold a commission.

Best regards.

Sincerely,

John Weitz

*Letter from John Weitz to the author. When the war ended Dachau was used as
a holding area for German Military personnel. John Weitz, a German born
American member of the OSS, went undercover into Dachau posing as a
German officer. His mission was to assess the strength of the insurgent German
Werewolves organization.*

By ___R̲C̲D̲ ̲/̲⟶⟶̲___   NARA, Date _3̲/̲1̲8̲/̲9̲2̲_ ✝

Testimony of: Lt. Rene J. Giraud, 1325565, Infantry OSS Detachment, ETO.

Taken at: Dachau, Germany.

Date: 3 May 1945.   By: Lt. Col. Joseph M. Whitaker, IGD,
                                         Asst. Inspector General, Seventh Army.

    The witness was sworn.

19 Q Please state your name, rank, serial number and organization.

    A Rene J. Giraud, 1st Lieutenant, 1325565, Infantry OSS Detachment, ETO.

       (The witness was fully advised of his rights under the 24th Article of
       War.)

20 Q You were interned at and present in the Dachau Camp when the American
       forces liberated it?

    A That is right, sir.

21 Q Did you witness the death of any of the prison guards?

    A No, sir, I did not witness the method of death or shooting.

22 Q Did you witness the mistreatment of any of the prison guards?

    A No, sir.

23 Q Where were you when the American troops came?

    A I was inside the camp, in fact in the hospital. I went to the gate and
       through the crowd to get to the commanding officer. By that time every-
       thing was over except the prisoners trying to get out.

24 Q Do you remember the commanding officer's name?

    A I am afraid not. There was a brigadier general from the 42nd or 45th
       Division.

25 Q What day was that?

    A That was on April 30th, approximately at 2:15 in the afternoon.

26 Q Can you give me an estimate of the time you met these two brigadier gener-
       als with reference to the time the camp was liberated?

    A The troops arrived approximately at 2:00 and I met the generals about :15.

27 Q Did you stay with these generals after that?

    A I placed myself under their disposition and asked that I help with the in-
       structions, and after that time I walked around as Major Giraud and helped
       with the camp protection.

EXHIBIT "B"   - 4 -   GIRAUD

*Inspector General's interrogation of Lt. Rene J. Giraud, the only American
prisoner in Dachau on the day of liberation (see also next two pages).*

Testimony of: Lt. Rene J. Giraud (Contd)

28 Q Were you inside the stockade or outside after your conversation with these generals?

A Outside, sir.

29 Q Did you see any guards in the hands of American troops?

A Yes, sir, I did.

30 Q Where were they when you saw them?

A They were sitting on the siding just in front of the camp gate.

31 Q About how many?

A Very roughly I would estimate about twenty.

32 Q Do you know what the American troops die with them?

A They were marched away, sir. I don't know where or what they did.

33 Q Do you know anything about the subsequent shooting or killing of guards by either troops or inmates?

A No, sir, I don't know anything in particular.

34 Q Do you know of any persons being killed here after the initial taking of the camp?

A Yes, sir, I do.

35 Q Will you tell me about those matters?

A Only one incident that I know of. That was the 2nd of May, just after the general's party inspection of the camp. Prisoners of the camp chased out three individuals whom they claimed to be SS. The individuals climbed over the wire enclosure at the same time the enclosure guards came out immediately to see what the trouble was and maintain order. That is all that I saw up to that point, and afterwards I saw that the men had been shot in the pillbox just in front of the enclosure.

36 Q Could you tell from where you were whether they were shot by inmates or by American guards?

A I couldn't because I didn't see them shot. I just heard the shots.

37 Q Do you know whether or not they were SS or guards?

A No, sir, I do not know whether or not they were SS.

38 Q I believe that is all unless you have something else?

A I believe not, sir.

EXHIBIT "B"   - 5 -   GIRAUD

Rene J. Guiraud - 5 October 1920 - F.A.M.E. #167

Block 12 Supplemental Sheet

a.   After undergoing intensive specialized training and operational testing, I was parachuted into Nazi-occupied France, accompanied by a radio operator. Upon arrival in France, we assumed identities and posed as French citizens who had been in Occupied France throughout the war. My mission was to organize a secret organization capable of collecting intelligence, harassing German Military units and occupation forces, sabotaging critical war materiel facilities, and protecting certain key military features for use by Allied Forces when they reached the area.

b.   Though arrested on a charge unrelated to my activities, the mission was successful. Prior to my arrest, 1500 guerrillas had been organized, equipped from "Local" stocks, trained and led in operations; intelligence and counter-intelligence networks had been developed; numerous resistance cells for passive sabotage had been brought under our control and direction, and had been trained and "security weeded" of penetrations; and my radio operator had been established with a secure system of transmission sites, couriers, etc. Upon my arrest, he carried on.

c.   After undergoing two months of "forceful" interrogation by the Gestapo, and having successfully avoided compromising the mission, I became the permanent "guest" of the Nazis in the Concentration Camp of Dachau in Germany, where I remained until liberated by U.S. Forces in April 1945. While in Dachau, I fostered and participated in a prisoner resistance movement which went undetected until liberation. At the moment of liberation, I was placed in command of the Dachau Camp and post area, pending arrival of U.S. Civil Affairs, etc., authorities. After orienting three difference G-5's in two weeks, I "escaped" the "assignment," accompanied by five fellow-"ex-prisoners" (all British agents). Commandeering a disabled U.S. C-47 and crew, we arrived in Paris in time for the "V-E" celebrations that evening.

d.   In July 1945, I was decorated with the Legion of Merit, as a 1st Lieutenant. I "recuperated" for my next assignment until August 1945.

D A C H A U

By Tec. 3 James W. Creasman

Dachau is no longer a name of terror for hunted men. 32,000 of them have been freed by the 42D Rainbow Division. The crimes done behind the walls ot this worst of Nazi concentration camps now live only to haunt the memories of the Rainbowmen who tore opein its gates and first saw its misery, and to accuse its SS keepers of one of the worst crimes in all history.

When Infantrymen of the 42D Division fought their way into Dachau against fanatical SS troops who met deserved violent deaths along the moats, behind the high fences and in the railyards littered with the bodies of fifty carloads of their starved victims, these hardened soldiers expected to see horrible sights.

But no human imagination fed with the most fantastic of the tales that have leaked out from the earliest and most notorious of all Nazi concentration camps, could have been prepared for what they did see there.

The keen descriptive powers of a score of ace correspondents who entered the camp while the battle of liberation was still in progress, and through whose eyes the whole world looked upon that scene, could not do justice to this story. Seasoned as they were by long acquaintanceship with stark reality, these trained observers gazed at freightcars full of piled cadavers no more than bones covered with skin and they could not believe what they saw there with their own eyes.

Riflemen accustomed to witnessing death had no stomach for rooms stacked almost ceiling-high with tangled human bodies adjoining the cremation furnaces, looking like some maniac's woodpile.

And when an officer pressed thru mobs of the forgotten men of all nations inside the electric barbed wire enclosure and entered a room where lay the dying survivors of the horror train, he wept unashamedly as limp ghosts under filthy blankets, lying in human excreta, tried to salute him with broom-stick arms, falling back in deathly stupor from which most would never rouse.

Article from 42nd division newspaper by Jim Creasman giving an eye witness account of events as they unfolded at Dachau on April 29, 1945. The author of this letter was given a Battlefield Commission for this outstanding report (see also next two pages).

- 2 -

Ten days before the arrival of the Rainbow Division fifty carloads of prisoners arrived at Dachau from the Buchenwald concentration camp in a starving condition after 27 days without food. When Buchenwald was threatened by advancing American troops the Nazis hurriedly crowded about 4,000 of their prisoners into open flatcars unfit even for cattle. 27 days later--days of exposure to freezing weather without anything to eat, a trainload of human suffering arrived at Dachau only to be left to die in the railyard leading into this extermination camp.

In those stinking cars were seen the bodies of those prisoners too weak even to get out. A few tried, and they made a bloody heap in the door of one of the cars. They had been machine gunned by the SS. A little girl was in that car.

In another car, sitting on the bodies of his comrades, his face contorted with pain frozen by death, was the body of one who completed the amputation of his gangrenous leg with his own hands and covered the stump with paper. Underneath was one with a crushed skull. "He's better off now" was the comment of one newsman. Close by was one who had been beaten until his entrails protruded from his back.

But most of them had simply died in the attitudes of absolute exhaustion that only starving men can assume. Curled up with their faces resting in fingers tipped with blue nails. With naked buttocks angling up to pivot on a skeletal pelvis. Or twisted over to show an abdomen stretched drum-tight against the spine with ribs making an overhanging bulge.

Some of the cars had been emptied and the bodies carted to the crematory. In one room adjoining the furnace-room on the left they were neatly stacked. The stripped corpses were very straight. But in the room on the right they were piled in complete disorder, still clothed.

With the help of a husky Yugoslav inmate who worked at the furnaces and

- 3 -

who told that all four of them had been going "tag und nacht"———"day and
night" with a capacity of 7 bodies each, the explanation was partially unfolded.
The straight neat ones had probably been brought in alive, showered in the
"Brausebad" or shower-room, then gassed or hanged from hooks on the rafters in
front of the furnaces. Those on the right were just as they were dumped out of
the freight cars where they had died of starvation.

It was incredible that such things could happen today, but there was the
visible proof.

It was unbelievable that human beings were capable of perpetrating such
unspeakable atrocities, but there were the men who did it. The SS.

At least 25 and perhaps 50 were beaten to death by inmates who struck with
all the fury of men who suddenly release years of pent-up hate.

Someone said there were 14 in the canal. One was lying beside his own
bloody artificial limb with which his brains had been exposed. One in a railroad car had no face left.

These once-swaggering Hitler-worshippers would pocket no more of the pro-
fits from the hair-oil, shoe-polish, thermos bottles, notebooks, stationery,
brushes, porcelain works of art, and cigarette paper manufactured there by men
and women from all of Europe who slaved until starvation and disease made them
worthless and then they were burned. Now the SS guards were dead. But their death
could not avenge the thousands dead and dying there in Dachau.

Those tortured dead can only be avenged when our world is aroused so much
by what the 42D uncovered at Dachau and by what others have found at all the
other Dachaus scattered throughout Germany, that never again will any party,
any government, any people be allowed to mar the face of the earth with such
inhumanity.

DEPARTMENT OF THE ARMY
THE U.S. ARMY CENTER OF MILITARY HISTORY
103 THIRD AVENUE
FORT LESLEY J. McNAIR DC 20319-5058

REPLY TO
ATTENTION OF   AUG 2 1 2000

Historical Resources Branch

Thank you for your recent letter regarding remarks that Secretary of the Army, Louis Caldera, made during the recent ceremony awarding the Medal of Honor to Asian Americans for heroism during World War II. You state that Secretary Caldera credited some of the medal recipients with having liberated the concentration camp at Dachau. I have been tasked to determine the facts in this case and to respond directly to you.

As you know, the 442d Regimental Combat Team (RCT) consisted of the 442d Infantry, the 522d Field Artillery Battalion, and the 232d Engineer Combat Company, and incorporated the 100th Infantry Battalion, originally organized in Hawaii. With the exception of the 522d, the 442d RCT was serving in Italy on April 29, 1945, the date on which the Dachau concentration camp was liberated. None of the units of the 442d RCT was involved in the liberation of Dachau concentration camp proper. The main camp at Dachau was liberated by the 42d and the 45th Infantry Divisions, and the 20th Armored Division.

However, the Nazi concentration camp system consisted of over 5,000 camps and subcamps. In April of 1945 the 522d Field Battalion of the 442d RCT was attached to the 4th Infantry Division fighting its way through south-central Germany. The 4th Division did liberate an outlying subcamp of Dachau at Grossaitingen on April 28, 1945. With no intent to deceive being involved, it is easy to see how the liberation of the subcamp could have been confused with the liberation of the camp proper in unit lore. As you graciously acknowledged, the veterans of the 442d RCT did deserve the recognition they recently received and played an important role in the hard-fought liberation of Europe. These seem the most important points to remember at this point in time.

Thank you very much for your letter and for your continuing interest in keeping the historical record straight. Our military heritage remains a great source of pride for all of us, and is at its best when straightforward and accurate.

Sincerely,

John S Brown

John S. Brown
Brigadier General, U.S. Army
Chief of Military History

Department of Army Military History reply to a request for clarification concerning day of liberation, Dachau.

COMITÉ INTERNATIONAL DE LA CROIX-ROUGE

Geneva, 8th July 1997
GEN/ARCH 97/178 - FBS

Dear Mr Israel,

We refer to your letter of 10 May and apologize for the delay in our reply.

In response to your request, we enclose a copy of the report by ICRC delegate Victor Maurer on his visit to Dachau in April and May 1945 (French and German versions).

We have not found any information in our archives enabling us to identify the Dachau camp commandant at that time. However, Konnilyn G. Feig's book *Hitler's death camps: The sanity of madness*, Holmes & Meier, New York, 1983 (2nd edition), suggests that the person in question must have been Wilhelm Weiter. You would no doubt find this book well worth reading.

As regards Lt. Marcel Jean Guiraud, we have found no trace of him in our Central Agency for Prisoners of War archives.

We hope that this information proves useful and wish you every success in your research.

Yours sincerely,

Fabrizio Bensi
Archives Division

Encl.

Mr David L. Israel
1200 Mira Mar Suite 1001
Medford, Oregon 97504
USA

19, AVENUE DE LA PAIX - CH-1202 GENÈVE - TÉLÉPHONE: (022) 734 60 01 - TÉLEX: 414 226 CCR CH - TÉLÉFAX: (022) 733 20 57

Red Cross reply to information request

HEADQUARTERS 116TH EVACUATION HOSPITAL (SEM)
Office of the Commanding Officer
APO #758, U S Army

20 May 1945

Subject: Unit History 1 - 10 May 1945.

To   : Commanding General,
           Seventh Army,
           APO #758, U S Army.

ATTENTION: Historian.

     1 May 1945 the hospital was in operation at Ottingen, Germany, in support of the 15th Corps, which consisted of the 42nd and 45th Infantry Divisions, the 20th Armored Division, and Corps troops. That day we stopped receiving patients at midnight preparatory to a move. 2 May 1945 the unit moved into the notorious Dachau Concentration Camp at Dachau, Germany. The camp had been liberated from the SS troops and the camp was in a most depressing condition. There was a daily death rate from disease and starvation of about one hundred and forty (140) daily. Added were the SS dead, which were increasing for two or three days. The principal causes for deaths were starvation, tuberculosis, typhus, and dysentery. Typhus had been epidemic since December 1944. There were over four thousand (4,000) in the prison hospital and unknown number of sick in the prison barracks, where they were dying at the rate of about seventy (70) daily, without the benefit of medical treatment.

     The SS barracks were assigned to us for hospital use. These consisted of eighteen (18) one-story frame buildings, which were full of trash and very disorderly. They were convertible, by removing partitions, into large wards with latrines and washrooms. This work, which was considerable, was done by us with the aid of ex-prisoner help. Fortunately there was a large mess hall with excellent cooking facilities, cooler, and steam from central plant.

     The medical personnel was housed in the SS administrative building which was fairly easy to convert.

     All personnel received 1 cc dose of typhus vaccine and DDT dusting (daily). The Typhus Commission arrived and the delousing and vaccinating of the prison personnel was started.

     3 May 1945 we started receiving patients. They were brought from the prison compound by a team of litter bearers and ambulances after being tagged by our prison liaison officer, and were received in our receiving department established in double ward tents near the ward section. There they were bathed, old clothing burned, pajamas put on, and dusted well with DDT powder.

- 1 -

Medical Corps history (Dachau)

Thirteen·wnet

356 West 58th Street
New York NY 10019

212.560.2000
FAX: 212.582.3297

September 8, 1993

Mr. David L. Israel

Dear Mr. Israel:

When Thirteen/WNET withdrew the documentary LIBERATORS: FIGHTING ON TWO FRONTS IN WORLD WAR II in February, we promised you and the viewing public that we would undertake a comprehensive review to evaluate allegations that portions of the film were inaccurate. That review has been completed, and it has concluded that the film contains factual inaccuracies. Because of your interest in this matter, I want to share these findings with you.

Based on extensive oral testimony and a detailed analysis of the historical record as found in the National Archives, which include the battalion's own morning reports, operational journals and after-action reports, and research at other institutions concerned with documentation of the Holocaust, the review findings concur with critics of the film who have asserted that the 761st Tank Battalion and the 183rd Engineer Combat Battalion did not liberate Buchenwald and Dachau. However, as stated in the review team's report, "the review team can substantiate the presence of the 183rd Engineer Combat Battalion at Buchenwald sometime within the week following April 11, 1945" and does acknowledge the possibility that some members of the 183rd Engineer Combat Battalion may have been at Buchenwald within the 48-hour period that defines liberation.

Historical records place Company A of the 761st Tank Battalion at the liberation of the Gunskirchen Lager camp, a subcamp of Mauthausen near Lambach, Austria. Some survivors of Mauthausen have also reported to the review team that African-American soldiers offered them food and medicine at the time of their liberation or in their first days of freedom. G-2 intelligence reports suggest the possible involvement of the 761st in the liberation of Kircheim by Pocking, a subcamp of Flossenburg, northeast of Nuremberg, Germany. Although the film makes passing reference to a camp at Lambach, the role of the

Letter from PBS concerning the documentary film "The Liberators." Efforts of veterans helped get PBS to withdraw sponsorship of the controversial film.

Continued on next page.

761st in liberating Gunskirchen Lager and Kircheim by Pocking is not described in the documentary. However, the participation of the 761st in these liberations supports the general thesis of the film that African-American soldiers in segregated battalions assisted in the liberation of Nazi concentration camps.

The review also found a substantial number of less egregious errors, ranging from incorrect dates for military events and the misattribution of still photographs and film footage of concentration camps. We are very disturbed that a documentary addressing such an important time in history was not supported by appropriate journalistic rigor during its research and development stage. We have also determined that the producer's advisory panel of experts was inadequately utilized to monitor the factual content of the film.

Thirteen/WNET regrets that we did not detect these deficiencies prior to broadcast. We recognize that we must reevaluate our working relationships with independent producers to better ensure the accuracy of any programs that we put our name on and present to the public in the future.

Thirteen/WNET will continue to suspend broadcast of LIBERATORS on public television stations until such time as the documentary is corrected. The filmmaker's independent production company, Miles Educational Film Productions, Inc., holds the copyright to the film, and is the only party that can alter it. Thirteen has also asked Miles Educational Film Productions, Inc. to remove our name from the film's credits for any non-broadcast distribution.

Thank you for your interest in Thirteen/WNET's programs. We hope we have been responsive to your concerns.

Sincerely,

Harry Chancey, Jr.
Vice President and Director
Program Service

HC:cp

Megan MacPherson
January 27, 1992
EDIT C-80 Magazine Writing
Personal Profile

At first, Ed Gorak took pictures during World War II for personal remembrances. He developed them in his helmet in trenches when the sun went down-- a sort of crude darkroom. The technique is one he taught himself from a pamphlet the Eastman Kodak Co. handed out at the 1933 World's Fair in Chicago when he was 13.

His parents bought him a camera for high school graduation, not knowing the atrocities he later would see through its viewfinder. The camera accompanied him through basic training, but he had to send it home before going to fight in Europe. His mom later sent it to him when he was in Italy along with half a pint of Wilken Family whiskey. "It didn't break. She wrapped it real well," he says about the whiskey.

His sky blue eyes wander as he tells the story. His full head of white hair, which he's had since age 28, gives him an air of authority. He's been 6'-1" all of his life, but now admits to shrinking an inch. He constantly adjusts his belt so it's not too tight around his waist. He's fit and active and proud that he weighs the same today as he did when he was discharged from the Army in 1945. He straightens up in his chair as he talks about his pictures.

He took more than 600 pictures overseas to help him relate scenes to his family that words alone couldn't fully describe. Holocaust museums in California and New York display his photographs. They are in a holocaust documentary film, and they are also part of the collection at the U.S. Army Military History Institute in Carlisle, Pa. He has sold and given away more than 300,000 of them to friends, collectors and history buffs.

The scenes he captured on film at the concentration camp in Dachau, Germany, are the most horrific. His division, the 45th Infantry, was the first to arrive at Dachau to liberate it from the Nazis. He counted 39 boxcars loaded with dead bodies at the site, and he photographed one of them.

Most of the 35,000 inmates were Polish, which is also the first language Ed learned from his immigrant parents in Chicago. He approached the fence that separated him from the inmates and spotted two inmates that

A grandaughter's tribute to a liberator.
(continued on next page)

weren't "skin and bones" like the rest of them. He learned that they ate better because they did the dirty work of cremating the bodies from the gas chamber. He asked them for a tour.

Before entering the chamber, inmates had to undress. "I have pictures of the shed where their clothes were hanging," he says.

Before the Allied troops arrived, the camp ran out of power to run the ovens and bodies were piling up. He asked the men to pose, putting bodies in the oven. He didn't have a flash for the camera, so he asked them to be still. He held the camera steady against his forehead, letting light into the open lense. At the same time, he held a handkerchief over his nose. "They could stand the stench better than me."

After developing a sort of immunity to the death and destruction he saw, it was easier to photograph the scenes. "It didn't seem real that anyone could be so cruel." He shakes his head and his insightful blue eyes gloss over with tears. "And I can't hold the camera that steady anymore."

****

Ed's girlfriend, Lillian, supplied him with the film and chemical solutions he needed. He married her when he returned from the war in 1945, and they spent the first four months of their marriage developing, reprinting, catalogging and mailing sets of pictures to his buddies. "I let him talk when he wanted to about what he went through. I didn't prod him," she says. The pictures helped because she found it hard to believe and understand what the war was really like.

He and Lillian have been attending the 45th Infantry reunion every year since 1984. He finds the event therapeutic. "Only we who were there can relate to each other. And we're dying out," he says. He leans back in his chair and sighs. "We were victorious. We thought it was the war to end all wars."

Ed Gorak was a Polish Catholic from Chicago. When he entered Dachau with the 45th Division he was able to converse freely with many Polish inmates. He was a prolific photographer and took more than 600 pictures documenting the Nazi atrocities.

March 24, 2001

Dear General Foster,

I was most pleased to receive your warm note and the accompanying information about The Comanche Codetalkers.

Over the years I have read 200 to 300 books about WWII without ever seeing a reference to the role of the Codetalkers in Europe. The PR man for the Navajos in the Pacific seems to have done a much better job. Many people know about the Navajos. Few people I am in contact with ever heard of the exploits of the Comanches.

In searching for more information I came across information about the roles played by the Mohawks as well as the Sioux. A also followed up on your information and took the liberty of speaking with Charles Chibitty in Tulsa. He is alive and well and still quite feisty.

I thank you again for your help. While in service I never had the opportunity to communicate with any officer above the rank of Captain. I found it very liberating at this age to have been able to write to you, Gen. Sparks, Gen. Quinn, Gen. Wickham, Gen. Eschenberg and Colonels Bartlett and Hugh Foster III. I feel sure you must have come in contact with all of these men during the war. I was even fortunate enough to be able to speak with Gen. Patch's daughter, Mrs. Chandler Diehl of San Antonio, Texas. She gave me one of the final lines for my book. Her father in speaking of his 7th Army as well as all the other GI's in the ETO asked, Where did we get such men?"

I never heard anyone say it better.

Sincerely,

David

Letter thanking General Hugh Foster, Jr. for information concerning his role in training the Comanche code talkers.

Fact Sheet

Total U.S. War Deaths		Peak strength of Armed Forces	
Civil War	497,000	U.S.	12,364,000
WWII	406,000	USSR	12,500,000
WWI	116,000	Germany	10,000,000
Vietnam	109,000	Japan	6,095,000
Korea	55,000	England	4,683,000

From the Desk of . . .
Felix L. Sparks

David:

Thanks for the clipping. A Japanese film crew interviewed me last week. I told them that there were no Japanese at Dachau. They probably did not believe me. They are making a documentary.

Sparks

Note from General Sparks to author

August 20, 2002

David Israel

Dear David,
Your story on the 150th Panzer Brigade is very interesting. I am of course familiar with much of it and have some other facts to add. Though the Army continued to use Pass words and send up to us, much of the rest of the war we resorted to the G.I. method of recognition. When someone asked me about Baseball, I was at a loss, but one or more of my men answered quickly. I could ask about Boston and its districts & many cities I traveled to for the government. Many GIs would OK me saying OH!, we know you are from BARSTEN... because of my Harvard accent then. No Jerry could do that, they said.

When we were dug in at Elsenborn in the deep snow, one day a guy in American uniform came walking out of the woods to my positions and went from hole to hole asking my men & I questions such as where the BN HQ was. I followed him and checked the men about what he was asking etc and realized that he was not American and drew down on him. Checking him carefully we knew that he was German and brought him to company. We shot him after making sure. Often the combat troops took care of them right there. Some times they were taken back to the MP's. Capt. Pat wouldn't screw around with them at all. We didn't have time or men to take them back at that period. (only 18 of us left.) OH! Ya, what bothered me was that Jerry had a carbine and a Garand ammo belt. He was supposed to be a GI but only officers on line carried a carbine then or a pistol as Capt. Pat. After the Bulge, our officers carried better weapons such as a Thomson sub.

I have an interesting story from our POWs and will dig it up and copy. This story was told in like by other POWs.

Any info you find on the CIC history and men, pass along as I like that history.

OK, I looked through many papers but haven't found the story yet in the Checkerboard years ago. The gist and there are several ex POWs who tell this
Many units were over run in the Bulge and taken prisoner in my Bn & Regiment. They were taken back to a town behind German lines and herded into a building like an old theater. Certain German soldiers were matched by rank to POWs and taken into small rooms and the POWs were told to strip after these Germans asked them many questions about where they lived in the states. This was the very beginning of the Bulge.
These Germans took their uniforms, dog tags etc and then they were sent back to the rest of the prisoners minus their clothing and shoes. They were left in their underwear. Later

they were given prisoner clothing of sorts in the Stalag but these guys now had frozen limbs and other problems from the cold to start their imprisonment for the duration.

In "G" company, by a road, a jeep approached them with four men in it. Only one spoke up and answered questions and was tripped up. They were shot right there as the two in back began to draw down their weapons. GI's all talk together under such conditions. It was useless to ask for someone's Dog Tags, that we knew for sure, but some Germans still had on their own shoes for some reason. Then again, some uniforms were too clean for combat troops and we didn't wear ranks in combat, except a sgt wore a horizontal white stripe on the back of his helmet and we covered them with mud with our netting on top...if we had one. Ya, because we carried our fuse & caps in the netting as in a pocket, body heat would set off the caps. An officer wore a vertical stripe and did the same. It's been a long time.

Younger readers may not be aware of the horrors American servicemen faced on a daily basis. This letter was written to the author by a veteran who had been a combat infantry squad sergeant in Germany during World War II. The life expectancy of a squad sergeant was estimated to be 4 1/2 seconds.

SURVIVORS OF THE
SꜧHκOₗAʊH
VISUAL HISTORY FOUNDATION.

14 November 1996

Winfield Rosenberg

Dear Mr. Rosenberg,

In sharing your personal testimony as a survivor of the Holocaust, you have granted future generations the opportunity to experience a personal connection with history.

Your interview will be carefully preserved as an important part of the most comprehensive library of testimonies ever collected. Far into the future, people will be able to see a face, hear a voice, and observe a life, so that they may listen and learn, and always remember.

Thank you for your invaluable contribution, your strength, and your generosity of spirit.

All my best,

Steven Spielberg
Chairman

Letter from Steven Spielberg to Winfield Rosenberg, American soldier, survivor of Berga concentration camp.

FELIX L. SPARKS, Secretary

FAX: (202) 488-2693

To: Ralph Grunewald, United States Holocaust Memorial Museum.

Subject: Remarks of Felix L. Sparks to be given on May 8, 1995.

I have before me a document prepared by the Institute for Historical Review, Costa Mesa, California. It can be purchased from that so-called historical institute at a price of $2.00 for ten copies. This document professes to prove that the Holocaust never happened. It asserts that there is no evidence to prove that any member of the Jewish faith was ever persecuted or died at the hands of the Nazi Government of Germany. Among other things, it is claimed that gas chambers and crematoriums were constructed after the war as tourist attractions. The document contains a total of 66 questions and answers to prove that the Holocaust never happened.

I beg to disagree with authors of this totally sick and false literature. I am in a good position to disagree. On the morning of April 29, 1945, I was a lieutenant colonel commanding an infantry battalion of the United States 45th Infantry Division, with the mission of breaching the defenses of the city of Munich, Germany, in my assigned combat sector. Shortly after I had launched an attack against the outer defenses of Munich, I received an order to immediately proceed to the Dachau Concentration Camp. I knew nothing about the camp, nor had I ever heard of it.

Our first experience with the camp came as a traumatic shock. The first evidence of the horrors to come was a string of about forty railway cars on a railway spur leading into the camp. Each car was filled with emaciated human corpses, both men and women. A hasty search by the stunned infantry soldiers revealed no signs of life among the hundreds of still bodies, over 2,000 in all.

It was in this atmosphere of human depravity, degradation and death that the soldiers of my battalion then entered the camp itself. Almost all of the SS command guarding the camp had fled before our arrival, leaving behind about two hundred lower ranking members of the command. There was some sporadic firing of weapons. As we approached the confinement area, the scene numbed my senses. Dante's Inferno seemed pale compared to the real Hell of Dachau. A row of small cement structures near the prison entrance contained a coal-fired crematorium, a gas chamber, and rooms piled high with naked and emaciated corpses. As I turned to look over the prison yard with unbelieving eyes, I saw a large number of dead inmates lying where they had fallen in the last few hours or days before our arrival. Since all of the many bodies were in various stages of decomposition, the stench of death was overpowering. The men of the 45th Infantry Division were hardened combat veterans. We had been in combat almost two years at that point. While we were accustomed to death, we were not able to comprehend the type of death that we encountered at Dachau.

Many of the prisoners were still alive, but many were dying as we arrived and continued to die at the rate of over a hundred a day for about two weeks after our arrival. There were over six hundred troops from the 45th Infantry Division who were in Dachau on the day of liberation, along with some troops from the 42nd Infantry Division. During the month of April, 1945, several hundred other slave labor and death camps were liberated by American, British and Russian soldiers.

Most certainly, there were well over a hundred thousand Allied soldiers who were eyewitnesses to the unspeakable horrors of the Holocaust, along with a considerable number of Holocaust survivors. To those sick people in our society who say that it never happened, I say: Tell us who were there that it never happened, instead of trying to disseminate your bigotry and hatred by a total revision of the Holocaust history. Your efforts will never prevail. This remarkable United States Holocaust Memorial Museum in which we are assembled today will always stand as a living monument to remind us forever that caring men and women must always actively resist those forces of evil which practice intolerance, bigotry, hatred and slavery.

Felix L. Sparks
Brigadier General, AUS (Ret.

Glossary

Aktion (German) – During the Holocaust, Aktion could have one of several meanings. It could mean either a mass assembly, deportation or murder.

Allies – The nations bound together in their fight against Germany, Italy and Japan. The Allied nations were the United States, Great Britain and the Soviet Union.

Aryan Race – People of Northern European racial background.

Auschwitz – Concentration and extermination camp in Poland.

Axis – The Axis powers were Germany, Italy and Japan who were later joined by Bulgaria, Croatia, Hungary and Slovakia in the war against the Allies.

Belzec – One of six extermination camps in Poland. An estimated 600,000 souls were murdered here between the years 1941 to 1943.

Chelmno – An extermination camp in Poland. An estimated 320,000 souls were exterminated at Chelmno.

Churchill, Winston – British Prime Minister 1940 to 1945.

Concentration Camps – The Nazis established concentration camps for the imprisonment of all "enemies" of their regime.

Eichmann, Adolf – Head of the Jewish section of the Gestapo. Implemented the "Final Solution" by organizing the transportation of Jews from all over Europe to extermination camps.

Einsatzgruppen (German) – Mobile killing units of the Security Police that followed the German armies in the Soviet Union and Poland.

Euthanasia – Referred to by the Nazis using their code word "special treatment." This was a program for killing insane, permanently disabled, deformed and incurable individuals. It was designated by the Nazis as the T4 Program.

Evian Conference – Conference convened by the United States in 1938 to discuss the problem of refugees. 32 countries met in Evian, France. Nothing was accomplished as the Western countries refused to accept Jewish refugees.

Extermination Camps – Nazi camps established for mass killing. All Nazi extermination camps were located in Poland.

Final Solution – The Nazi code name for Hitler's plan to destroy all the Jews of Europe. The Jews were told they would be resettled in the East and went willingly, not knowing these were code words for extermination.

Genocide – The systematic destruction of a religious, racial, national or cultural group.

Ghetto – Section of a city surrounded by barbed wire or walls where the inhabitants were sealed in and prevented from leaving.

Goering, Hermann – Created the German Air Force and was made Air Minister of Germany. Committed suicide by taking poison while on trial as a war criminal.

Heydrich, Reinhard – Organized Einsatzgruppen which systematically murdered Jews in Russia and Poland.

Holocaust – The destruction of 6 million Jews by the Nazis and their collaborators between the years 1933 and 1945.

Jehovah's Witnesses – A religious sect considered to be enemies of the state by the Nazis. They were persecuted and sentenced to death.

Jewish Badge – A yellow star of David which Jews were compelled to wear in Germany and Nazi-occupied countries.

Judenrat – Counsels of Jewish representatives set up by the Nazis charged with carrying out Nazi instructions and directives.

Judenrein (German) – Areas where all Jews had been murdered or deported. The area was then declared Judenrein or cleansed of all Jews.

Kapo – Prisoner in charge of other prisoners in concentration camps.

Krystallnacht (German) – Known as the night of the broken glass, November 9, 1938. Synagogues, Jewish institutions and stores were destroyed and their contents looted.

Lidice – As a reprisal for the assassination of Reinhard Heydrich, the Nazis liquidated the entire population of this village in Czechoslovakia.

Mauthausen – Concentration camp in Northern Austria where an estimated 125,000 prisoners were killed.

Majdanek – Extermination camp in Poland where an estimated 250,000 men, women and children were exterminated.

Mein Kampf (German) – The autobiographical book by Adolf Hitler. Meaning my struggle, it laid out Hitler's blueprint for the future of Germany.

Mengele, Josef – Medical doctor who specialized in experimental operations on twins and gypsies. He selected his patients by pointing a finger to the left or right.

Musselmann (German) – Word used by prisoners in the concentration camp system for those prisoners who were unable to fight for life any longer.

Night and Fog – Prisoners with the designation, "nacht un nebel," were selected to disappear without a trace into night and fog.

Righteous Among the Nations – Term of honor applied to those non Jews who at the risk of their own lives saved others from Nazi persecution.

SA (German abbreviation for the word stormabteilung) – Storm troops of the Nazi party.

Selection – Code word the Nazis used for the process of choosing victims to be gassed.

Sobibor – Extermination camp in Poland. An estimated 250,000 Jews were killed here.

SS – German schutzsteffel. Hitler's personal bodyguard.

Swastika – Nazi symbol associated with the worship of Aryan sun gods.

Treblinka – Extermination camp in Poland. An estimated 870,000 people were murdered here.

Wannsee Conference (January 20, 1942) – Attended by 15 high ranking Nazi officials. The plans for the Final Solution of the "Jewish question in Europe" were ratified.

Wallenberg, Raoul – Swedish diplomat in Hungary who, in 1944, saved the lives of an estimated 30,000 people.

Warsaw Ghetto – An uprising by the Jewish inhabitants of the

Warsaw Ghetto was the first revolt against the Germans in an occupied territory. It lasted from April 19 to May 16, 1943.

Wehrmacht – The regular German army.

Wiesenthal, Simon – Holocaust survivor who has dedicated his life to identifying and capturing Nazi war criminals.

Timeline

1933

January 30th- - - - - - Adolf Hitler appointed Chancellor of Germany

March 15th - - - - - - Dachau concentration camp opened

April 1st- - - - - - - - Boycott of Jewish businesses announced

April 7th - - - - - - - Jews barred from holding civil service or state positions

May 10th - - - - - - - Burning of "Non-Aryan" books

1934

August 2nd - - - - - - Adolf Hitler proclaims himself Fuehrer. Armed forces swear allegiance to Hitler alone.

1935

September 15th- - - - Nuremberg laws promulgated. Jews no longer considered German citizens. Forbidden from marrying Germans. Jew defined as anyone having three Jewish grandparents.

1936
March 3rd - - - - - - - Jewish doctors prohibited from practicing in German institutions

March 7th - - - - - - - Germany invades the Rhineland which had been de-militarized by the Versailles Treaty.

October 25th - - - - - Italy and Germany form the Rome-Berlin Axis.

1937
July 15th - - - - - - - - Buchwenwald concentration camp opens

1938
March 13th - - - - - - Germany incorporates Austria (Anschluss)

September 30th- - - - England and France agree to German occupation of the Sudetenland, previously called Western Czechoslovakia.

October 5th - - - - - - The government of Switzerland requests a "J" be imprinted on passports of Jews in Germany in order to restrict their immigration to Switzerland.

November 9th - - - - Night of the Broken Glass (Kristallnacht). "Spontaneous outbreaks" of death and destruction on Jews and their businesses throughout Germany and Austria. An estimated 30,000 Jews arrested and sent to concentration camps

November 12th- - - - All Jews required to transfer retail businesses to German citizens

December 12th - - - - A fine of 1 billion marks imposed upon Jews for the destruction of property during Kristallnacht

1939

March 15th - - - - - - Germany invades Czechoslovkia

August 23rd - - - - - - Russia and Germany- sign non-aggression pact

September 1st - - - - - Germany invades Poland. This date officially recognized as the beginning of World War II

November 23rd - - - - Jews forced to live in ghettos in Poland and to wear armbands indicating their nationality

1940

April 9th - - - - - - - - Southern Norway and Denmark are occupied by Germany.

May 10th - - - - - - - - France, Luxemburg, Belgium and Holland are invaded by Germany.

June 22nd - - - - - - - France surrenders

1941

April 6th - - - - - - - - Yugoslavia and Greece invaded by Germany

June 22nd - - - - - - - Soviet Union invaded by Germany

September 22nd - - - 34,000 Jews slaughtered at Babi Yar

December 7th - - - - - Pearl Harbor attacked by Japanese

1942

January 20th - - - - - - Wannsee Conference in Berlin. "Final Solution" of Europe's Jews is announced

March 17th - - - - - - Extermination program begins in Belzec extermination camp

1943

April - - - - - - - - - - - The revolt of the Warsaw Ghetto begins. The Jewish fighters battle the German army until June.

October 14th - - - - - Prisoners in the Sobibor extermination camp revolt

1944

March 19th - - - - - - Germany occupies Hungary

June 6th- - - - - - - - - Allies invade Normandy

July 20th - - - - - - - - Assassination attempt on Hitler's life by German officers.

1945

April 4th - - - - - - - - Ohrdruf, first concentration camp liberated by American forces.

April 6th - - - - - - - - Evacuation of prisoners from the Buchenwald concentration camp

April 12th - - - - - - - Buchenwald liberated by American forces

April 29th - - - - - - - Dachau concentration camp liberated by American forces

April 30th - - - - - - - Hitler and his wife commit suicide

May 8th - - - - - - - - - Allied victory in Europe is announced

Bibliography

Abzug, Robert, Inside the Vicious Heart (Oxford University Press, 1985)

Bakels, Floris B., Nacht und Nebel (Lutterworth Press, 1993)

Baldwin, Harrison W., Battles Lost and Won (Harper and Row, 1966)

Benz, Wolfgang and Barbara Distel, eds., Dachau and the Nazi Terror, Vols. 1 and 2 (Comite Intl. de Dachau, 2002)

Benz, Wolfgang and Barbara Distel, eds., Dachau Review, Vols. 1 and 2 (Comite Intl. de Dachau, 1985)

Berben, Paul, Dachau (Norfolk Press, 1975)

Berenbaum, Michael, The World Must Know (Little, Brown and Co., 1966)

Bird, Kay, The Chairman (Simon and Schuster, 1992)

Bradley, Omar W., A Soldier's Story (Henry Holt and Co., 1951)

Bridgman, Jon, The End of the Holocaust (Areopagitica Press, 1990)

Buechner, Howard A., The Hour of the Avenger (Thunderbird, 1986)

Carlson, John Roy, Under Cover (P. Dutton, 1943)

Cave Brown, Anthony, Background of Lies (Harper and Row, 1975)

Chamberlin, Brewster and Marcia Feldman, eds., The Liberation of the Nazi Concentration Camps 1945 (United States Holocaust Memorial Council, 1987)

Chang, Thelma, I Can Never Forget (Sigi Productions, Inc., 1991)

Cohen, Roger, Soldiers and Slaves (Knoph, 2005)

Conot, Robert, Justice at Nuremburg (Carroll & Graf, 1983)

Daniels, Roger, The Bonus March (Greenwood Publishing Co., 1971)

Dann, Sam, Dachau 29 April 1945 (Texas Tech. Univ. Press, 1998)

Dawidowicz, Lucy, The War Against the Jews (Holt Rinehart Winston, 1986)

Distel, Barbara, ed., Dachau Review Vol. I, History of Nazi Concentration Camps, Studies, Reports and Documents(Dachau Comite, Brussels, 1965)

Eisenhower, Dwight D., Crusade in Europe (Doubleday and Co., 1948)

Eisner, Jack, The Survivor (William Morrow, 1980)

Ellach, Yaffa and Brana Gurewitsch, The Liberators (Futurama Printing Corp., 1981)

Farago, Ladislas, Ordeal and Triumph (G.P. Putnam's Sons, 1955)

Fest, Joachin, Speer (Harcourt, Inc., 1999)

Foy, David, For You the War Is Over (Stein and Day, 1984)

Friedman, Philip, ed., Martyrs and Fighters (Praeger, 1954)

Fussell,Paul, Doing Battle, (Little Brown and Company,1996)

Gehlen,Reinhard, The Memoirs of Reinhard Gehlen (World Publishing, 1972)

Gilbert, Martin, Atlas of the Holocaust (MacMillan Press, 1982)

Green, Joshua M., Justice at Dachau (Broadway Books, 2003)

Gunn, Nerin E., The Day of the Americans (Fleet Publishing Corp., 1986)

Higgins, Marguerite, Witness to War (Beau Fort Books, Inc., 1983)

Holt Giles, Janice, The Damned Engineers (Office of Chief of Engineers, Washington, D.C., 1970)

I.C.R.C., The Role of the I.C.R.C. in German Concentration Camps

(I.C.R.C., 1973)

Ingersoll, Ralph, Top Secrets (Harcourt, Brace and Co., 1946)

Karst, George M., The Beasts of the Earth (Unger Press, 1942)

Kaufman, Henry, Vertrauensmann (Rivercross Publishers, Inc., 1994)

Kennan, George, Memoirs (Little, Brown and Co., 1967)

Kennett, Lee, G.I. (Broadway Books, 2003)

Kogon, Eugene, The Theory and Practice of Hell (Octagon Books, 1973)

Lachene, Evelyn, Mauthausen (Methuen, 1971)

Langbein, Hermann, Against All Hope (Paragon House Press, Inc., 1994)

Laqueur, Walter, The Terrible Secret (Penguin Books, 1980)

Leber, Annedore, Conscience In Revolt (Vallentine, Mitchell, 1957)

Lenz, John M., Christ In Dachau(Published with church approval, Vienna, 1960)

Levin and McDevitt, Hate Crimes (Plenur Press, 1993)

Levy, Alan, The Wiesennthal File (Erdmans Publishing Co., 1993)

Linden, John H., Surrender of the Dachau Concentration Camp(Sycamore Press, 1997)

Lipman, Steve, Laughter In Hell (Jason Aronson, Inc., 1991)

Lipstadt, Deborah E., Denying the Holocaust (The Free Press, 1993)

Loftus, John, The Belarus Secret (St. Martins Press, 1989)

Loftus, John and Mark Arrons, The Secret War Against the Jews (St. Martins Press, 1994)

Lubitsky, Larry, AJDC Berlin Tracing Office (AJDC Berlin AJDC Tracing Office, 1948)

Manchester, William, The Arms of Krupp (Little, Brown and Co., 1968)

Marcuse, Harold, Legacies of Dachau (Cambridge University Press, 2001)

Martin, Gilbert, Atlas of the Holocaust (MacMillan, 1982)

Mauldin, Bill, Back Home (William Gloan Association, 1945)

McDonald, Charles B., The Mighty Endeavor (Oxford University Press, 1989)

Mendelsohn, John, The History of the Counter Intelligence Corps (Garland Publishing, Inc., 1989)

Meyer, Robert, Jr., The Stars and Stripes (David J. McKay, Co., Inc., 1960)

Miller, Nathan, Spying For America (Paragon House, 1989)

Overduin, Jack, Faith and Victory in Dachau (Paideia Press, 1978)

Patton, George S., War as I Knew It (Houghlin, Miflin Co., 1947)

Perry, Michael W., ed., Dachau Liberated (Inkling Books, 2000)

Pratt, Sherman, Autobahn to Berchtesgarden (Gateway Press, 1992)

Segev, Tom, Soldiers of Evil (McGraw Hill, 1997)

Shirer, William L., The Rise and Fall of the Third Reich (Simon & Schuster, 1960)

Simpson, Christopher, Blowback (Weidenfeld and Nicolson, 1988)

Smith, Marcus J., Dachau, The Harrowing of Hell (University of New Mexico Press, 1985)

Snyder, Dr. Louis L., The Third Reich (Marlowe and Co., 1976)

Sofsky, Wolfgang, The Order of Terror: The Concentration Camp (Princeton University Press, 1993)

Stanberg, Robert H., From There to Here and Back Again (Carlton Press Corp., 1995)

Stein, Kenneth S., A Force Upon the Plain (Simon and Schuster, 1996)

Steiner, John, Power Politics and Social Change in National Socialist Germany (Mouton Publishers, 1976)

Vidal-Naquet, Pierre, Assassins of Memory (Columbia University Press, 1992)

Wyant, William K., Sandy Patch (Praeger, 1991)

Weber, Louis, The Holocaust Chronicle (Publications International, 2000)

Whiting, Charles, Hitler's Werewolves (Stein and Day, 1948)

Wyman, David, The Abandonment of the Jews (Pantheon Press, 1984)

Index

Eicke, Theodor 117, 122,
123, 136
Eisenhower, General Dwight
D. 39, 53, 77, 99, 150, 162,
166, 169, 209, 225, 226,
243, 295
electrified fences 110, 137
escape equipment 189
espionage 7, 8, 18, 51
European Theatre of
Operations 35, 38, 42, 190,
194
Euthanasia Program 13
extermination camps 124,
135, 208, 285, 286

F

Faulkner, William 1, 15
FBI 7, 8, 50
Federal War Victims Act 142
Feingold, Sol 178
Fellman, Norm 195, 197
Final Solution 124, 135
fishermen 8, 214, 215
Five Points 42, 219
Flanders 74, 75
Fort Ritchie 26
Foster, Lt. Col. Hugh 24, 25,
178, 215, 216, 278
Fox, John 80, 81, 82
France 6, 20, 21, 22, 32, 35,
38, 45, 51, 69, 74, 89, 112,
124, 132, 183, 199, 212,
216, 229, 234, 244
Freiheit Action Bavaria 112
BAV 112, 113
French 6, 20, 21, 22, 23, 32,
39, 127, 128, 140, 141, 148,
158, 185, 211, 212, 213

French resistance 22
French Revolution 32
Fry, Varian 229, 232
Fu-Go Project 234, 235
Fuehrer 14, 45, 46

G

gas chambers 94, 109, 253
Gaulle, Charles de 20
Gearhart Mountain, Oregon
236
Genovese, Vito 10
German Constitution 15
German Industrial complex
140
German Sabotage Service 45
German Tiger and Panther
tanks 211
Gerngross, Ruprecht 112
Gestapo 46, 65, 103, 104,
106, 122, 135, 136, 201
Giraud, Lt. Rene J. 127
Go for broke 96
Goebbels 18
gold star banners 234
Golden Lions 37, 38
Greece 124, 183
Greeks 140, 158
Guadalcanal 234
Guerisse, Albert 127
guillotine 103, 104
Gypsies 12, 130, 140, 240,
248

H

Hadamar 4, 12, 230
Haffenden, Charles H. 8
Haislip, General 175
Hammelburg Prisoner of War

45
Waters, Col. John 84, 86
Waters, Walter W 222, 223
Wehrmacht 26, 85, 146
Weiss, Martin Gottfried 117,
    182, 183, 184
Weitz, John 186
Werewolf Organization 185,
    186
Western Defense Command
    237
Western forests 236
White Rose 101, 103, 104
Whiteway, Curtis 65, 178,
    230, 232
Whitwell Middle School 248
Wicker, Heinrich 149
Willis, Everett, 43
Wise, Rabbi Stephen S. 17
Wicker, Heinrich 149
Watkins, Pfc. James 198
Weiskircher, General Russ
    178
West Point 183
Willie & Joe 98, 99
wolf packs 214

Y

Yad Vashem Memorial
    Museum 228
Yevtushenko, Yevgeny 242
Yiddish 118

Z

Zachary, Otis 80, 81
Zill, Egon 114, 115, 116, 117
Zyklon B gas 140

X

"X" 189